Where in the world is the best place to be today, tomorrow or for your next birthday?

My, I felt smug. The sky was too blue to be true, a spread of cobalt I thought only existed in Technicolor or Photoshop. The historic trail – largely empty, it being before the peak hiking months – was fringed by a golden fuzz of gorse, while surrounding meadows nodded with purples, pinks and fresh greens. Birds were in good voice, singing and zinging from the leafy treetops on a quest to secure a mate. And the days were endless! The sunshine hours stretched beyond 10pm, encouraging late nights on warm-enough outdoor terraces, savouring tapas dishes of (in-season) padrón peppers and a vino tinto or two. Yes, it seemed walking a smidgen of Spain's Camino de Santiago pilgrimage trail in late May (26 May, to be precise), when it was all wildflowers and long days and holiday-horde free, was the embodiment of right time, right place.

This, of course, is where all travellers want to be, no matter what their cultural or geographical preferences: right time, right place. We all want that sweet serendipity of being there when the Northern Lights are most likely to dance (but, ideally, it's not too chilly); when the sleepy scruff-bucket town transforms for its once-a-year fabulous fiesta; when a mass mob of whales gathers at the nearby reef; when the climate is just perfect for whatever our chosen adventure. And that's why this book exists – to help you focus your travels, zooming in on precise dates or periods to ensure some of the very best experiences, be they wildlife migrations, active escapades, raucous festivals or cultural showstoppers.

Perhaps you want to know when to pack your picnic for the prettiest Japanese cherry blossom party (26 March, in case you're wondering). Or when best to raft the Colorado River through the Grand Canyon (try 16 September, the day after motorboats are prohibited for the year). Maybe you want to spend your Christmas break with baby warthogs rather than baby Jesus (try Kenya, 27 December), ride a bobsled in summer rather than winter (Austria, 2 July) or be sure not to miss a biggie, such as Glastonbury (England, 28 June) or messy Tomatina (Spain, 26 August).

We all want that sweet serendipity of being there when the Northern Lights are most likely to dance...

Or maybe you want to be there (with a good waterproof coat) when the rain is gushing in biblical torrents, thus ensuring waterfalls are at their most spectacular and most other people have stayed away (think Iguaçu Falls, 9 December). Perhaps 'right' is being there in shoulder season – say, tramping New Zealand's Milford Track on 10 March – to best balance still-decent weather with fewer crowds.

When you drill down into the calendar year, you can find the world's seasonal secrets, like Vanuatu's land-divers marking the start of the yam season or the brief window of opportunity to trek while listening to the sound of mating pandas. Organising the planet this way helps you pick a destination for that June honeymoon or your October annual leave. You can even use it to inspire your whereabouts on your next birthday.

There's an idea here for every day of the year. Some suggestions are date specific – a religious holiday, a festival, an annual seasonal opening. Some give an indication of the best week, month or timeframe when perhaps it's driest, coolest, quietest or most full of wildebeest. For the date-specific events, we've

There's an idea here for every day of the year. Some suggestions are date specific, others give an indication of the best week or month

pinned them to their 2015 occurrences where possible, with dates given for the following years where known.

Of course, there are myriad options. On any given day, there are many best places to be, many destinations ripe for adventures. But here are 365 goodies to get you started. Now, stop reading this – you shouldn't be HERE. Why not flick forward to 'today' and start planning tomorrow?

SARAH BAXTER

CONTENTS

**Celebrate St
Patrick's Day**
PAGE 63

17
MAR

09
JUL

**Run with bulls
in Pamplona**
PAGE 141

27
OCT

**Mountain
bike in Moab**
PAGE 221

15
FEB

**Dress up
for Venice
Carnevale**
PAGE 40

09
NOV

**Dive into
cenotes**
PAGE 230

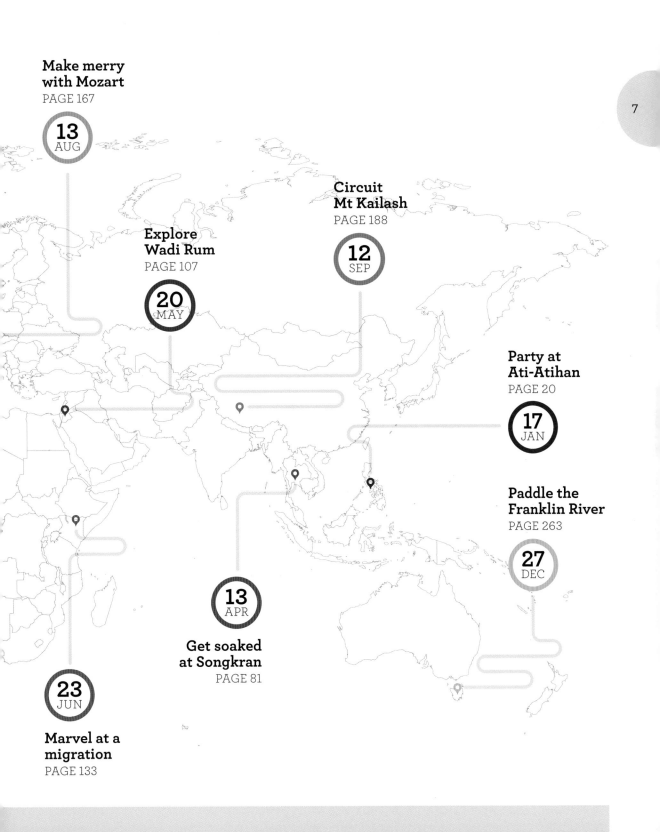

**Make merry
with Mozart**
PAGE 167

13
AUG

**Circuit
Mt Kailash**
PAGE 188

12
SEP

**Explore
Wadi Rum**
PAGE 107

20
MAY

**Party at
Ati-Atihan**
PAGE 20

17
JAN

**Paddle the
Franklin River**
PAGE 263

27
DEC

13
APR

**Get soaked
at Songkran**
PAGE 81

23
JUN

**Marvel at a
migration**
PAGE 133

Join Junkanoo

THE BAHAMAS

WHY NOW To join in the national fiesta

WHERE Nassau

DATES 1 January (and 26 December)

01 JAN More funk than junk, the Bahamas' national festival is a mass of energy and colour that roars through two nights of the year. Celebrated across the country, Junkanoo is at its wildest best in the capital, Nassau, where the first 'rush' (as the parade is known) takes place on Boxing Day, the second on New Year's Day. The latter parade attracts the largest crowds, with up to 50,000 people lining the streets.

The parades begin at 2am and finish at 8am. Standing on Bay or Shirley Sts you'll feel the music before you see its source – a frenzied barrage of whistles, horns, cowbells, drums and conch shells. Then the costumed revellers stream into view, whirling and gyrating in rhythm with the cacophony.

Most elaborate is the human parade. Marchers spend all year planning their costumes, keeping their designs secret – it is fiercely competitive. — *www.bahamas.co.uk.*

January

Cheer at Kaapse Klopse

SOUTH AFRICA

WHY NOW To partake in the party of the year in the shadow of Table Mountain

WHERE Cape Town

DATES Starts 2 January, lasts for a month

02 JAN Kaapse Klopse (the Cape Minstrel Carnival), Cape Town's largest carnival, is a joyous affair featuring marching troupes adorned in every colour of satin, sequin and glitter. The festival dates back to the 19th century, when slaves in the city were allowed their only day off for the year on 2 January. However, the look of today's carnival was actually inspired by visiting American minstrels in the late 19th century, hence the make-up and ribald dances.

The main parade begins at midday on Darling St, in front of Old City Hall, finishing at Green Point Stadium. It attracts tens of thousands of spectators, so be sure to stake a place early.

The actual Cape Minstrel competition, when troupes are judged on a variety of criteria, including costume, singing and dancing, runs each Saturday night throughout January and early February. If you miss the main parade, there are chances to catch the minstrels in action on these nights at Green Point Stadium, Athlone Stadium and Vygerkraal Stadium – it makes for a unique Capetonian experience.
— *www.capetown-minstrels.co.za*

Fly to the South Pole

ANTARCTICA

WHY NOW You have a short window of opportunity to stand at 90° south

WHERE Antarctica

DATES 3 January (2015 expedition); Union Glacier Camp is open November to January

Once upon a time you had to be prepared to eat your dogs if you wanted to set foot on the South Pole. Today, you need only endure a bumpy 6-hour flight, and you can be making the world's most southerly snowman. That is, as long as you have US$46,000 to spare...

Air journeys to the South Pole begin with a flight from the Chilean town of Punta Arenas to your base at Union Glacier Camp. It's a further 5-hour flight to the Amundsen-Scott Research Station and the Geographic South Pole. Here, 360 lines of longitude meet and the temperature is likely to be -30°C as you stand atop the 3000m-thick ice. — *www.adventure-network.com*

LEFT: **You won't miss the marching troupes at Kaapse Klopse**

BELOW: **Storm clouds on the horizon are a regular occurence on Vancouver Island**

Ride the Cresta Run

SWITZERLAND

WHY NOW To toboggan at terrifying speed on one of the few runs open to the public

WHERE St Moritz

DATES The run is open from a few days before Christmas until the end of February

The Cresta Run was first built in 1885, and is reconstructed each winter. This most famous of skeleton (head-first tobogganing) runs is used for both fun and competition, though visitors can only play on non-race days (and women cannot ride at all).

The best reach speeds of up to 130km/h, but beginners have trouble just mastering braking (done with rakes on your boots). Fail in this and you're bound to come a cropper on the run's most famous corner, the Shuttlecock. This at least grants you entry into the Shuttlecock Club and the right to wear the special Shuttlecock tie. — *www.cresta-run.com*

Watch the storms roll in

CANADA

WHY NOW The winter weather is wild

WHERE Vancouver Island, British Columbia

DATES November to March (peak months are December to February)

Each winter, Vancouver Island's west coast becomes a front-row seat to the most spectacular storms on the North American west coast.

With nothing but the Pacific Ocean between the island and Japan, these well-travelled storms – driven here by a persistent low-pressure system in the Gulf of Alaska – roar ashore, bringing high winds and waves that hit harder than a boxer.

Wander the beaches to experience the storms' full fury, follow the aptly named Wild Pacific Trail for a cliff-top view, take a storm-watching tour from the town of Tofino or simply watch the action from the window of your hotel room. — *www.tofino-bc.com; www.my-tofino.com*

Join the Blacks & Whites Carnival

COLOMBIA

WHY NOW To make merry – and messy

WHERE Pasto, Nariño

DATES 2–7 January; 6 January is the day of the Grand Parade

06 JAN One of South America's oldest festivals, Pasto's Carnaval de Negros y Blancos (Carnival of Blacks and Whites) dates back to the time of Spanish rule, when slaves were allowed to party on 5 January, with their masters showing approval by painting their faces black. In turn, the slaves painted their faces white the following day. The tradition is faithfully maintained, and the city goes wild, with everybody painting or dusting one another with grease, chalk, talc, flour and any other available substance even vaguely black or white in colour. You're free to dust down whoever you like and, in turn, you can expect to be a mother's nightmare of a mess by the carnival's end.

Wear the oldest clothes you own and buy an *antifaz*, a type of mask to protect your face (these are widely sold for the occasion). Pasto is 2500m above sea level, so pack a sweater because days can be cool and nights are downright chilly. Or fire up your festival spirit with a meal at Pasto's Salón Guadalquivir, where the walls are lined with carnival posters.
— *www.colombia.travel*

RIGHT: ANDREW WATSON – GETTY IMAGES

Surf the Superbank

AUSTRALIA

WHY NOW In cyclone season, incoming storms see super-big swells line up

WHERE Gold Coast, Queensland

DATES January to April

Until a few decades ago, there was no such place as Superbank, the great white sandbar off Queensland's Gold Coast that's now home to the world's longest waves and barrels. In 1999 a 'sand bypass' project aimed to move northerly flowing sand past the mouth of the Tweed River and on to the Gold Coast. Instead it resulted in the creation of Superbank – all praise to failed bureaucracy! – which stretches in a ruler-straight line from Snapper Rocks to Kirra, with summer cyclone swells creating tubes as long as an oil pipeline.

Indeed, Superbank – which is located at Tweed Heads, just north of the New South Wales–Queensland border – is so good at this time of year that you'll even find a handful of surfers still riding their fortune at night. The waters are always packed, but don't fret – there are waves enough here for everyone. — *queenslandholidays.com.au*

Bird-watch in Rajasthan

INDIA

WHY NOW To watch winter migrants join the resident birds at Keoladeo Ghana National Park
WHERE Bharatpur, Rajasthan
DATES November to March

08 JAN Once considered the premier duck-hunting destination in the British Empire, the wetlands at India's Bharatpur were elevated to national park status and renamed as Keoladeo Ghana National Park in 1982. Gone are the days of royal hunting parties, and wildlife populations have soared in response, making this one of the finest birdwatching destinations in the world. Even better, the park is ridiculously easy to visit. From Bharatpur, 180km south of Delhi, you can just hop on a bike and ride the flat roads that weave among the ponds and marshes. Wildlife is so densely packed into this relatively small park that your foremost problem will be identifying everything you see.

From August to October the park's trees are chock-full of nesting herons, storks and egrets, with up to nine species per tree. From November to March bird diversity soars as countless migrants arrive from Asia and Europe – you might see 180 species in a day. Also, with 40 species of raptor and seven species of owl, Bharatpur is one of the best places on earth to see birds of prey.

Mixed among the birds, handsome blackbucks, chital deer, sambar and nilgai wade in the shallows or wander nearby grasslands. You shouldn't have any problem spotting pythons, monkeys or one of the park's several species of cat. — *www.rajasthantourism.gov.in*

Ride the Tour d'Afrique

EGYPT–SOUTH AFRICA

WHY NOW Start the most epic cycle expedition

WHERE Cairo to Cape Town

DATES Tour runs early January to May each year; 2015 ride starts 9 January

09 JAN

The Tour d'Afrique is an 11,900km bike race starting at the pyramids of Giza, outside Cairo, and finishing in Cape Town, South Africa. For four months cyclists average 120km a day, pedalling past some of Africa's greatest sights – Luxor, the Blue Nile Gorge, Mt Kenya, Mt Kilimanjaro, Lake Malawi, Victoria Falls – and even more of its wildlife.

The Tour d'Afrique is foremost a race but you can also cycle as an 'expedition rider' and ride individual sections – there are eight, ranging in distance between 1000km and 2000km. There are particularly brutal sections and there are more open sections, such as the all-sealed route from Iringa (Tanzania) to Lilongwe (Malawi). Fees start from US$1500; to do the whole thing costs around US$14,500. — *www.tourdafrique.com*

View the Voodoo Festival

BENIN

WHY NOW Dance, sing and stick pins in things at offbeat Benin's biggest bash

WHERE Ouidah

DATES 10 January

10 JAN

For millions of Beninese, voodoo is a skulduggery–free part of daily life. It does have a dark side – it's hard to miss the voodoo dolls riddled with nails – but this is only one aspect of it. Ouidah's Voodoo Festival, Benin's most vibrant party, showcases its other qualities.

Since 1997, one year after the government decreed voodoo a religion (practised by 60% of Benin's 7.4 million residents), thousands have flocked to Ouidah, the historic centre of voodoo, to receive blessings from the city's voodoo chief. The celebrations begin when the supreme voodoo priest slaughters a goat to honour the spirits; there follows much singing, chanting, dancing, drum-beating and drinking of gin.

Ouidah is 42km west of Cotonou, Benin's major city. — *www.benin-tourisme.com*

LEFT: **A white-throated kingfisher waits for lunch in Keoladeo Ghana National Park**

BELOW: **An early start for this Tour d'Afrique rider in Sudan**

Explore Patagonia

ARGENTINA/CHILE

WHY NOW Come when it's at its approachable best – snow-topped not snowbound

WHERE Far south South America

DATES December to February

11 JAN

Patagonia is the literal end-of-the-earth, a rugged place where South America tapers away to a chilly nothing. The star feature is the tail end of the Andes, the longest mountain chain on the planet. Assaulted by wind and ice for millennia, the Patagonian Andes are not especially high – they average 2000m – but they've been blasted into an array of shapes, such as the Torres del Paine, which look like a hand of broken fingers, and the 1.2km-high domed summit of Monte FitzRoy. Hidden beneath FitzRoy is the South Patagonian Icecap; from it springs the pin-up of world ice, 60m-high Moreno Glacier. Stand in awe as it noisily calves seracs into the milky waters of Lago Argentino.

The Andes separate two different landscapes. To their east is the arid Argentine steppe, which extends to the wildlife wonderland of Península Valdés, populated by Magellanic penguins and elephant seals. To the west is the fjord-slashed Chilean coast, where rivers such as Río Serrano provide kayakers with access to iceberg-choked lakes. For a more turbulent experience, consider a rafting trip on Chile's Río Futaleufú, one of the world's wildest white-water experiences.

Patagonia's full stop is Tierra del Fuego. The Chilean side is an expanse of sheep farms and mountains. Argentina's half is home to Ushuaia, the departure point for Antarctica-bound ships.
— *www.chile.travel; www.turismo.gov.ar*

RIGHT: **GARETH MCCORMACK – GETTY IMAGES**

Waltz around Vienna

AUSTRIA

WHY NOW It's ball season – your chance to whirl with the Viennese elite

WHERE Vienna

DATES January to March

12 JAN If Rio owns the samba, then Vienna owns the waltz. And as Rio marks Carnaval with bootie-shaking parades, Vienna does so with balls. Indeed, the city hosts around 450 balls, from January to March; the season kicks off in grand style with the Imperial Palace's Le Grand Bal on New Year's Eve, and continues through to spring with the Flower Ball, Jaegerball, Bonbon Ball and more.

Venues include the Hofburg Palace, a symphony of marble columns and vast chandeliers, various concert halls, and the State Opera House. One quirk of the season is that many of the most popular balls are hosted by the associations of various professions, so you might be surrounded by lawyers or the owners of the city's coffee houses.

Anyone can buy a ticket, but you need a fancy outfit – tux or ballgown – and you need to be able to dance. Take a lesson, even if you've waltzed before: the Viennese variety is breathtakingly fast. Elmayer's Studio offers drop-in tuition sessions for tourists.
— *www.vienna.info*

Snorkel Jellyfish Lake

PALAU

WHY NOW For the most surreal swim, during the driest months of the year
WHERE Palau, Micronesia
DATES January to March

13 JAN Palau is a spectacular dive spot, with coral reefs, blue holes, WWII wrecks, hidden caves and more than 60 vertical drop-offs. The epicentre is the Rock Islands, where more than 200 jungly knobs of limestone dot the waters.

The seas around the Rock Islands teem with more than 1500 varieties of reef and pelagic fish. Divers might see manta rays, turtles, moray eels, giant clams, sharks and dugongs. But the real fish-of-the-day is jellyfish. Among the Rock Islands' 80 marine lakes – former sinkholes – is Jellyfish Lake. Here, millions of harmless, transparent jellyfish swim. Diving is not allowed but snorkelling in this pulsating mass is an unearthly sensation. — *www.visit-palau.com*

LEFT: **Waltz this way for the Opera Ball in Vienna, Austria**

BELOW: **Share Jellyfish Lake with two species of jellyfish, neither will sting**

Ski the Alborz Mountains

IRAN

WHY NOW To make the most of mid-winter's coolest conditions and the region's best snow
WHERE Near Tehran
DATES Mid-January to mid-March

14 JAN It might sound an unlikely spot for getting piste but Iran has several ski resorts. The country's Alborz mountain range is higher than the European Alps, with slopes suitable for beginners and powder hounds. Four resorts lie within day-trip distance of Tehran: Dizin is the largest of Iran's ski fields and, thanks to its altitude – its loftiest run begins at around 3500m, making it one of the highest in the world – it gets about a six-month season.

Another ski field worth a look is Shemshak, nearer to Tehran. This offers steep runs, plenty of moguls and even night skiing. Just be aware that if you come to ski in the Alborz it's about the snow, not the parties. — *www.tourismiran.ir*

Spot James' flamingos

BOLIVIA

WHY NOW This is when flamingo numbers peak
WHERE Laguna Colorado, 600km from La Paz
DATES November to January

15 JAN It is testament to the allure of flamingos that over 40,000 people a year now sojourn to the remote Laguna Colorado in southern Bolivia to see these magical birds. Here, at nearly 4300m, the sun is fierce and the air thin but seeing this ethereal landscape of barren hills and shifting light is more than enough reason to visit. Three species of flamingo gather by the thousands in November to nest in this red-stained lake.

Because nesting colonies are easily disturbed and the ecosystems are so fragile, it is advisable to travel with guides from the local towns of Uyuni or San Juan and check in with the tourism office in Uyuni before entering the Eduardo Avaroa Faunal Reserve. — *www.enjoybolivia.com*

Delight in Art Deco

USA

WHY NOW Miami's Art Deco Weekend takes over the town
WHERE Ocean Drive, Miami
DATES 16–18 January 2015 (usually mid-Jan)

16 JAN Pin those curls, put on your cat-eye sunglasses and get ready to shake your jazz hands – on one weekend a year, Miami celebrates its Art Deco heritage as if it was still 1922. Sunny South Beach comes alive with period-sound bands, vintage cars, dashing pinstripe gangsters and ladies looking lovely in flapper dresses and pearls.

Go shopping for antique furniture and fittings, get nostalgic about old toys, watch *The Great Gatsby* at the alfresco cinema screen, listen to live jazz at the 10th Street Stage, coo over the beads and spats at the Art Deco fashion show and finish up in a speakeasy, sipping Champagne. — *www.artdecoweekend.com*

Watch camels wrestle

TURKEY

WHY NOW Watch warring camels in winter sun
WHERE Pamucak Beach, near Selçuk
DATES Third Sunday in January (18 Jan 2015; 17 Jan 2016; 15 Jan 2017; 21 Jan 2018)

18 JAN Uniquely Turkish, camel wrestling has a devoted following along the Western Mediterranean, with the greatest event taking place in Selçuk, where the eve of the festival is celebrated with feasting. Camel owners across Turkey marshal their males for the bouts, which are governed by ancient rules. First and foremost, camels must use their heads, necks and bodies to overcome opponents, forcing them to flee the ring or pushing them over; judges and referees preside over each match.

While you're there, visit Ephesus – the well-preserved classic city is 3km from Selçuk; its Temple of Artemis is one of the seven ancient wonders of the world. — *www.goturkey.com*

Party at Ati-Atihan

PHILIPPINES

WHY NOW To be joyfully dragged into the country's biggest street party
WHERE Kalibo
DATES Third week of January

17 JAN Ati-Atihan is the biggest and best Mardi Gras in the Philippines. It's a week-long street party that rages from dawn to dusk, peaking on the third Sunday in January. Honouring Santo Niño (the infant Jesus), it's a religious celebration cloaked in secular sequins.

The festival runs for a week, but celebrations fire up in the final three days. A Friday morning mass gives way to mass hysteria in the streets, and people dance their way into Saturday. Sunday begins with the transfer of the Santo Niño icon from Kalibo Cathedral to Pastrana Park, where an open-air mass is conducted. The festival culminates late Sunday afternoon with an enormous parade. — *www.ati-atihan.net*

RIGHT: **Orthodox church priests during Timkat at Lalibela**

BELOW: **Art deco meets neon in Miami**

Join the faithful at Timkat

ETHIOPIA

WHY NOW To have an Eastern Christian Epiphany in 'Africa's Camelot'

WHERE Fasilidas' Bath, Gonder

DATES 18–20 January

19 JAN

Ethiopia's most colourful festival commemorates Jesus' baptism in the River Jordan and is celebrated around the country, though it's most spectacular in the former capital of Gonder. On the eve of Timkat, the church tabots (replicas of the Ark of the Covenant) are taken to Fasilidas' Bath. During the night, the priests and faithful participate in a vigil around the tabots. The following morning (19 January) the crowds gather around the water, which is blessed then splashed onto them, and religious vows are renewed. The tabots are then paraded back to the church accompanied by much singing and dancing. A unique sight at the Gonder Timkat is of the faithful leaping into the baths for a full-immersion 'baptism'.

Known as 'Africa's Camelot', Gonder is evocative year round. Visit the World Heritage–listed Fasil Ghebbi (Royal Enclosure) and the Debre Berhan Selassie church, which has 104 cherubs on the ceiling and a mass of artworks on the walls. Consider flying into Gonder from Addis Ababa – buses take two days.
— *www.tourismethiopia.gov.et*

Admire red-crowned cranes

JAPAN

WHY NOW Watch these elegant birds perform their wonderful winter courtship

WHERE Kushiro, Hokkaido

DATES January to February

Despite being mythological symbols of eternal life, red-crowned cranes were hunted into extinction in Japan by the late 1880s. So it was regarded as a miracle when one reappeared in a Japanese field in 1910, and after a remnant band of cranes was discovered starving to death during the legendary winter of 1952, farmers and children began a tradition of feeding cranes that has continued ever since.

Today you can see several hundred cranes gathered on snow-covered fields outside Kushiro on the Japanese island of Hokkaido, where they are something of a national treasure. One of the best observation points is the Tancho no Sato reserve, adjacent to the Akan International Crane Center. It's interesting to watch majestic 1.5m-tall cranes striding back and forth across the fields. But the reason visitors line up by the dozens and risk freezing their fingers off is because red-crowned cranes have the most spectacular courtship dances of any of the world's cranes (all of which are renowned dancers).

The excitement is palpable as flocks swoop in, their cries ringing off the hills with mounting ardour. Although pairs mate for life, it does little to dampen their enthusiasm for each other; before long they're bowing, leaping and prancing. It's said human dance evolved from watching cranes, and if you catch yourself bobbing up and down you'll see why. — *www.lake-akan.com/en*

Explore Dogon Country

MALI

WHY NOW See this weird world at its coolest: north-east winds keep temperatures in the 30°Cs

WHERE Dogon Country

DATES November to January

21 JAN Mali's Dogon Country resembles Tolkien's Middle Earth: there are granaries with witch-hat straw roofs, shocked-looking baobab trees and perfect, small fields like something out of Hobbiton. What sets it apart is the 150km-long, copper-red and wrinkled Bandiagara Escarpment towering over the scene.

The best way to see the Pays Dogon is to trek along this dramatic escarpment, walking between villages along truly ancient tracks. Guides aren't essential, but are highly recommended: they will show you the route, help with translation and stop you stumbling over sacred sites. The central area between Dourou and Banani is the most spectacular. The southern section from Dorou to Djiguibombo is also very beautiful.
— *www.dogoncountry.com*

Cycle an island

CUBA

WHY NOW To ride around cool Cuba during its coolest and driest time of year

WHERE Cuba

DATES January to April

22 JAN See the land behind the politics as you pedal across the Caribbean's largest island. Fly into the capital, Havana, and stretch out your legs with a ride along the waterfront Malecón, where you'll have waves on one side and colonial grandeur on the other. Park the bike for an evening spent hopping between salsa and son joints, sampling the local rum cocktails.

Continue east out of Havana for the tropical treats of the Varadero beaches. After that, cross to the island's eastern tip to pit yourself against the 300km-long Sierra Maestra, Cuba's highest range. Alternatively, head west, to pedal around the lush Viñales Valley, a region of leafy tobacco plantations, rounded *mogotes* (haystack-like hills) and tranquil tracks that seem made for exploration by bike. — *www.travel2cuba.co.uk*

LEFT: **The dances of Hokkaido's red-crowned cranes include bowing, jumping and synchronised strutting**

BELOW: **Cycle through Vinales valley in Cuba**

Track mountain gorillas

UGANDA

WHY NOW To meet the relatives in the middle of the rainforest's dry(er) season
WHERE Bwindi Impenetrable National Park
DATES December to February

23 JAN It's estimated that there are only about 800 mountain gorillas remaining in the world, and half of these live in Uganda's Bwindi Impenetrable National Park. Seeing them is one of Africa's magic moments.

Nine gorilla groups are habituated to human presence in the so-called Impenetrable Forest, and they change location daily. They may be only 15 minutes' walk from the park entrance, or they may be hours of hard hiking away, up hillsides and slippery paths. Only eight people are permitted to visit each group each day, and each person requires a permit (US$600). Permits are snapped up fast, so plan ahead. Children under 15 years of age, and people with a cold or other illness, are not allowed. Once you finally join a trekking group, the chance of finding the gorillas is excellent, though the time you spend with them is limited to 1 hour.

Adult male mountain gorillas – silverbacks – can weigh more than 160kg, but they're usually placid unless they feel threatened. Their reaction to danger (and sometimes strangers) is to scream and charge at the intruder. If this happens, don't lose your nerve: stay still and look away; he may come close but there's little chance he'll actually hurt you. — *www.uwa.or.ug*

Celebrate Yamayaki

JAPAN

WHY NOW To honour a fiery feud

WHERE Mt Wakakusa-yama, Nara

DATES Fourth Saturday in January (24 Jan 2015; 23 Jan 2016; 28 Jan 2017; 27 Jan 2018)

24 JAN

Winter in the Japanese region of Kansai would seem a good enough excuse for one of the world's biggest bonfires, but in Nara they point to history as the reason for setting alight an entire hill each year. The event commemorates a feud from many centuries ago between the monks of two of Nara's Buddhist temples – Tōdai-ji and Kōfuku-ji – during which mediation went so badly that 342m Mt Wakakusa-yama ended up being torched. Today, in commemoration, a torch is lit with sacred fire at the Kasuga Taisha shrine, and carried by monks in a procession to the foot of Wakakusa-yama, where the hill is set on fire. It usually burns for 30 minutes before a show of fireworks. The burning begins at 6pm.

The average temperature in Nara in January is 8°C, so rug up. The best viewing is in Nara-kōen, a park on the east side of the city.

While you're there, don't miss Tōdai-ji and Kōfuku-ji – both are World Heritage–listed temples. Tōdai-ji contains the world's largest wooden building. Kōfuku-ji has Japan's second-tallest pagoda. — *www.jnto.go.jp*

Hear the rally roar

MONACO

WHY NOW Watch as a range of really fast cars race around the posh principality

WHERE Monte Carlo, Monaco

DATES 20–25 January 2015 (usually mid/late Jan)

25 JAN

The Rallye Monte-Carlo has been running since 1911, originally designed as a tourism stunt. Cars from across Europe converge on the money-loaded enclave of Monaco and its spectacular surrounding countryside. They must cover almost 1400km, split across 15 treacherous stages – including snow-crusted sections in the Hautes-Alpes, the challenging Sisteron test and a nighttime loop in the mountains above Monaco.

Be there when it all ends in Monte Carlo on the Sunday. There's plenty of fanfare and a traditional awards ceremony at the Prince's Palace, with monarch Prince Albert handing out the prizes. — *www.acm.mca*

LEFT: **Fireworks... in a region noted for its wooden buildings**

BELOW: **Monte Carlo, glitzy setting for one of the world's classic car rallies**

Trek to Roraima

VENEZUELA

WHY NOW Be thankful it's the dry season – at other times of year it *really* rains

WHERE Canaima National Park

DATES December to March

26 JAN

Sir Arthur Conan Doyle's *Lost World* was a place frozen in time, a plateau so removed from the world that dinosaurs continued to roam atop it. The inspiration for Sir Arthur's tale was the sandstone *tepuis* (mesas) of the South American jungles.

Stretching 34 sq km across the borders of Venezuela, Guyana and Brazil, Roraima is the highest of the tepuis but the easiest to ascend. Its scenery is a dreamscape of blackened rocks, gorges, creeks and pink beaches. A few organisms have adapted to the inhospitable conditions, including the little black frog that crawls instead of jumps and the carnivorous plant that traps unwary insects. — *www.venezuelaturismo.gob.ve*

Get fired up at Up-Helly-Aa

SCOTLAND

WHY NOW Celebrate in incendiary style

WHERE Lerwick, Shetland Islands

DATES Last Tuesday in January (27 Jan 2015; 26 Jan 2016; 31 Jan 2017; 30 Jan 2018)

27 JAN

Under Norse rule until 1469, the Shetland Islands choose to honour their heritage each year by setting fire to a replica Viking longship. In the evening, hundreds of wannabe Vikings (or guizers) parade towards the galley with lit torches, pitching them aboard and burning the ship to ashes. Job done, they head off to let down their hair. Through the night the guizers visit many parties; at each they're obliged to dance with at least one lady and drink a dram – by morning their heads are more sore than Thor.

To get there, catch the ferry from Aberdeen. Flights also connect Lerwick to major Scottish cities, including Edinburgh and Glasgow. — *www.visitshetland.com*

Encounter kea

NEW ZEALAND

WHY NOW To meet and marvel at larger gangs of these cheeky birds
WHERE Arthur's Pass National Park, South Island
DATES January and February

28 JAN As soon as you come across kea on New Zealand's South Island, you'll see why these remarkable alpine parrots are described as playful, inquisitive, tame and extremely bold. Their favourite pastimes include rolling in the snow or tumbling gleefully through the air but you may just as easily discover that a gang of kea has stripped the wiper blades from your car. The gangs are at their biggest in January and February, when kea form flocks of up to 20.

In part, these 1kg parrots are merely using their curiosity to test out their world. It's difficult to find food in their alpine environment so they've evolved to try new, sometimes odd food sources. — *www.keaconservation.co.nz*

Climb Adam's Peak

SRI LANKA

WHY NOW To make the walk with local pilgrims in the dry season
WHERE Central Highlands
DATES December to May, the pilgrimage season

30 JAN Adam's Peak (2243m) has fired imaginations for centuries. Sri Lanka's holiest peak has a huge 'footprint' on its summit, which is variously claimed to be the place where Adam first set foot on earth, a sacred footprint left by Buddha as he ascended to paradise, or the indent of St Thomas or Shiva. Little wonder it's become a haunt for pilgrims.

Pilgrimage season, which coincides with hill country's driest months, runs December to May. A steady stream of people make the climb up the countless steps from the settlement of Dalhousie, which is illuminated by lights at this time; this means you can climb at night to summit for a dreamy dawn. — *www.srilanka.travel*

Find culture in Cartagena

COLOMBIA

WHY NOW The Latin outing of the bookish Hay Festival hits the comely colonial city
WHERE Cartagena
DATES 29 January – 1 Feb 2015 (usually late Jan)

29 JAN It all started in Hay-on-Wye, a small riverside town on the Wales–England border. Now the name is synonymous with literary gatherings: Hay Festivals have spread worldwide – and maybe most exotically, to colourful Cartagena in Colombia.

Now one of the most important literary events in the Hispanic world, Cartagena's Hay Festival sees big names in the spheres of literature, visual arts, music, politics, cinema, journalism and the environment get together for lively debates and inspirational lectures. Past attendees have ranged from Hollywood star Gael García Bernal to a troupe of Scottish bongo players.
— *www.hayfestival.com/cartagena*

RIGHT: **Yellowstone's wolf packs are easier to track in the winter**

BELOW: **The cathedral of San Pedro Claver in cultural Cartagena**

Watch wolves in Yellowstone

USA

WHY NOW It's a sublime time for wolf tracking
WHERE Yellowstone National Park, Wyoming
DATES January to March

31 JAN As soon as you reach Yellowstone's Lamar Valley you realise why it's referred to as the Serengeti of North America. Along this sweeping river valley in the northeast corner of the world's oldest park there are clusters of elk, bison, moose and pronghorn antelope, as well as predators ranging from bald eagles to grizzly bears. Convenient viewing lookouts guarantee crowds of tourists in summer, but arrive in winter and you'll find a very different scene.

Set on the slopes of the Continental Divide, Yellowstone is a complex landscape of geysers, hot springs, forests and wilderness. Snow-bound winters can bite the end off a thermometer, so a drive into Lamar may feel suicidal on a January morning. But the laybys will be full of wildlife groupies, all here for the same reason – wolves.

Since wolves were reintroduced here in 1995, the Lamar Valley has become the world's top site for watching wild wolves. And in snow, their paw-prints are easier to track. But winter Yellowstone has many other highlights, from frost-covered bison gathered around hot springs to elk wandering among ghostly trees, the air sparkling with ice crystals. — *www.nps.gov/yell*

Gawp at the Ice & Snow Festival

CHINA

WHY NOW Be dazzled by the most spectacular ice art, accessible via the most epic train

WHERE Harbin, Hēilóngjiāng province

DATES Early January to late February

01 FEB China's northern Hēilóngjiāng province may be cursed with one of the coldest climates in Asia, but its capital Harbin has made the best of a bad thing with its International Ice & Snow Festival. Held in the depths of winter, the festival revolves around an array of elaborate ice sculptures, including re-creations of famous buildings and structures. Past displays have included a scaled-down Forbidden City and a Great Wall of China that doubled as an ice slide.

Most of the sculptures are in central Zhaolin Park and Sun Island Park, while the hardiest of festival-goers can join Harbin's winter swimmers (*brrrrrrr!*) for a dip in the frozen Songhua River.

There are plenty of attractions to take your mind off the cold: admire Harbin's Russian heritage in the Dàolǐqū area and the Church of St Sophia. Don't miss the city's Siberian Tiger Park, which has a mission to breed, release and ultimately save the Siberian tiger from extinction.

And the best way to get here or get away? Travellers taking the Trans-Siberian Railway to or from Moscow can start or finish in Harbin.
— *www.cnto.org*

RIGHT: **SINO – GETTY IMAGES**

February

Whale watch in Baja California

MEXICO

WHY NOW To greet grey whales, the friendliest cetaceans in the seas

WHERE San Ignacio Lagoon, Baja

DATES December to March

02 FEB

The grey whale nearly became extinct back in the 1850s but happily made a remarkable recovery to a stable population at its historic level of around 20,000 of the leviathans. Today it is again possible to witness them return each December to their calving grounds on the coasts of Baja California. This experience is made all the more compelling because the whales have begun responding positively to human presence, with countless tales of mother whales bringing their calves over to boatloads of visitors so the babies can be petted. And it seems that San Ignacio Lagoon, on the Pacific Ocean side of this wild peninsula, has the friendliest whales of all.

Grey whales make the most extraordinary migration of any mammal, travelling 10,000km from the Bering Sea to Baja California for the sole purpose of finding a warm, safe place for their 600kg calves to be born. Males tag along to mate with the many gathered females. And lucky tourists in small boats get to have very close encounters indeed. — *www.visitmexico.com*

Wince at Thaipusam

MALAYSIA

WHY NOW Pierced penitents parade the streets
WHERE Batu Caves, near Kuala Lumpur
DATES Full moon day in tenth Tamil month
(3 Feb 2015; 23 Jan 2016; 9 Feb 2017; 31 Jan 2018)

03 FEB Malaysia's most arresting Hindu festival is an orgy of body piercings, marking the day when Lord Shiva's son, Murugan, was given a lance to vanquish three demons. The greatest sight is the kavadi carriers, the devotees who subject themselves to masochistic acts. Many of the faithful carry offerings of milk in *paal kudam* (milk pots), often connected to their skin by hooks. Even more striking are the *vel kavadi* – great cages of spikes that pierce the skin of the carrier and are decorated with peacock feathers, pictures of deities and flowers. A trance-like state stops participants from feeling pain; the wounds are treated with lemon juice and ash to prevent scarring. — *www.tourism.gov.my*

LEFT: **Watch graceful grey whales at Baja California, Mexico**

BELOW: **Cigar smoking is customary among Thaipusam's devotees**

Spot cheetahs

TANZANIA

WHY NOW Avoid the crowds that come for the Great Migration, but still see great game, in the dry
WHERE Serengeti National Park
DATES January and February, the short dry season

04 FEB While you're almost guaranteed to see a big cat on a safari, the one you're most likely to see bringing down a kill is the cheetah. This is because the cheetah is a diurnal hunter, making it easy to spot on the open plains of the Serengeti. Targeting only the fastest antelopes – impalas and gazelles – a cheetah springs from cover, reaching speeds of 110km/h and making 7m-long bounds to snag its prey. The Wandamu River area in Serengeti National Park has a high cheetah density. Look out for hunting cheetahs during the cooler hours of early morning or late afternoon, when you might spy a cheetah perched atop a termite mound, scanning the horizon. —*www.serengeti.org*

Windsurf at Cabarete

DOMINICAN REPUBLIC

WHY NOW Because the waves are at their best
WHERE Cabarete, north shore
DATES December to March

05 FEB Cabarete's bay seems custom-made for windsurfing. A reef on the bay's upwind side protects it from waves and currents, leaving a huge area of shallow, flat water. With light morning winds and mellow seas, the bay is ideal for beginners. In the afternoon, thermal winds pick up, blowing east to west and reaching speeds of between 25km/h and 40km/h. About 1km out, waves break over a second coral reef, and expert windsurfers head here to practise their 360° spins and end-over-end flips.

Don't come to Cabarete expecting to discover a secret. Its single road is crammed with hotels and shops catering to wind-sport enthusiasts; kiteboarding is also a mainstay here.
— *www.activecabarete.com*

Trek on the Zanskar River

INDIA

WHY NOW Trek while the remote Zanskar River has become a frozen footpath
WHERE Ladakh, accessible via Leh
DATES December to February

06 FEB

The extreme cold in Ladakh means that it's little visited in winter. The mountain passes close and the only way in and out is by air. However, for those hardy souls who want to do something outlandish, there's the chance to trek along the frozen Zanskar River from Chilling to Padum. For Zanskaris this is the only way in and out when the high passes are snowed in. But for trekkers it means about eight days of walking and sleeping in rock shelters.

Conditions are unpredictable: you can expect severe cold, though Ladakh does receive 300 days of sun a year, making for crisp, clear conditions. Also, you'll visit remote Himalayan villages, gain insight into local culture and get to test yourself on one of the region's toughest trekking challenges. — *www.ladakh-tourism.net*

Enjoy the Winter Carnival

CANADA

WHY NOW Join the world's biggest winter bash
WHERE Québec City, Québec
DATES Usually first two weeks of February (30 Jan–15 Feb 2015)

07 FEB

Billing itself as the world's largest winter carnival, the 17-day Carnaval de Québec was first created in 1894 as a way to beat the winter chills.

You'll find night parades, ice slides, dog-sled races, an outdoor cinema and dance parties in the snow. For the bravest Carnival-goer there's the snow bath, requiring three dips into the snow in your swimsuit. However, the carnival's showcase event is the canoe race, in which competitors must paddle 3.2km across the St Lawrence River through a mass of ice.

Bring lots of warm clothes and organise your trip early, as accommodation fills up fast. While there, wander the old walled city; just about every building inside the old walls has some historical interest. The best views are from Terrasse Dufferin. — *www.carnaval.qc.ca*

RIGHT: **An Adélie penguin regards trespassers in the icy Antarctic**

BELOW: **Partying in the snow at Québec's Winter Carnival**

Waddle with Adélie penguins

ANTARCTICA

WHY NOW Chicks must make a solo dash for the sea through a gauntlet of predators
WHERE Cape Adere, north of McMurdo Station
DATES Mid-February

08 FEB

It must be fun to be a penguin. First of all you get to wear a handsome suit. Then you get to hang out in big noisy groups with all your buddies. And, let's face it, you get to be really cute. It's no wonder these comical creatures have always been perhaps the premier attraction for most Antarctic travellers.

As the most common and widespread penguin in the world, the Adélie is readily observed by visitors throughout the Antarctic region, especially from December to March when these 70cm-tall birds gather to nest on the ice-free slopes of rocky coastlines. In the Ross Sea region alone, there are an estimated five to seven million Adélie penguins, including the largest known colony – 250,000 pairs – on Ridley Beach at Cape Adere. There is no feeling like standing among a chaotic sea of squabbling penguins sitting on their little pebble nests or tending their fuzz-ball chicks.

One of the most interesting behaviours occurs in the first half of February when all the Adélie chicks line up in preparation for making a mad dash to the ocean to join their departing parents. It is a terribly anxious and raucous time because their number-one predator, the leopard seal, waits for them at the surf's edge hoping to snag a meal. — *www.antarctica.ac.uk*

Tour skate
on Mälaren

SWEDEN

WHY NOW The ice is excellent, plus you might
catch the legendary Vikingarännet skate race
WHERE Lake Mälaren, West of Stockholm
DATES December to March

09
FEB

Sweden is a heartland for the
pursuit of touring on ice skates.
Whenever the ice is thick enough,
Stockholm's lake and canal system
is exploited by skating enthusiasts
seeking the longest possible 'run'.

Stretching west from Stockholm, Mälaren
is Sweden's third-largest lake and a prime
Nordic skating venue. A short ride on public
transport and you can be skating across the
frozen freshwater, covering up to 100km a day
and stopping at towns and landmarks as you
go – such as the Viking trading centre of Birka,
home to the largest Viking Age cemetery in
Scandinavia.

Mälaren also hosts the Vikingarännet. Started
in 1999, this marathon event sees skaters race
80km from Uppsala to Stockholm – the record
is 2 hours 35 minutes. Vikingarännet is only
held when the lake ice is very thick; the most
probable date is during February.

Stockholm offers extra thrills when the Baltic
Sea freezes. When it does – which happens
about once or twice every 10 years – fantastic
tours of the archipelago are possible. But never
skate alone. — *www.sssk.se/english; www.
vikingarannet.com*

RIGHT: FRANS LEMMENS – GETTY IMAGES

Cruise the Nile

EGYPT

WHY NOW The mighty river is full to bursting, and the weather is wonderfully mild

WHERE Cairo to Aswan

DATES February to April

10 FEB

It's the most timeless of river journeys. The scenes on the banks of the Nile – swaying palms, oxen-ploughed fields, mudbrick farmhouses, ancient stone temples – have changed very little for centuries, if not millennia. Also, the Nile is so much more than a river – it is the lifeblood of Egypt, the water-wall that's believed to divide the land of the living (east) from the land of the dead (west).

To sail along the Nile is the most iconic of Egypt experiences. And February, when temperatures range from around 18°C in Cairo to 25°C in Aswan (see *above*), has the perfect climate for it. February is also when the river is at its fullest, so the floodplains look lush, and there's plenty of water to ensure easy sailing – if you come when the water-level is low, mooring options could be restricted and you may need to be bussed about. And where's the Ancient Egyptian romance in that? — *www.egypt.travel*

Dive Glover's Reef

BELIZE

WHY NOW For lovely weather – it's dry season, between the Christmas and Easter tourist peaks
WHERE 45km offshore, southern Belize
DATES December to May

Named after 18th-century English pirate John Glover, Glover's Reef is the southernmost of Belize's three atolls. Six small cayes of white sand and palm trees are dotted along the atoll's southeastern rim, supporting a handful of low-key resorts and diving bases.

The reef sits atop a ridge on the edge of the continental shelf, surrounded by huge drop-offs. On the east side, where visibility is usually more than 30m, the ocean floor plummets to 800m. Divers regularly see spotted eagle rays, southern stingrays, turtles, moray eels, dolphins, sharks, groupers, barracudas and tropical reef fish. Coral patches in the central lagoon are brilliant for snorkellers. — *www.gloversreef.org*

Climb Aconcagua

ARGENTINA

WHY NOW To stand atop the Americas in the Andean region's best trekking season
WHERE Mendoza
DATES December to March

At 6960m, Aconcagua is the highest mountain outside the Himalayas, but it yields to fit trekkers. It requires at least 15 days, including time to acclimatise to the altitude.

The traditional ascent is the Northwest Route, approached on a 40km trail from Laguna los Horcones; the Polish Glacier Route is longer (76km) and harder but more scenic and less crowded. A third route, the South Face, is a demanding technical climb.

Only experienced climbers should tackle Aconcagua without the relative safety of an organised tour; even skilled climbers often hire guides who know the mountain's Jekyll-and-Hyde weather. — *www.aconcagua.mendoza.gov.ar*

RIGHT: **A wintry Terni. birthplace of Valentine, by night**

BELOW: **Exploring Belize's reefs, one of the world's top scuba-diving destinations**

Look out for platypuses

AUSTRALIA

WHY NOW For the best chance of seeing babies make their first forays into the world
WHERE Eungella National Park, Queensland
DATES December to February

Australia has a lot of odd creatures, but none so hard to fathom as the platypus. Early biologists thought they were a hoax and it didn't help doubters when it was discovered that this semi-aquatic anomaly also laid eggs and possessed poison-bearing spurs on its hind legs.

It is easy to see this animal for yourself. In Queensland's Eungella National Park there are viewing platforms looking down on the Broken River – in which a number of platypuses like to swim. Between December and February you may even glimpse baby platypuses paddling along behind their mothers. Most platypus sightings are made in the early morning or late afternoon, when they feed. — *www.nprsr.qld.gov.au*

Feel the love on Valentine's Day

ITALY

WHY NOW Revel in romance in the hometown of St Valentine

WHERE Basilica di San Valentino, Terni, Umbria

DATES 14 February

14 FEB Where better to swing hands with a loved one on St Valentine's Day than at the St Valentine's feast in the eponymous saint's Umbrian hometown? It is said that in Terni, Valentine would often give gifts of flowers from his own garden to young visitors. Two such visitors fell in love and married, forever linking St Valentine with love. Chocolate-makers and florists have been forever grateful.

Terni dedicates itself to romance throughout February, but you will want to be here for the big day: 14 February. Terni knows this and celebrates St Valentine's Day with a feast around the basilica where the matchmaking saint's remains are interred. The festival includes the 'A Year of Loving' award, which honours a special act of love – a Nobel Prize for Passion.

Ideally, visit Terni with your beloved. Then, hand in hand, pay a visit to St Valentine himself (or at least his enshrined remains) in the 17th-century Basilica di San Valentino, before finding beauty at the artificial Marmore Waterfalls (created by the Romans), 7km out of town.
— *www.umbria-turismo.it*

Dress up for Venice Carnevale

ITALY

WHY NOW To don a mask amid the canals
WHERE Piazza San Marco, Venice
DATES 17 days, from two Fridays before Ash Wednesday to Shrove Tuesday (31 Jan–17 Feb 2015)

15 FEB The world's best-known baroque fancy-dress party, Carnevale Venizia is as extravagant as Rio's Carnaval is riotous. Venetians have celebrated Carnevale since at least the 15th century, when private clubs organised masked balls, and entertainment included bull-baiting and firing live dogs from cannons. By the 18th century Venice was in the grip of hedonism, and Carnevale lasted two months. After years of decline, it was abandoned when Mussolini banned masks. It was revived in 1979, retaking its place among the world's finest festivals.

The official opening is on Saturday, when a masked procession leaves Piazza San Marco around 4pm. Highlights include the Doge's Ball (anyone with a costume and dance skills can go) and a parade of decorated boats and gondolas down the Grand Canal. Plenty goes on outside the main events. Street performers fill the squares and an ice rink is sometimes set up in Campo San Polo. Buy a mask and soak up the Carnevale spirit. — *www.carnevale-venezia.com*

Dance like the devil

BOLIVIA

WHY NOW To watch a cultural 'masterpiece'
WHERE Oruro
DATES 10 days around Ash Wednesday (18 Feb 2015; 10 Feb 2016; 1 Mar 2017; 14 Feb 2018)

16 FEB Listed by Unesco as a Masterpiece of the Oral and Intangible Heritage of Humanity, the Oruro Carnaval is Bolivia's largest annual celebration. Its centrepiece is La Diablada, the 'Dance of the Devils', an extraordinary parade that takes place on the Saturday before Ash Wednesday and features 20,000 dancers and 10,000 musicians. It's led by a costumed San Miguel character. Behind him come the famous devils and a host of bears and condors. When the archangel and the devils arrive at the city's stadium, they dance a story of the battle between good and evil. After good triumphs over evil (hurrah!), the dancers retire to the Santuario de la Virgen del Socavón. — *www.orurocarnaval.com*

Get messy in Binche

BELGIUM

WHY NOW To see Belgium at its most bizarre
WHERE Binche, Province of Hainaut
DATES Shrove Tuesday (17 Feb 2015; 9 Feb 2016; 28 Feb 2017; 13 Feb 2018)

17 FEB Come prepared for a bruising at Belgium's most bizarre carnival, which sees local men, known as *Gilles*, stomp around the town of Binche wearing strange green-eyed masks and shaking sticks to ward off evil spirits.

The *Gilles* slow-dance through town, decked out in all their finery, including enormous headdresses, and accompanied by lads carrying baskets of oranges. From here, things get messy as the crowd is pelted with oranges to bless the forthcoming summer. No matter how tempting, don't hurl one back – it's a gift!

The rituals surrounding the carnival date back centuries; some of the *Gilles*' costumes are up to 150 years old. — *www.carnavaldebinche.be*

Safari in Kgalagadi

BOTSWANA & SOUTH AFRICA

WHY NOW The rains arrive this month
WHERE Kgalagadi Transfrontier Park
DATES February

18 FEB Kgalagadi means 'land of thirst'. The two river courses in this 52,000 sq km park flow only once every 10 years. It's a harsh place, but rich in wildlife. Widely considered a desert, it's technically semi-arid savannah. This becomes clear when the rains arrive in February and transform the landscape with a flush of brilliant-green grasses. It's hard to overstate the excitement: male antelope stake out territories and fight each other for access to harems; predators, including cheetahs and black-maned lions, lurk on the perimeter.

Travel is easiest from the South Africa side of the park. Along the routes, pumps create water holes where some of the best wildlife watching can be found. — *www.sanparks.org*

LEFT: **The mystery of Venice's Carnevale**

BELOW: **Botswana's lions await the wet season in Kgalagadi**

Celebrate Maslenitsa

RUSSIA

WHY NOW Pig out on pancakes before Lent

WHERE Vassilyevsky Spusk, Moscow

DATES Week before Orthodox Great Lent (Great Lent starts 23 Feb 2015; 14 Mar 2016; 27 Feb 2017)

19 FEB

Akin to Mardi Gras, Russia's only surviving pagan festival celebrates the end of winter and the beginning of spring, kicking off Orthodox Lent on a very full stomach. The word 'Maslenitsa' comes from the Russian for butter, which is a key ingredient in the festive treat, bliny. As well as bingeing on Russian pancakes, the week-long festival features horse-drawn sledges, storytelling clowns and beer-drinking bears.

It culminates with the burning of a scarecrow to welcome spring, as well as with Forgiveness Day, in which people ask family and friends for forgiveness for wrongdoings in the past year.

In truth, it's a little early to call this a spring rite, with temperatures in Moscow continuing to hover around -10°C for weeks, so come with plenty of warm clothing.

Maslenitsa is celebrated across Russia but has been truly revived of late in Moscow, where a 'Maslenitsa town' is created in Vassilyevsky Spusk. While there, wander through the Kremlin for a brush with Cold War powerbrokers, and then marvel at onion domes (and an embalmed Lenin) in Red Square.
— *www.moscow.info*

RIGHT: ALAN MARSH – GETTY IMAGES

◉ See monarch butterflies

MEXICO

WHY NOW Monarchs become increasingly active as the days get sunnier
WHERE El Rosario Butterfly Sanctuary, Michoacán
DATES February to March

20 FEB Local Mexican villagers call them *las palomas* – 'souls of the lost children' – because as long as they can remember, monarch butterflies have arrived in time for the Mexican holiday of the Day of the Dead (1 November). The villagers didn't know that they held the answer to one of the great wildlife mysteries of the 20th century: where do the 120 million monarchs of North America go each winter? It wasn't until 1975 that the incredible story of Mexico's wintering monarchs reached the world.

For four to five months the butterflies remain nearly motionless, but on the first warming days in February they begin to stir. Soon, their short flights turn the air into a flurry that resembles a snowstorm of orange flakes as they drift to the ground in search of water and nectar.

Buses run from Mexico City to Angangueo, from where you can access El Rosario by vehicle or on foot. — *www.monarchwatch.org*

Strip at the Naked Festival

JAPAN

WHY NOW See a surreal sumo scrum
WHERE Kannon-in Temple, Okayama
DATES Third Saturday in February (21 Feb 2015; 20 Feb 2016; 18 Feb 2017; 17 Feb 2018)

 21 FEB Saidai-ji Eyō is Japan's most extraordinary naked festival. It looks part sumo, part scrum, part orgy, with thousands of men in loincloths fighting for two sacred *shingi* (wooden sticks), while freezing water is poured over them. Fuelled by alcohol, fights are common. Japan's mafia even fields competitors (look for the black loincloths). There's also a decent chance of hypothermia: average February lows in Okayama are around 1°C.

At 11pm the combatants enter the temple; at midnight, the *shingi* are thrown into the crowd and a frenzy ensues. To claim victory, and a year of good fortune, the sticks must be delivered back to the temple gates. — *www.jnto.go.jp*

Swim with whale sharks

PHILIPPINES

WHY NOW Take to the water with the world's biggest fish
WHERE Donsol, Luzon Peninsula
DATES November to May

 23 FEB Until 1998 Donsol was a sleepy, little-known village. Then a local diver shot a video of the whale sharks that were swimming in the area. Days after a newspaper story about the 'discovery' was published, poachers arrived. Thankfully, hunting whale sharks has since been banned – but now travellers flock here to see the gentle giants.

Today, Donsol is one of the world's top spots to float with the largest fish in the sea – it's truly exhilarating to swim or snorkel alongside them (scuba diving is prohibited). During the peak period of late February to April, the question isn't whether you'll see a shark, but how many. — *itsmorefuninthephilippines.com*

Climb Kilimanjaro

TANZANIA

WHY NOW To stand on the roof of Africa in good weather, and with fewer people
WHERE Northern Tanzania
DATES February

 22 FEB Looming over wildlife-rich plains, Mt Kilimanjaro (5895m) is Africa's highest mountain. It's also one of the continent's most popular trekking challenges. Avoid New Year peak-season crowds, but take advantage of the best weather by climbing in late February.

There are a range of routes up the mountain. The oldest and busiest is the Marangu Route. Of the others, Umbwe is the most direct, Lemosho the longest, Rongai the wildest and Machame arguably the most scenic. It's not an easy hike. The altitude makes every step feel like a mile. The reward from the summit at Uhuru Peak is unforgettable – a sunrise view over what seems like half of Africa. — *www.tanzaniaparks.com*

RIGHT: **Watch out for red-eyed tree frogs in Monteverde's forests**

BELOW: **Fighting for the sacred sticks in Okayama, Japan**

Go wild in Central America

COSTA RICA

WHY NOW To make the most of the drier season for hiking, rafting and wildlife adventures
WHERE Countrywide
DATES Mid-February to April

24 FEB

For number of species per 10,000 sq km, Costa Rica tops the country list with 615. It's a naturalist's nirvana. More than 850 animal species have been recorded, but birds are the big draw. The best time to see the star species, the resplendent quetzal, is November to April.

Not all that's wild in Costa Rica is wildlife. The drier season (December to April) is great for hiking among fumaroles and tropical dry forest in Parque Nacional Rincón de la Vieja, or in the cloud forest reserves of Santa Elena and Monteverde. Those with higher ambitions can scale Costa Rica's highest peak, Cerro Chirripó (3820m), on a 16km trail. Or you could bungy jump from the Río Colorado bridge in San José, find legendary surf at Witches Rock and raft world-class white-water on the Río Pacuare.

Unsurprisingly, the country is busiest in the dry season, but by late February Costa Rican kids will be back in school, making this natural wonderland that little bit quieter.
— *www.visitcostarica.com*

Spot Tasmanian devils

AUSTRALIA

WHY NOW For the best chance to see devils – youngsters are on their own for the first time

WHERE Cradle Mountain-Lake St Clair NP

DATES January and February

25 FEB

Despite its sensational name, Australia's largest marsupial carnivore has a notoriety that is largely undeserved. True, there are the threatening growls, gnashing teeth and blood-chilling screams that can be heard several kilometres away as a horde of devils devour a carcass. And even more unnerving is the sight of a dead wombat bulging and heaving as a devil emerges from inside the body covered in gore – they commonly eat large corpses from the inside out. However, in general Tasmanian devils are shy and solitary creatures rather than the demons of lore.

Life is a struggle from birth for Tasmanian devils. As many as 50 offspring are born at the same time, each about the size of a rice grain, and they must scramble 8cm from the birth canal to their mother's pouch where they battle for access to four teats. There are only four winners and it seems that evolution favours devils that are particularly fierce and strong.

The best way to see these nocturnal carnivores is to drive along forest roads an hour or two after sunset. Newly independent young that are too inexperienced to avoid detection can be spotted in January and February, especially around Cradle Mountain (see *right*). As a bonus, it's Tassie summertime too! — *www.parks.tas.gov.au*

RIGHT: **AUSCAPE – GETTY IMAGES**

Surf the Pipeline

USA

WHY NOW Your best chance to catch a big wave outside pro surfing conditions

WHERE Oahu, Hawaii

DATES February and March

26 FEB Hawaii lies smack in the path of the major swells that race across the Pacific Ocean, with the biggest waves rolling into the north shores of the islands in winter, from November through to February. On Oahu's north shore, the glassy tubes of Banzai Pipeline have become the unofficial world mecca of surfing. Winter swells can bring in 10m waves that break onto a shallow reef, while equally hazardous currents pull at the surfers and boogie boarders.

If you're experienced, your best bet for snagging any space on a wave is to come at dawn, slightly after the peak surf season. Alternatively, wait until the summer when the Pipeline will have mellowed into a swimmers' delight. To find the Pipeline, head for Ehukai Beach Park and walk about 100m to the left. — *www.gohawaii.com*

RIGHT: **It's no lemon – Menton's festival of citrus fruit**

BELOW: **Surfing the Pipeline is for experienced surfers**

Heli-bike the high peaks

NEW ZEALAND

WHY NOW To pedal down from the mountain tops when they're still snow-free

WHERE Countrywide

DATES November to April

27 FEB In New Zealand, they don't like to keep their adventures simple; white-water rafting became black-water rafting. For mountain bikers, the Kiwis upped the ante to heli-biking, a pursuit that sees riders and bikes choppered into the mountains, deposited on the tops and left to freewheel through alpine lands back into town. The views are always spectacular.

This high-adrenalin activity is doable during the summer months, when the routes aren't covered in snow. There's plenty of choice – heli-biking is available in Twizel, the Coromandel Peninsula, Nelson, Rotorua, Taupo and the country's twin adventure capitals, Wanaka and Queenstown. You'll get access to routes usually offlimits to everyone, bar the birds. — *www.helibike.com*

Suck a whole lot of lemons

FRANCE

WHY NOW Find a new zest for life in the south of France at the Fête du Citron

WHERE Menton, French Riviera

DATES Mid-February to early March

28 FEB Citrus is taken seriously in the south of France. The town of Menton – which sits on the Mediterranean, a short hop from the Italian border – is known for its lovely lemons. The fruits thrive in Menton's subtropical microclimate, and chefs worldwide desire them for their dishes; they are known to be rich in essential oils and extremely bright yellow. Consequently, the town has been celebrating its citrus since the 1930s; what started as a few carts of fruit trees being wheeled through the streets has burst into a fantastically fragrant carnival. Around 250,000 people a year flock here for three weeks, from mid-February to early March, to worship the world-class wares.

These days floats are festooned with fruit that's been fashioned into everything from garden gnomes to Ganeshes, from Eiffel Towers to octopuses, from Taj Mahals to tyrannosaurs – each year has a different theme. Some of the citrus sculptures tower up to 10m tall and are made from 140 tonnes of lemons (and oranges too). A crack team of 20 citrus-saviours is on standby to replace any rotten fruit, to keep all the sculptures looking good.

Visitors can wander the sweet-smelling fantasy gardens, watch parades day and night, and raise a glass of lemon-flavoured libation to the fabulous fruit. — *www.fete-du-citron.com*

Spot leopards in Yala

SRI LANKA

WHY NOW It's the best time to see Yala National Park's leopards and elephants
WHERE Yala National Park
DATES February to June

01 MAR

On Sri Lanka's southeast coast, Yala is 1270 sq km of scrub, plains, lagoons and outcrops. And within this diverse park lurks an array of animals, including one of the world's densest leopard populations.

Despite the quantity of wildlife, the forest can make sightings quite hard. Fortunately there are small grassy clearings and lots of waterholes around which the wildlife congregates. The end of the dry season (March to April) is the best time to visit: when it's still dry, the leopards and other animals stay near the remaining water, whereas during the rains they disperse. Other creatures to look for include elephants, sloth bears, fox-like jackals, boars, crocodiles, buffaloes, mongooses and monkeys. Also, a whopping 150 species of birds have been recorded here.
— *www.sltda.lk*

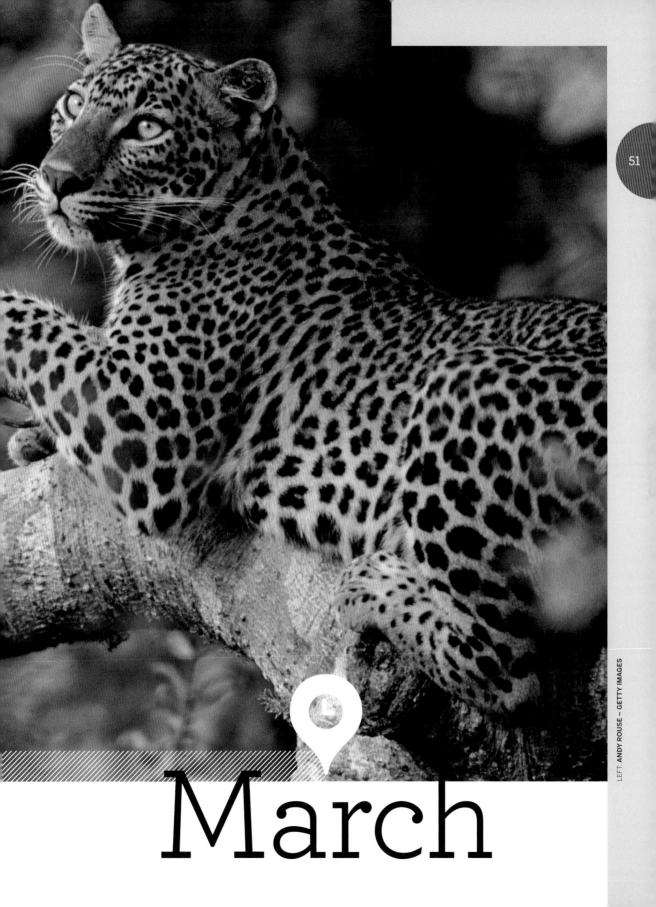

March

Trek the Ruwenzoris

UGANDA

WHY NOW For the best (driest) trekking in the 'Mountains of the Moon'
WHERE Western Uganda
DATES November to March

02 MAR Straddling Uganda's border with the Democratic Republic of Congo, the Rwenzori Mountains (or 'Mountains of the Moon') contain six massifs, culminating in Margherita Peak on Mt Stanley (5109m), Africa's third-highest point.

If you want your wilderness easy this is not the place: the paths are narrow, the bush dense and the bogs deep. To reach the three main peaks requires technical skill, ropes and crampons. The highest point normally reached by trekkers is Elena Hut (4540m), at the snout of Elena Glacier, where the technical routes up Mt Stanley begin. The main access town for treks is Kasese, about a 500km drive west from the capital, Kampala.
— *www.ugandawildlife.org*

Try river-tubing

BELIZE

WHY NOW The low-difficulty, high-fun sport of tubing is best in the dry season
WHERE Caves Branch River
DATES February to April

03 MAR River-tubing – sitting in an inflated inner-tube and floating or paddling along a river – is brilliant in Belize, a country blessed with many gentle, not-too-cold watercourses wending through gorgeous scenery. You go downstream most of the time; the only technique that needs to be learned is to avoid getting beached, eddied or snagged on rocks while continuing to face in roughly the right direction.

The Mopan River near San Ignacio is a popular tubing river, but the mother of Belizean tubing adventures is the float in and out of a sequence of caves on the Caves Branch River, inside the Nohoch Che'en Archaeological Reserve.
— *www.travelbelize.org*

RIGHT: **Turtles reproduce on Sabah's secret beaches**

BELOW: **Pacific Islander culture is celebrated at the Auckland Festival**

Enjoy Kiwi culture

NEW ZEALAND

WHY NOW The Auckland Festival brings amazing local and global arts to the city
WHERE Auckland, North Island
DATES March, biennially (4–22 Mar 2015)

04 MAR Every two years, for most of the month of March, Tamaki Makaurau (the Maori name of Auckland) celebrates cultural diversity in some style. Indeed, the 2013 event featured 300 events and over 1000 artists

The festival programme is diverse, featuring a profusion of performances from Maori and Pacific groups, as well as city favourites such as the Auckland Philharmonia Orchestra and Choirs Aotearoa. There are concerts, art works, drama and a Festival Garden, where the music is free and the vibe always friendly. Don't miss the White Night, when many of the city's museums stay open after hours.
— *www.aucklandfestival.co.nz*

See hawksbill turtles in Borneo

MALAYSIA

WHY NOW Gawp at hawksbills schlepping ashore to lay their eggs en masse

WHERE Pulau Gulisan, Sabah, Borneo

DATES February to April

05 MAR The name 'Borneo' is synonymous with the word 'wild'. And nowhere is it wilder than in the Malaysian province of Sabah, a region of high mountains (including the highest peak between the Himalaya and New Guinea), beautiful coral reefs and a profusion of birds, animals, trees and plants.

Sabah's trademark critters are orang-utans – marvel at these unruly bundles of red hair at the Sepilok Orang-Utan Rehabilitation Centre. But, come March, head out to tiny Pulau Gulisan, one of the three small islands that comprise Turtle Islands National Park. Here, on this 1.6-hectare scrap of sand and trees, you'll see hawksbill turtles plodding ashore to lay their eggs. The females haul themselves up the beach, above the high-water mark; then, using their powerful rear flippers, they dig a chamber, lay their eggs and cover them carefully with sand, hoping to keep their precious load safe until its time for them to hatch.

— *www.sabahparks.org.my*

Throw a paint party on Holi

INDIA

WHY NOW It's Holi, India's rainbow-fest
WHERE Countrywide
DATES Three days around March full moon
(6 Mar 2015, 23 Mar 2016, 13 Mar 2017, 2 Mar 2018)

06 MAR The most boisterous of Hindu festivals, Holi waves goodbye to winter and welcomes in spring in a rainbow of colours. In India it's predominantly celebrated in the north of the country, and is known as the Festival of Colours for the raucous events on Holi's final day, when children and adults take to the streets throwing colourful *gulal* (powder) over each other. Dyed water is shot from syringes, thrown from buckets and poured into balloons, which are then tossed at people. It's sanctioned anarchy and, as a visitor, you'll be a particular target – expect to end up looking like *gulab jamun* (a red, sticky Indian sweet).

Though it runs for three days, Holi is mostly condensed into this final mad day. The night before, huge bonfires are lit at major crossroads in towns and cities and effigies of the demon Holika are burned to symbolise the triumph of good over evil.

Holi's origins are little known but references to it have dated back to around the 3rd century BC. There are many places to witness huge Holi celebrations. In Udaipur, the royal family hosts an elaborate function at the City Palace, while the Uttar Pradesh towns of Mathura, Nandgaon, Vridavan and Barsana are linked with the birth and childhood of Krishna, giving them special Holi significance. — *www.holifestival.org*

RIGHT: **PORAS CHAUDHARY – GETTY IMAGES**

Cheer on the Iditarod

USA

WHY NOW See off the top husky-sledders
WHERE Nome–Anchorage (or vice versa), Alaska
DATES First Saturday in March (7 Mar 2015; 5 Mar 2016; 4 Mar 2017; 3 Mar 2018)

07 MAR Billed as the 'last great race', the Iditarod is one of the planet's most incredible endurance events. First held in 1973, the 1850km race along the Iditarod National Historic Trail between Anchorage and Nome actually commemorates a 'serum run' that saved Nome from diphtheria in 1925, when mushers relayed medical supplies.

Most visitors catch the race at the start – the corner of 4th Ave and E St in Anchorage – but that is strictly ceremonial. The mushers run their teams for only a few miles and then truck them up to Wasilla for a restart of the event. On even-numbered years they race north, and on odd-numbered years they sled south, following one of two routes, crossing two mountain ranges, following the frozen Yukon River and passing through dozens of native villages. The winner usually takes around nine or 10 days.

It's tough to follow this race, so best to cheer the competitors at the start or finish. Also, visit the Iditarod Trail Headquarters in Wasilla, where you can see race memorabilia, as well as take your own dog-sled ride. — *www.iditarod.com*

Ski Niseko

JAPAN

WHY NOW The powder is perfect while the days are getting warmer
WHERE Niseko, Hokkaido
DATES March (ski season Dec–May)

08 MAR

Niseko, on the far-north island of Hokkaido, is a vast ski resort. And it gets a lot of snow – wonderful powdery dumps of the stuff, so it's like skiing through icing sugar. Only cooler. And, by March, the weather isn't quite so chilly, and days are generally sunnier and snow-storm free.

As Niseko is popular with Australian pisters, it means there's an English-speaking infrastructure well in place. That said, when it comes to the end of a great day on the slopes, spurn the Fosters; opt for a hot *sake* and a soak in a steaming *onsen* (thermal spring) to experience apres ski, Japanese style. Or head out on the floodlit runs and keep skiing all night. — *www.jnto.go.jp*

LEFT: **There's no time to pause for breath in the Iditarod race**

BELOW: **Skiing another blue-sky powder day in Niseko, Japan**

Watch blue whales

CHILE

WHY NOW For some of the most reliable sightings of the world's largest creature
WHERE Gulf of Corcovado
DATES December to April

09 MAR

When a team of marine scientists surveyed 4000km of Chilean coast in 1997 they found only 40 of these giant mammals. However, when they hopped a ride back home on a cruise ship crossing the Gulf of Corcovado, a miracle occurred – they found 60 blue whales in 4 hours and discovered what may turn out to be their most important nursery ground.

The pristine waters of the gulf appear to be an ideal haven for nursing whales, who come here to calve during the Chilean summer. The calves grow an astonishing 90kg a day and require prodigious quantities of shrimplike krill.

A Blue Whale Center has been set up in the island town of Melinka. — *www.ballenazul.org*

Tramp the Milford Track

NEW ZEALAND

WHY NOW The holiday crowds have gone but the good conditions have not
WHERE Milford Track, Fiordland, South Island
DATES Late October to April

10 MAR

So popular is the 53.5km Milford Track that in the tramping season (late October to April) permits are required and strict conditions are placed on walkers: only 40 may start each day; accommodation is only in huts; you must follow a set four-day itinerary; and you must walk in one direction. In return, you're treated to a wild (and invariably wet) piece of the World Heritage-listed Fiordland National Park.

The tramp climbs to the crest of Mackinnon Pass. The descent follows the headwaters of the Arthur River, passing by 580m-high Sutherland Falls (the country's highest), before arriving at Milford Sound, where you can kayak out for a multisport ending. — *www.doc.govt.nz*

View nesting leatherbacks

TRINIDAD

WHY NOW It's the start of the nesting season for these vulnerable creatures
WHERE Matura Beach, 50km from Port-of-Spain
DATES March to August

11 MAR

In the sad story of sea turtle conservation, the village of Matura is a ray of hope. In response to plummeting turtle numbers, the Trinidad government acted to protect the world's largest leatherback nesting colony at Matura Beach in 1990. When patrols shut off the area, locals protested the loss of their favourite beach and formed a group called Nature Seekers, taking charge of safeguarding the turtles themselves.

Each night during egg-laying season, these majestic 900kg turtles lumber out of the ocean to nest; sometimes there are up to 150 animals. The Nature Seekers will be out too, measuring, monitoring and guarding against egg-poachers; it's possible to volunteer with them.
— *www.natureseekers.org*

Hike the National Trail

ISRAEL

WHY NOW Hit the desert for a hike before the summer heat arrives
WHERE Tel Dan to Taba
DATES March to May

12 MAR

The country-traversing Israel National Trail was inaugurated in 1995. It rambles for 900km through Israel's least-populated and most scenic areas, from Tel Dan, near the Lebanese border in the north, to Taba on the Red Sea in the south. It is remarkably varied and beautiful.

It takes around 45-60 days to complete the trail. For a short taster, head to the Eilat Mountains at the route's southern end. From the waterfall at Ein Netafim, 1km off the main road, follow the trail to Shehoret Canyon, 15km away. Near the mouth of Shehoret sit the Amram Pillars, where there's a campsite. Keep walking south for a few hours to the trail's end, passing through the Nakhal Gishron gorge to the Egyptian border. — *www.israeltrail.net*

RIGHT: **Austin is the cultural capital of Texas, USA**

BELOW: **Route-finding on Israel's National Trail, with Mt Eilat in the background**

Go music mad at South by Southwest

USA

WHY NOW Listen your ears off at the top Texas tune-fest that is South by Southwest (SXSW)

WHERE Austin, Texas

DATES Early to mid-March (13-21 Mar 2015)

13 MAR Here's further proof that things really are big in Texas, with a music festival so large it has almost single-handedly earned Austin the title of 'live music capital of the world'. Started in 1987, the South by Southwest Music & Media Conference brings the music industry and performers together for 10 days – bands come to be discovered and music execs come to discover them. During the day, industry buffs head to the Austin Convention Center to talk shop at a trade show, and by night more than 1200 acts perform at 50 or so venues across the city.

Coupled with the music festival, SXSW has swelled considerably in recent years to include a film festival and conference, and a festival for interactive media.

Registering for a Platinum Badge gets you into all three trade shows, conferences, screenings, clubs and VIP lounges; it costs less if you buy it in advance. A cheaper Music Badge allows entry into the music conference, trade show and nightly gigs. It's not possible to buy single session or single day passes to the event.

If you want even more live music (really, *more*?!) just spend an ordinary day roaming around appealing Austin, where bands regularly play at supermarkets, record shops – even at the airport. — *sxsw.com*

Raise a glass at Starkbierzeit

GERMANY

WHY NOW It's Strong Beer Time!
WHERE Paulaner Keller, Munich
DATES Two weeks around St Joseph's Day
(19 March)

 14 MAR Meet Oktoberfest's little brother, the down-to-earth sibling whose company can be enjoyed without the crowds. For Bavarians, Starkbierzeit (Strong Beer Time) marks a new season of beer drinking, coming just as summer begins to peep over the horizon.

Starkbierzeit is when brewers parade their most lethal ales, the *doppelbocks* (alcohol content: 7%+). The festival harks back to Paulaner monks in the 17th century, who brewed the first *doppelbock* to help them through their Lent fast. Starkbierzeit's first keg is tapped at the Paulaner Keller. You'll also find stone-lifting contests taking place in the Löwenbräukeller beer hall. Just follow the grunts.
— *www.muenchen.de*

View a violent volcano

MONTSERRAT

WHY NOW March is a marginally cooler month – plus the islanders love St Patrick's Day!
WHERE Montserrat, Leeward Islands
DATES March

 16 MAR Montserrat was given a big how-do-you-do by the Soufrière Hills Volcano on 18 July 1995, ending 400 years of dormancy. Its capital, Plymouth, was abandoned and tourists all but disappeared. In 1997 the volcano erupted again. It still lets off the occasional puff, but life has regained some normalcy, with 5000 people living in the northern third of the island.

The volcano itself isn't accessible, but there are good viewing points, and you can visit the Montserrat Volcano Observatory. Although much of the ocean surrounding the southern part of the island is off-limits, what is left of Montserrat's diving is legendary, and remains in near pristine condition. — *www.visitmontserrat.com*

Sail down the Amazon

BRAZIL

WHY NOW The fine weather coincides with high water levels, putting you eye-level with animals
WHERE Anavilhanas Archipelago
DATES November to April

 15 MAR The ultimate Amazon fantasy trip is to set sail on an expedition up the world's mightiest river. Many boats on such a mission – complete with captain and crew, living quarters and kitchen – are available from Manaus.

Manaus offers access to rivers and minor tributaries, but there's no better option than to motor 60km up the Rio Negro and weave into the 80km-long web of channels and islands of the Anavilhanas Archipelago Ecological Station.

From November to April the river is at its highest, flooding swathes of igapo forest. This protects the archipelago from human encroachment, making it a haven for wildlife.
— *www.visitbrasil.com*

RIGHT: **Wear some green to mark St Patrick's Day, wherever you are**

BELOW: **Monserrat smoulders**

Celebrate St Patrick's Day

IRELAND

WHY NOW Raise a glass of the black stuff to Ireland's patron saint

WHERE Dublin

DATES 17 March

17 MAR Wherever there's a Plastic Paddy, there's a St Patrick's Day festival, complete with green beer, blarney and craic. But the most authentic way to celebrate Ireland's patron saint is in the country's capital, Dublin. The mother of all Irish festivals, it sees hundreds of thousands gather on city streets and in venues throughout the centre to 'honour' the saint who apocryphally drove out Ireland's snakes. You'll find street theatre, a fairground and a music festival, with the famous St Patrick's Day street parade on 17 March to round out the festivities. The parade begins at midday, starting on Parnell Sq before heading down O'Connell St, through College Green to an appropriate end at St Patrick's Cathedral. If you want the best view of proceedings, it's possible to purchase grandstand seating.

Don't fancy the parade? Head to the Temple Bar area's eateries and drinking holes – an equally traditional way to spend St Pat's Day. And while you're in town, go to the source of much of the merriment: join a tour of the city's Guinness Brewery. — *www.stpatricksfestival.ie*

Be dazzled by the Northern Lights

SCANDINAVIA

WHY NOW The most awesome aurora displays often occur around the spring equinox
WHERE Far north Scandinavia
DATES September to April; equinox is 20 March

18 MAR

The Finns call them *revontuli* – fox fires – believing the phenomenon to be snow-spray swept up by the tail of a magical beast. Norwegians reckon they're the spirits of old maids performing a dance. The Sami people of Lapland thought of them as the energy created by the souls of the dead. In short, the Northern Lights have fascinated humans for centuries.

The scientific explanation is more prosaic. Auroras are formed from solar particles thrown out by explosions on the sun; when these particles near earth they're drawn to the magnetic poles, where they collide with atmospheric gases to emit photons of myriad shapes and colours. Most common are green aurora, but reds, yellows and purples can be seen. Their movement is mesmerising – on an aurora-active night, the lights shift into luminous whirls and streams.

Viewing is best in the auroral zone, close to the Arctic Circle. This includes the upper reaches of Norway, Sweden and Finland, as well as Alaska, northern Canada, Russia, Iceland and Greenland. Visit September–April, when the nights are dark; the warmer spring equinox is perhaps the very best time. And keep your fingers crossed for clear skies. — *www.gi.alaska.edu/AuroraForecast*

LEFT: ANTONY SPENCER – GETTY IMAGES

Feel the fire
at Las Fallas

SPAIN

WHY NOW Throw yourself headlong into spring's most flammable festivities
WHERE Valencia
DATES 12–19 March

19 MAR Exuberant and anarchic, Las Fallas is Europe's wildest spring party – not bad for what is essentially a glorified puppet show, thought to have been first held in the late 15th century. These days Valencia is taken over by the *fallas* – huge sculptures of papier-mâché on wood, built by local artists. Each neighbourhood sponsors its own *falla*, and when the town wakes after the *plantà* (overnight placement of the fallas) on 16 March, more than 350 have been erected. Reaching up to 15m in height, and costing up to €350,000 to build, these grotesque effigies satirise celebrities and current affairs.

Though the festival begins on 12 March, it doesn't really get going until after the *plantà*. The *fallas* are placed at various locations around the city and you have four days to wander about checking out the displays as well as revelling in the around-the-clock festivities, which include street parties, paella-cooking competitions, parades, open-air concerts and bullfights.

Las Fallas prides itself on its fireworks: each day at 2pm a *mascletà* (five minutes of deafening thumps and explosions) shakes the city. At midnight on the final day – 19 March, St Joseph's Day – each *falla* goes up in flames in another fiery explosion, with months of work turning to ash in seconds. Thirty minutes after midnight, it's the turn of the *falla* judged the festival's best to be burned. — *www.turisvalencia.es*

See in the spring equinox

MEXICO

WHY NOW Witness a Mayan masterstroke

WHERE Chichén Itzá, Yucatán

DATES 20 March, spring equinox

20 MAR At the ruined city of Chichén Itzá, the Mayan creators of the El Castillo pyramid devised a quirk that would live for centuries. Such is its architectural precision that during the vernal equinox – when night and day are of almost equal length – the morning and afternoon sun produces a light-and-shadow illusion of a serpent ascending or descending the side of El Castillo's staircase. It's a spectacular moment, with the only drawback being the fact that the site is mobbed. The illusion is almost as good in the week preceding and following each equinox, and these times draw smaller crowds.

If you've got a car you can do the double by catching the equinox dawn at Dzibilchaltún, where the sun aligns with the main door of the Templo de las Siete Muñecas, making the doors light up. — *www.visitmexico.com*

Respect Nyepi (New Year)

INDONESIA

WHY NOW See in New Year in silence

WHERE Bali

DATES The first new moon after mid-March (21 Mar 2015; 9 Mar 2016; 28 Mar 2017; 17 Mar 2018)

21 MAR If you don't like riotous New Years, then Bali has the do for you. The day before Nyepi, Tawur Agung Kesanga, is the 'Day of Great Sacrifices'. At 4pm villagers gather in town centres, playing music and offering gifts to the *ogoh-ogoh*, huge monster dolls with menacing fingers and bulging eyes. This is followed by the *ngrupuk*, when the *ogoh-ogoh* are paraded through the streets to frighten away evil spirits. After prayers, the dolls are burnt in a final symbolic gesture. Much revelry ensues.

Nyepi is a day of utter inactivity, so that when the evil spirits descend they will decide Bali is uninhabited and leave the island alone. It is the 'Day of Silence', and all human activity stops – venues close and no-one is allowed to leave their home or hotel. — *www.bali-tourism-board.com*

LEFT: **Fiery figurines burn during Las Fallas in Spain**

BELOW: **Look for the serpentine shadows down Chichén Itzá's steps around the spring equinox**

Swim out to Ningaloo Reef

AUSTRALIA

WHY NOW There's a good chance of seeing spawning coral and the world's biggest fish
WHERE Ningaloo Marine Park, Western Australia
DATES March and April

22 MAR You're likely to come to Ningaloo to see its biggest animal, but if you're lucky you might see its smallest too. Each year, on a single night a few days after the full moons in March and April, the entire reef gives 'birth'. This mass coral spawning happens suddenly, without warning. For a few hours the ocean turns pink as trillions of packets of coral sperm and eggs flood the waters.

Not only is the synchronised release beautiful to watch, but it attracts swarms of zooplankton and bait fish for a massive feeding frenzy. This in turn draws in large numbers of whale sharks, jellyfish and manta rays. The 12m-long whale sharks hang around in good numbers until June, making this the best time of year to see this behemothic freight-train of a fish.

Ningaloo is Australia's largest fringing coral reef, spanning 260km of coastline; it's a reef you can easily swim to from shore (as opposed to a barrier reef that you'd have to take a boat to see); and everywhere you look there are profusions of corals and fish.
– *www.tourism.wa.gov.au*

Giggle at meerkats

SOUTH AFRICA

WHY NOW There's a good chance of seeing adorable meerkat youngsters
WHERE Addo Elephant National Park
DATES February to April

23 MAR Few animals have the charisma of the diminutive meerkat. To properly appreciate their antics, head to a park such as Addo, in South Africa.
Meerkat social life is built around a pack of 10 to 30 members. The day starts with a session of grooming before a foraging expedition. A sentry is posted to cry out if a hawk flies over, but if a ground predator appears the pack jumps up and down together to give the illusion that they're charging. Otherwise their day is spent tousling, rolling around and playing 'follow the leader'. Everyone pays attention to the pups that emerge from the burrows after January, and the pack takes turns at nursery duty.
— *www.sanparks.org/parks/addo*

LEFT: **Meet giant whale sharks over the Ningaloo Reef**

BELOW: **Savour Swedish waffles with lingon berries**

Climb Fansipan

VIETNAM

WHY NOW Hike in the driest months, when the wildflowers are in full bloom
WHERE Lào Cai Province, northwest Vietnam
DATES February and March

24 MAR Technical skills are not required to reach the summit of Vietnam's highest peak, 3143m Fansipan – the 'Roof of Indochina' – but endurance, and a guide, are helpful. Despite the short distance (19km), the round-trip hike will take around three to four days. There are no mountain huts so you'll need to be self-sufficient.
The region is rich in minority villages, but after the first morning you won't see any signs of civilisation; just the forest, striking mountain vistas and crashing waterfalls. You might also spot local wildlife such as monkeys, mountain goats, birds and beautiful orchids – almost 2000 species of plants and 320 species of animals have been recorded here. — *www.vietnamtourism.com*

Gorge on waffles

SWEDEN

WHY NOW Celebrate (and scoff) on Waffle Day!
WHERE Sweden
DATES 25 March

25 MAR Sweden in March: the south is just about warming up for spring, the north is still icy (albeit with ace aurora and more daylight). But the improving weather is not the reason to visit today. It's because this is Våffeldag – Waffle Day. Yes – a day celebrating the waffle.
It sounds like a scheme cooked up by a big-brand batter-magnate, hoping to make more dough. But the real root of it is far more unlikely. On 25 March it's the Feast of the Annunciation, when the Angel Gabriel told Mary she was pregnant with Jesus; in Swedish 'Or Lady' (*Vår Fru*) sounds a bit like *Våfflor* – waffle. A linguistic mix up that's turned a holy day into a hotcake one. There's nothing for it: you must worship the waffle. — *www.visitsweden.com*

Have a hanami

JAPAN

WHY NOW Hold the perfect picnic party under a blossoming cherry tree
WHERE Across Japan
DATES March and April

26 MAR One of the most beautiful natural sights in Japan is groves of cherry trees in full bloom, giving the appearance of earthly clouds of flowers. Viewing the blossoms is such a big event that national news services carry maps of its progress. It's a time when the Japanese throw away their reserve and decide to party.

Hanami (blossom party) tradition is to have a picnic amid the trees; parties begin with the arrival of the earliest buds and endure to the last clinging blooms. Both daytime parties and moonlit soirees are standard, as crowds flood the parks to enjoy beer and good humour.

You can enjoy hanami anywhere there's blossom, but a few places have become faves. In Tokyo, Ueno-kōen has 1000 flowering cherry trees and is ground zero for the hanami explosion. In Kyoto, try Maruyama-kōen, where the centrepiece is a massive weeping cherry tree. The top blossom spot, however, is the mountain-top Kansai town of Yoshino, where thousands of cherry trees form a floral carpet gradually ascending the mountainsides.
— *www.jnto.go.jp*

RIGHT: **OLIVER J DAVIS – GETTY IMAGES**

Go to the Galápagos

ECUADOR

WHY NOW The sea is warm, the turtles are
nesting and seal pups line the shores
WHERE 1000km west of mainland Ecuador
DATES March and April

27 MAR The Galápagos Islands guarantee
close encounters of the wildlife
kind – above *and* below the sea.
This remote archipelago was known
to early explorers as Las Islas
Encantadas (the Enchanted Isles) and none of its
enchantment has been lost down the centuries.

Visitors continue to fall under the islands'
spell as they step over dozing sea lions to
come face-to-face with abundant birdlife and
lumbering giant tortoises.

Large marine mammals are abundant. Sea
lions and fur seals thrive in the rich waters of
the Humboldt Current and visitors are almost
guaranteed close interactions. While cruising
between islands keep an eye out for dolphins
and whales. Reptiles are the islands' pin-up
inhabitants, with giant tortoises, land iguanas
and marine iguanas in abundance.

In March and April, look out for the
curious courtship dances of the albatross and
blue-footed boobies. — *www.galapagos.org*

View hunting killer whales

ARGENTINA

WHY NOW The killer whales arrive to burst onto the beaches and eat seal pups
WHERE Valdés Peninsula
DATES Late March

Killer whales (orcas) are one of the world's most spectacular animals, and of all their behaviours nothing beats the show they put on at Argentina's Valdés Peninsula. This World Heritage site is a desolate thumb of land jutting into the Southern Atlantic Ocean. From December, sea lions gather to mate and give birth here. Towards the end of March, pups line up on the beach and make their first forays into the ocean. This is when killer whales arrive. These 10m-long predators catch seal pups by ramming forward with such speed that the whales actually launch themselves out of the water in an explosion of foam, land on the beach, grab a pup, and slide back into the ocean. — *www.pnor.org*

Have a lot of laughs

AUSTRALIA

WHY NOW Go for a right giggle at the Melbourne International Comedy Festival
WHERE Melbourne, Victoria
DATES Late March, for three weeks

Laugh your ruddy socks off, cackle until you cry, guffaw so much your belly aches: antipodean autumn sees Melbourne host the world's third-largest comedy festival (behind Montréal and Edinburgh). And it will tempt a titter from even the most miserablist onlooker.

For three weeks the Aussie city is taken over by stand-up comics, cabaret artists, actors and street performers as well as film screenings and multimedia broadcasts. The Melbourne Town Hall precinct becomes a huge comedy hub, and acts – both big-name and undiscovered talents – pop up all over the city Mostly, it's just a lot of fun. — *www.comedyfestival.com.au*

RIGHT: **A paraglider soars above the Cape peninsula, South Africa**

BELOW: **Spruiking the Melbourne Comedy Festival, Australia**

Climb El Capitan's Nose

USA

WHY NOW Spring and autumn are the best times to climb on El Cap
WHERE Yosemite National Park, California
DATES March to May

The most famous route on the most famous climbing rock in the world, El Capitan's Nose is where big-wall climbing was born. Guarding the entrance to the sublime Yosemite Valley, El Capitan is an imposing granite monolith rising 1000m above the Merced River.

The first ascent of the Nose was made in 1958 and took the combined efforts of 45 days of climbing. Most climbers now take five days to make the 31-pitch ascent. The elite scale it in a single day; the very quickest do it in 3 hours.

The Nose is not regarded as being technically difficult but it is long and exposed. If unsure, enjoy standing at the bottom and just watching the daredevils instead. — *www.nps.gov/yose*

Paraglide in Western Cape

SOUTH AFRICA

WHY NOW The thermals are strong but suitable for gliding beginners
WHERE Cape Town and beyond
DATES March and April

31 MAR South Africa is one of the world's top paragliding destinations. For experienced pilots, airspace restrictions are minimal and the potential for long-distance, cross-country flying is tremendous. Your own transport is essential to reach the best sheltered sites in Porterville (a ridge site), Hermanus (a coastal site) and at Sir Lowry's Pass (a ridge site). When conditions permit, it's possible to fly from Table Mountain, Lion's Head and Signal Hill and land on the beach at Clifton or Camps Bay. Soaring along the Twelve Apostles as the tablecloth cloud forms around you is a near-biblical experience.

The strongest thermals in these parts blow from November to April; the months of March and April provide the best conditions for beginners to take a leap off Table Mountain, flying tandem with an experienced paraglider.

It's an easy and safe sport to learn – the South African Hang Gliding and Paragliding Association can provide names of tour operators, and plenty of schools offer a range of courses for beginners as well as for more advanced pilots.
— *www.sahpa.co.za*

Wade into the Pantanal

BRAZIL

WHY NOW Explore the World Heritage-listed wetlands during one of its two dry seasons

WHERE Pantanal

DATES April to May

01 APR The Amazon may attract more fame and glory, but the vast Pantanal wetlands in the centre of South America are a better place to see wildlife. They contain the greatest concentration of fauna in the New World, and while the Amazon's dense foliage hides its animals, the Pantanal's open spaces make the wildlife visible to the most casual observer.

The Pantanal is more than half the size of France. It has few people and no towns. Distances are so great and ground transport so poor that people get around in small airplanes and motorboats. The only road that runs deep into the Pantanal is the Transpantaneira. This raised dirt road was supposed to stretch to the Bolivian border but two-thirds of the intended route has been left incomplete for lack of funds.

April and May form one of the Pantanal's two dry seasons. The area floods in wet season (October to March). The waters teem with fish, and the ponds provide excellent niches for animals and plants. Later in the dry, the water recedes, lagoons and marshes dry out and fresh grasses emerge. — *www.pantanal.org*

RIGHT: **NATPHOTOS – GETTY IMAGES**

April

Go wet and wild in Sinharaja

SRI LANKA

WHY NOW The beginning of the rainy season in April brings everything back to life
WHERE Sinharaja National Park
DATES Early April

02 APR Sri Lanka's Sinharaja National Park is a real conservation success story. First set aside in the third century BC as a *thahanakelle* (protected forest) by tribal law, it held sway in local legend as the home of Sinharaja, 'the Lion King', a mythological lion who ruled the region until vanquished. In recognition of the forest's stellar biodiversity, Dutch colonists declared the area a reserve in 1875, and it was further protected by the new Sri Lankan government in 1977 after national outcry over logging activity.

Even though Sinharaja constitutes a mere 0.7% of Sri Lanka's land area, it is home to half of the island's endemic species. There's a vibrant mix of endemic birds, from red-faced malkohas to Ceylon hanging-parrots, plus spectacular dipterocarp trees. These forests, with their 45m-high canopies, are crisscrossed by clear streams and are home to many animals such as the slender loris, the purple-faced leaf monkey, the wrinkled frog and the torrent toad. You'd be lucky to spot a leopard, but can console yourself with seeing the world's largest butterflies.

Go at the very beginning of the rainy season to experience the resurgence of life, but don't linger too long: once the wet gets going, rainfall can reach 6m a year and the trails will be a bit of a slog. — *www.slwcs.org*

Lose your marbles

ENGLAND

WHY NOW See the World Marble Championships
WHERE The Greyhound, Tinsley Green, Sussex
DATES Good Friday (3 Apr 2015; 25 Mar 2016;
14 Apr 2017; 30 Mar 2018)

03 APR

You may have played marbles as a kid but did your parents ever tell you that if you knuckled down you could be a world champ? The championships are held in the car park of this West Sussex pub, where competitors vie for honours inside a 6ft concrete circle. The championships have been held here since 1932.

Competition marbles sees 49 of the glass balls placed in the ring; the first person or team to knock 25 out with their tolley (shooting marble) goes through to the next round. The event attracts players from Europe and the USA, with German teams winning a couple of world titles, something the Brits ruefully blame on their own excessive alcohol intake. Tinsley Green is very near Gatwick Airport if you're planning an international entrance. — *greyhoundmarbles.com*

Watch sea otters

USA

WHY NOW You can enjoy beautiful weather and observe the otter pups
WHERE Monterey Bay, California
DATES April and May

04 APR

The rugged beauty of California's coastline is greatly enhanced by the presence of the cutest marine mammal of all. Sea otters are a delight to watch, whether they are rolling around in play, banging on a crab with a rock or scrubbing their faces with deft hands.

It's fortunate that they're still around: it was thought that they'd been hunted into extinction by the early 1900s. However, a tiny group of 50 was discovered on California's Big Sur coast in 1911. Today the population hovers at around 2000.

There is no better place for observing sea otters than from the charming village of Pacific Grove, at Monterey Bay. Grab a seat on a shoreline bench to see them bob in undulating kelp beds.

For closer views, visit the otter exhibit at the Monterey Bay Aquarium. — *www.monterey.com*

LEFT: **An Agamid lizard in Sinharaja National Park, Sri Lanka**

BELOW: **Sea otters say 'hey!' at Monterey**

Observe
Semana Santa

SPAIN

WHY NOW To feel the heart of Holy Week

WHERE Seville, Andalucía

DATES Holy Week (29 Mar–5 Apr 2015; 20–27 Mar 2016; 9–16 Apr 2017; 25 Mar–1 Apr 2018)

05 APR Easter week is a big deal across the Spanish-speaking world but it's in Seville that it's celebrated with the most gusto. Here, Holy Week rites go back to the 14th century; they took their present form around 300 years later, when many of the images – some of them supreme works of art – were created.

For eight days (from Palm Sunday to Easter Sunday) floats with large, richly bedecked images and life-size tableaux of scenes from the Easter story are carried from Seville's churches, following the shortest route through the streets to the cathedral. There are around 115 floats, carried by about 60,000 hooded members of 57 religious brotherhoods, or *cofradías*. Each *cofradía* usually carries two floats, one containing a figure of Christ and the other with a statue of the Virgin. The processions are so long, and the floats so heavy (each bearer supports about 50kg), they take more than an hour to pass. Huge crowds line the routes to watch the spectacle.

The most important of Seville's Semana Santa processions takes place at midnight on Maundy Thursday. At this time there can be more than one million people lining the streets of the *carrera oficial*, watching as Seville's six oldest and most respected brotherhoods parade somberly through the streets until past dawn.

— *www.spain.info*

See the 'fifth' season

ESTONIA

WHY NOW Witness a unique climatic change in the Baltic wilderness
WHERE Soomaa National Park
DATES Late March to April

06 APR Spring, summer, autumn, winter – so passé! If you want to mix up the regular calendar a little, head for the boglands of Soomaa, southwest Estonia, in April – for a fifth season.

At this time, the melted snow waters gushing down from the uplands raise water levels (by up to 5m) and transform the landscape. This national park of rivers, wetlands and swamps is temporarily submerged under the deluge. Plains turn into lakes, tracks become waterways and tussock mounds morph into isolated islands.

The 'fifth' is the best time for watery fun in Soomaa (indeed, by boat is the only way to get around). Join a guided canoe trip for the unique chance to paddle on 'dry land'. Scull through the forest, looking out for eagles and beavers, and listening for wolves. — *www.soomaa.com*

Spy on a reclusive country

NORTH KOREA

WHY NOW It's a beautiful time in North Korea, with mild temperatures and flowers blooming
WHERE Pyongyang and beyond
DATES April and May

07 APR Off the beaten path is too slight a term for a nation that admits fewer than 2000 Westerners a year. North Korea is a place frozen in the Cold War. Visitors are escorted at all times by guides. There's no internet access for tourists and there are just a handful of flights into the capital, Pyongyang, each week. These zealous measures make North Korea a magnet for those seeking a cultural adventure.

Once through the North Korean red tape, trips here usually run like clockwork. A visit to the Demilitarized Zone (DMZ) is a must. To add some extra adventure, plan a trip to Mt Paekdu, the highest peak in Korea (2744m) and, according to official sources, the birthplace of Kim Jong-il – though Soviet records state he was born in Khabarovsk, Russia. — *www.korea-dpr.com*

LEFT: **Nazarenos, the 'penitent ones', in a Holy Week procession in Seville**

BELOW:
Neighbourhood Watch – looking over Myohyangsan, mountain in North Korea

Ski the Haute Route

FRANCE, ITALY & SWITZERLAND

WHY NOW Warmer weather and suitable snow

WHERE Chamonix to Zermatt

DATES April

08 APR

One of the world's top ski-touring trails, the Haute Route links the two most celebrated mountains of the European Alps, crossing from the French resort of Chamonix, at the foot of Mont Blanc, to the Swiss town of Zermatt, in the shadow of the Matterhorn.

Covering around 140km, the route was pioneered on foot by members of the Alpine Club in the 1860s. While it remains a popular summer trek (on a slightly different route), it's best known as a classic spring ski-mountaineering expedition. It's prized both for its challenging terrain and its parade of big-name mountains – Mont Blanc, Monte Rosa, Grand Combin and the Matterhorn will be your touring companions.

Ski tourers usually take six or seven days to complete this hut-to-hut route, which crosses more than 20 glaciers and follows a high line across the snow-plastered slopes of the Alps, rarely dipping into valleys. Pushing across a number of passes, including the spectacular Val d'Arpette, with its views down onto the fractured surface of Glacier du Trient, the route tops out on Pigne d'Arolla, at around 3800m – high enough to make your head spin from more than exertion.

You'll drag your ski-strapped feet over climbs totalling around 10,000m. Skiing days on the Haute Route can be difficult, so limber up on less gruelling tours before. — *www.chamonix.com*

Canyoneer in Paria Canyon

USA

WHY NOW Hit the slots in spring to avoid the prospect of summer or winter flash floods

WHERE Arizona–Utah border

DATES April and May

09 APR Much of Southwest USA's most stunning sights are within serpentine corridors of stone. Some of these narrow to become slot canyons, and offer some of the best canyoneering anywhere, with technical climbing, swimming in pools and shooting down waterfalls.

Paria Canyon, on the Arizona–Utah border, is one of the most beautiful. Its biggest attraction is Buckskin Gulch, a deep, 19km-long canyon only 5m wide for most of its length. Wire Pass and Buckskin are popular trailheads, and serious canyoneers can tackle the five-day, 61km trek through to Lees Ferry through this, the longest and most flash-flood-prone canyon in the world. — *www.utah.com*

Tree climb in Pemberton

AUSTRALIA

WHY NOW It's the least windy month, which you'll appreciate when you're 75m up a tree
WHERE Pemberton, Western Australia
DATES April

 10 APR Growing up to 90m tall, Western Australia's endemic karri tree is one of the giants of the wooden world. Eight karri trees were chosen in the first half of the 20th century as fire-lookout trees; platforms were built at their tops and metal spikes hammered into their trunks. Today, three of the trees have been designated as 'climbing trees', allowing visitors to ascend them. The rewards are views over hillsides thick with old-growth forest and a well-earned certificate.

The most popular is the 61m Gloucester Tree, 3km from the milling town of Pemberton. At 75m, the Dave Evans Bicentennial Tree is the tallest of the three. Bring good shoes and a head for heights. — *www.pembertonvisitor.com.au*

Walk the 88 Temple Circuit

JAPAN

WHY NOW It's a long walk and you want to be finished before the heat of summer fully kicks in
WHERE Tokushima, Shikoku
DATES April

 11 APR Japan's best-known pilgrimage is the lengthy 88 Temple Circuit on the island of Shikoku. Kōbō Daishi, Japan's most revered saint, is said to have chosen the 1400km route. Allow two months to walk it; it begins in Tokushima and is usually walked in a clockwise direction.

Some of the temples are only a few hundred metres apart; others more than 100km. Individually, none are that interesting; it's the whole circuit that counts. The 88 temples represent the number of evil human passions defined by the Buddhist doctrine; completing the circuit is said to rid you of these. — *www.shikokuhenrotrail.com*

RIGHT: **Enjoy Songkran in Bangkok**

BELOW: **Stay away, greys – red squirrels, such as this youngster, are most easily spotted in Scotland**

Seek out red squirrels

SCOTLAND

WHY NOW To see spring's baby squirrels
WHERE Abernethy Forest, near Nethy Bridge
DATES April and May

 12 APR If the number of devoted websites and working groups is any measure, the red squirrel ranks as one of Great Britain's most beloved creatures. These pointy-eared squirrels are charismatic, but their population is suffering from an influx of North American grey squirrels. The latest count was red squirrels 140,000 and falling; grey squirrels 2.5 million and growing.

One of the original denizens of the great pine woods felled more than 1000 years ago, about 85% of Britain's red squirrel population is in Scotland, with a sizable number surviving in the Scots pines at the Abernethy Forest Reserve. Here, watch them scamper and scold and chase, and introduce their babies to the world. — *www.forestry.gov.uk/forestry/Redsquirrel*

Get soaked at Songkran

THAILAND

WHY NOW Cool down at Thai New Year – the world's biggest water fight

WHERE Countrywide

DATES 13–15 April

13 APR The Lunar New Year in Thailand marks a time when the country literally goes to water. Part a time of respect and part riot, Songkran is an occasion when images of the Buddha are 'bathed' and young Thais seek the blessing of their elders by pouring scented water over their hands. After that, it's a water-throwing free-for-all – traditionally, the custom was to pour water gently over other people but it has evolved into an almighty water fight.

Held in the hot season, Songkran is a chance for the country to cool off. For the three days of the celebration nobody is safe from a dousing. Water balloons are launched at unsuspecting passers-by, water guns are fired from bicycles, motorbikes and cars. Songkran is also when replica sand stupas are built in the courtyards of monasteries. Birds and fish are also set free.

Songkran is best witnessed in the northern city of Chiang Mai, where it's enthusiastically celebrated. Revellers line up along the city's moats, and pumps are installed so that water can be sucked from the moats and sprayed with abandon. — *www.tourismthailand.org*

See in
Bisket Jatra

NEPAL

WHY NOW Celebrate New Year, Nepali style

WHERE Khalna Tole, Bhaktapur

DATES Start of the Nepali month of Baisakh (around 13/14 April)

14 APR Bisket Jatra heralds the start of the Nepali New Year and is celebrated with the most aplomb in Bhaktapur. In one of the most exciting annual events in the Kathmandu valley, a huge and ponderous chariot carrying images of the god Bhairab is hauled by dozens of villagers to Khalna Tole. The creaking and swaying chariot lumbers around town, pausing for a huge tug of war between the eastern and western sides of town. After the battle the chariots head to Khalna Tole, where a huge 25m-high *lingam* (phallic symbol) is erected in the stone *yoni* (female genital symbol) base.

In the evening of the following day (New Year's Day), the pole is pulled down, again in an often-violent tug-of-war. As the pole crashes to the ground, the New Year officially commences.

Variations on the Bisket Jatra theme can also be seen in the villages of Timi and Bode. In the former there's a parade of images of the gods, with villagers throwing red powder over them. In the latter, there's a piercing ceremony, with one villager spending the day with an iron spike through his tongue. — *www.welcomenepal.com*

Wander with wild bison

POLAND

WHY NOW Go after the snow but before the summer rains and mosquitoes take over
WHERE Bialowieza National Park
DATES Mid-March to early May

15 APR

The vast, ancient Bialowieza Forest, straddling the border of Poland and Belarus, is often overlooked even though it is the European wilderness equivalent of Africa's Serengeti or North America's Yellowstone.

This is primeval Europe, a snapshot of a time when howling wolves and mythological creatures roamed dark forests surrounding remote villages. Here, among the pines, firs, oaks and birches, live moose, grey wolves, elk, lynxes, beavers and otters.

Originally a royal hunting ground, it was the last stronghold for the European bison despite this protection. It's a conservation triumph that 12 captive individuals were bred into a current population of 3000 bison. — *www.bpn.com.pl*

LEFT: **Hauling on the ropes at Bisket Jatra**

BELOW: **Pandas need to eat bamboo for more than 12 hours per day**

Canyon at Wadi Mujib

JORDAN

WHY NOW The gorge is open from April – come before the sun boils your brain
WHERE Wadi Mujib
DATES April to October

16 APR

Stretching from the Desert Hwy to the Dead Sea – a distance of over 70km – is the vast and beautiful Wadi Mujib. There are four main walking trails in Mujib Nature Reserve, but the one through the gorge offers the most adventure. This trail follows the river as it slices through the earth. You'll abseil down a 20m-high waterfall and at times swim or submerge to squeeze under rock barriers.

The trail can take up to 12 hours and must be undertaken with a guide from the Royal Society for the Conservation of Nature. Other attractions in the reserve include a small population of rare Nubian ibex, a species of goat that was almost hunted to extinction. — *www.rscn.org.jo*

Track giant pandas

CHINA

WHY NOW It's your best chance of hearing the love songs of mating pandas
WHERE Wolong Nature Reserve, near Chengdu
DATES April

17 APR

The giant panda is one of the world's most iconic endangered animals. And according to a 2006 study, there may now be 3000 of them in central China's mountains.

About 100 pandas live in the mountain forests of the 2000 sq km Wolong Nature Reserve, the best known of China's 50 panda reserves. Because pandas are thinly dispersed and lead solitary lives it takes a supreme effort to spot one. April, however, is when females are fertile for a couple of days and dim-sighted males must leave their feeding places to seek them out. Even if you don't cross paths with a panda, this is a great time to visit because whole hillsides of rhododendrons will be in bloom. — *www.pandasinternational.org*

Dance in
the desert

USA

WHY NOW For Coachella, simply one of the
world's most A-list music-fests

WHERE Indio, southern California

DATES Two weekends in April (10–12 & 17–19 2015)

18 APR Some seriously big names play at the Coachella Valley Music and Arts Annual Festival – past notables include the Red Hot Chili Peppers, Radiohead, Pearl Jam, Jay-Z, Paul McCartney and the Beastie Boys. But, arguably, many attendees come to gawp at the assembled crowds as well as the acts on stage. Coachella has become beloved of incognito Hollywood stars and assorted hipsters who are as keen as regular Joes to brave the desert sun for two weekends of electronica, dance, trance, rock, pop, indie, jazz, blues, funk, laser shows, art installations and oversize mechanical spiders.

The festival ground – a few nondescript fields in a valley in the Sonoran Desert – is hot, even in April (think 30°C). However, the vibe is very cool – and very southern Californian. It's best to camp on-site, to better immerse yourself in the Coachella world.

As well as floating between gobsmacking gigs, there's lots to do: chance your arm at the Rock, Paper, Scissors Championship; learn a few yoga poses; bust some moves at the Not So Silent Dance Party; and stuff your face with everything from craft beer to Baja-style tacos at The Terrace. Oh, and don't forget to keep an eye out for the stars. — *www.coachella.com*

RIGHT: **ZUMA PRESS – ALAMY**

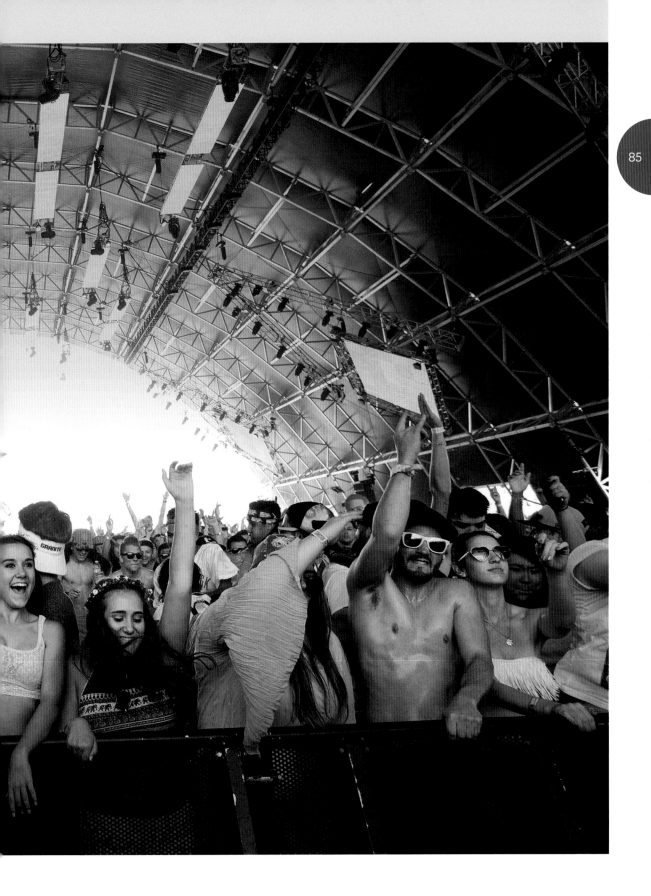

Hike the Coast Path

ENGLAND

WHY NOW It's a long walk, so get started early in the season, in warmer spring weather
WHERE Somerset, Devon, Cornwall and Dorset
DATES April and May

19 APR

Britain's National Trail system is unequalled. Its 15 long-distance paths cover 4400km; it's said that wherever you stand on the island, there's a national trail within 80km.

The longest, and arguably best, of the trails is the South West Coast Path, which rounds Britain's spectacularly rugged southwest extreme, from Minehead to Poole. It takes around eight weeks to hike its entire 1014km length.

The distance is only half the battle; the coast is very hilly, and following the path involves a lot of descents into valleys where rivers meet the sea, then steep climbs out. Ascents along the route total 27,000m – about three times the height of Mt Everest. — *www.southwestcoastpath.com*

Track chimpanzees

TANZANIA

WHY NOW Chimps are often easier to find during the rainy season
WHERE Gombe Stream
DATES February to June

20 APR

With an area of 52 sq km, Gombe Stream is Tanzania's smallest national park. It's also the site of the longest-running study of any wild animal population in the world. British researcher Jane Goodall arrived in 1960 to begin a study of wild chimpanzees, and her research is still going strong. Gombe Stream's 100-or-so chimps are accustomed to humans and there's nothing quite like encountering one of our closest relatives – chimpanzees share about 98% of their genes with humans.

Allow two days at Gombe. Accommodation options in the park are a matter of extremes: a run-down hostel, a resthouse or a luxury tented camp. — *www.tanzaniaparks.com/gombe.html*

RIGHT: **Land-diving in Vanuatu is a rite of passage for men**

BELOW: **Walking the South West Coast Path at Pentire Head in Cornwall, England**

Join the Feria de Abril

SPAIN

WHY NOW To dance, make merry, drink sherry
WHERE Seville
DATES Two weeks after Semana Santa (21–26 Apr 2015; 12–17 Apr 2016; 2–7 May 2017)

21 APR

A jolly postscript to sombre Semana Santa, the April Fair is the most colourful of Andalucía's festivals. A temporary city is set up, comprising 1000 *casetas* (bright striped tents). Most are private – it can feel a bit Secret Squirrel – but there are also some free public *casetas*. Inside it's all about chat, flamenco dancing and drinking *manzanilla* (dry sherry).

The feria opens on Monday night with the lighting-up of the fairgrounds. This marks the start of six nights of eating, drinking, talking, dressing up and dancing till dawn. In the afternoons, horses and carriages parade the streets. — *www.turismo.sevilla.org*

See the original bungy-jumpers

VANUATU

WHY NOW The land-diving towers should be finished and ready for vertiginous action

WHERE Pentecost Island

DATES Early April to June

22 APR Simply, the *naghol* (land diving) on the island of Pentecost is one of the world's most remarkable customs. Every year in early April, as the first yam crop emerges, the islanders in the south build tall wooden towers. A full-sized tower is vertical for 16m, then leans backwards.

Once completed, and until early June, men and boys dive from these rickety structures with only two springy vines to break their fall, a leap that is said to guarantee a bountiful yam harvest. Between 20 and 60 males per village will dive. As a diver raises his hands he tells the crowd his most intimate thoughts; the people stand quietly, for these could be his last words.

Finally the diver claps his hands, crosses his arms and leans forward. The vines abruptly stop his downward rush. Only his hair will touch the soil, to fertilise the yam crop. The crowd roars its appreciation. If it sounds vaguely familiar, it is – *naghol* was the inspiration for bungy jumping.

South Pentecost has many land-diving sites. Land-dive towers are erected in Lonorore and on the hills between Panas and nearby Wali.

— *vanuatu.travel*

Ride the Friendship Highway

CHINA & NEPAL

WHY NOW To see Mt Everest's north face at its best as you cycle past

WHERE Lhasa to Kathmandu

DATES Late March to early May

23 APR

This cycling route takes in most of Tibet's main sights, offering superb scenery and (for those leaving from Lhasa) featuring a roller-coaster ride down from La Lung-la (5124m) into the Kathmandu Valley. The journey is one of the most spectacular in the world.

The entire trip is 940km but most people start from Shigatse, Tibet's second-largest city, 300km west of Lhasa, knocking out the busiest section of the highway. It will take at least two weeks; to include stopovers at Gyantse, Shigatse and Sakya, allow 20 days.

This is the time to ride to see Tibet's star natural feature – the north face of Mt Everest – at its clearest. If you have a mountain bike, you can detour to Everest Base Camp, turning off the highway at Shegar. From here it's a two-day ride to Rongphu Monastery, with its fine views of Everest. Base camp is a few kilometres on; you might arrive with the first of the season's mountaineers. – *www.cnto.org*

LEFT: MONIKA LEWANDOWSKI – GETTY IMAGES

Wake up and smell the tulips

NETHERLANDS

WHY NOW To see and sniff millions and millions of bulbs a-bloom

WHERE Keukenhof, southern Holland

DATES Mid-March to mid-May

Imagine: a sea of seven million cheery tulips nodding their heads in the warming Dutch breeze... That's the sight that greets visitors to Keukenhof, the world's largest flower garden, when it opens for its annual spring season. From around 20 March until late May,

flora-fanciers can wander the garden's themed displays and buy bulbs to take home. The blooms tends to be at their best in mid-April.

Keukenhof – 'kitchen courtyard' in Dutch – was once a 15th-century hunting estate, where game was tracked and wild food foraged for the nearby castle. Now it is a floral fantasy, a cluster of perfectly tended and presented areas ranging from the Bee Happy Garden, where insects are encouraged, to the Dutch Cow Garden, where the black-and-white colour scheme mimics the famed Friesian cow.

While there, take a cycle ride into the countryside; or head to Amsterdam, only 35km away. — *www.keukenhof.nl*

Be cool at
Jazz Fest

USA

WHY NOW Chill out to the funkiest type of tunes in the city that invented jazz
WHERE Fair Grounds, New Orleans
DATES Last weekend in April, first weekend in May

25 APR
Where else would you want your jazz than in the city that spawned it? After Mardi Gras, the Jazz & Heritage Festival – Jazz Fest – is New Orleans' biggest reason to party, a feel-good musical smorgasbord served up on more than ten stages across two weekends.

Jazz Fest began as a celebration of the city's 250th birthday in 1968, an event that attracted musicians such as Louis Armstrong, Duke Ellington and Dave Brubeck. After struggling with poor attendance, it moved to the Fair Grounds in 1972 and began showcasing different musical forms in addition to its staple jazz. The event boomed and continues to do so, with past headline acts including Norah Jones, Van Morrison, Harry Connick Jr, Rod Stewart, ZZ Top and Steely Dan.

The Fair Grounds are open from 11am to 7pm, but Jazz Fest continues well into the wee hours in bars and clubs throughout the city. Jazz up your days further while you're here by visiting the New Orleans Jazz National Historical Park in the French Quarter, which recounts the history of the music. — *www.nojazzfest.com*

Run the London Marathon

ENGLAND

WHY NOW Lace up for a 26.2 mile jog around the UK capital – or join the spectating party
WHERE Greenwich to The Mall, London
DATES Mid-April (26 Apr 2015)

26 APR

It's not just a race – it's an inspirational surge of humanity. The London Marathon, first held in 1981, is a World Marathon Major, attracting elite athletes. But many of its 35,000+ field aren't there to break records; they're there for the challenge and, often, to make cash for charity – the London Marathon is also the world's largest single-event fundraiser. This means it's positively carnivalesque: runners wear everything from bright neon vests to enormous rhino costumes. Securing entry is tough – the ballot closes just hours after opening. But even if you can't run, go to watch, to soak up the feel-good atmosphere and the city sights. — *www.virginmoneylondonmarathon.com*

LEFT: **Jive to street performers in New Orleans, Louisiana**

BELOW: **Sealife is rich in the Poor Knights off New Zealand**

Rock climb a great gorge

CROATIA

WHY NOW Spring is the best climbing season, and attracts world-class scramblers
WHERE Paklenica National Park
DATES April and May

27 APR

Rising above the Adriatic, the stark peaks of the Velebit Massif stretch for 145km in a dramatic landscape of rock and sea. Paklenica National Park covers 36 sq km of the range, circling around two deep gorges. This karst landscape makes for one of Europe's premier climbing venues, offering a huge variety of routes. The firm, occasionally sharp limestone offers graded climbs, including 72 short sports routes and 250 longer routes.

The most advanced climbing is on Anića Kuk, which offers 100 routes up to a height of 350m. Nearly all routes have spits and pitons. Also, the International Speed Climbing competition is held here in April. — *www.paklenica.hr*

Dive the Poor Knights

NEW ZEALAND

WHY NOW Visibility can reach up to 50m in the austral autumn months
WHERE 20km off the east coast of Northland
DATES March to May

28 APR

Rated by the late Jacques Cousteau as one of the world's ten best dive sites, the Poor Knights Islands are the remnants of ancient volcanoes. Swept by the East Auckland current that brings warm waters from the Coral Sea, you'll find fish-filled caves, archways and underwater cliffs that offer spectacular diving against a backdrop of colourful invertebrate life. The range of dive sites at the Poor Knights offers something for everyone, including good snorkelling. These waters offer unparalleled biodiversity.

This is also a good time to visit New Zealand in general – for cool but settled weather, autumn colours, wine harvests and lower shoulder-season prices. — *www.doc.govt.nz*

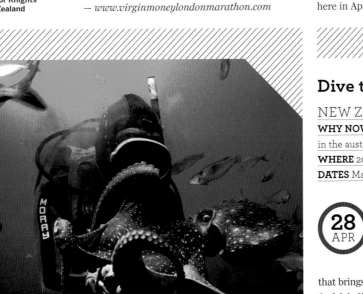

Hike the Lycian Way

TURKEY

WHY NOW Lycia gets so hot, it's best to walk
there before the summer punch

WHERE Lycian Coast

DATES March to May

29 APR

The Lycian Way was Turkey's first long-distance hiking trail, created in 1999 – although the history of this well-trodden region goes back far, far further. Sticking out into the Mediterranean, Lycia – the old name for the Tekke Peninsula – is a strategic spot and many colonialists have taken interest: the Persians, Alexander the Great, the Romans; evidence of these past civilisations can be seen en route.

The trail itself – using ancient footpaths and mule tracks – runs for 509km around the coast and mountains of Lycia, starting at Fethiye and finishing at Antalya. It gets more difficult as it winds into the mountain ranges, and a moderate level of fitness is required. It can be trekked in its entirety in about 25 to 30 days, or it can be walked in smaller chunks if you're short on time. Good places for starting out are Ölüdeniz, Kaş, Adrasan or Olympos.

Pensions and hotels along the route provide some relief from your tent and there are also homestay options. Look out for the abundant birdlife in April. — *www.lycianway.com*

Welcome in Walpurgisnacht

GERMANY

WHY NOW Dress up and climb a mountain to get ghoulish on Witches' Night

WHERE The Brocken, Harz Mountains

DATES 30 April

30 APR What better way to see out April than on a mountain top in the company of witches and warlocks. According to local mythology, they gather on Walpurgisnacht (which takes its name from Saint Walburga, whose feast day is 1 May) at locations throughout the Harz Mountains before flying off to the 1142m-high Brocken on broomsticks or goats. There they recount the year's evil deeds and top off the stories with a bacchanalian frenzy.

Frightened peasants used to hang crosses and herbs on stable doors to protect their livestock; ringing church bells or cracking whips were other ways to prevent stray witches from dropping by.

One of the best places to celebrate Walpurgisnacht is the town of Thale, where not-so-pagan hordes of 35,000 or more arrive for a colourful variety of events. People dress as witches and toss away all reserve as they dance around fires. — *www.harzinfo.de*

LEFT: **TIM BARKER – GETTY IMAGES**

Sing for spring
on May Day

ENGLAND

WHY NOW Welcome in the new month at the
university town's May Morning

WHERE Oxford

DATES 1 May

01 MAY Set your alarm clock to early: in Oxford, the shenanigans begin at 6am on May Morning. May Day has long been a day of traditional (and often raucous) celebration across the globe, as communities welcomed the warming weather; in the UK city of spires, they've been heralding the new month in a similar fashion for hundreds of years.

Festivities start with the tuneful choristers of Magdalen College choir singing 'Hymnus Eucharisticus' from the Great Tower. This is followed by 20 minutes of if-you-weren't-awake-before-you-certainly-are-now bell-ringing. Also, lots of cafes and bars in the city open early, to serve hearty breakfasts – useful fuel for the day's activities.

Tradition is still strong here: there is live music, horn-blowing and jangly, stick-clacking Morris dancing. There are also dare-devils with death wishes: the practice of leaping off Magdalen Bridge into the River Cherwell is popular, but if water levels are low, injuries can occur. It's best to enjoy the party atmosphere on dry land. — *www.oxford.gov.uk*

LEFT: **HOMER SYKES – ALAMY**

May

Trek through Tiger Leaping Gorge

CHINA

WHY NOW To hike amid hillsides afire with plants and wildflowers

WHERE Yunnan, southwestern China

DATES May to early June

02 MAY After making its first turn at Shígǔ, the mighty Yangtze River surges through Tiger Leaping Gorge, one of the deepest gorges in the world. The gorge measures 16km in length, and it's a giddy 3900m from the floor of the gorge to the mountain tops above. There are two trails through the gorge – the higher route is older and known as the 24-bend path (although it's more like 30), while the lower route is a new road replete with belching tour buses.

The trail can be completed in two days, but better to allow three or four, to properly take in the awesome landscapes. En route you'll pass rice fields, tiny villages, vertiginous mountain walls, sturdy oxen ploughing the fields and herds of agile goats. You'll stay in rustic guesthouses; the best have verandas with dramatic views, where you can rest with hot tea and homecooked food. Lìjiāng, 160km north of provincial capital, Dàlǐ, is the best base for the hike; Qiaotou, the start point, is 2 hours away. — *www.cnto.org*

Celebrate Waisak

INDONESIA

WHY NOW To view awe-inspiring Hindu feats
WHERE Borobudur, Java
DATES Full moon in 4th month of Chinese lunar calendar (3 May 2015; 20 May 2016; 10 May 2017)

03 MAY Waisak is the holiest day on the Buddhist calendar and celebrations are especially spectacular at Java's Borobudur, the world's largest Buddhist temple. Attracting thousands of pilgrims, Waisak marks the triple whammy of the Buddha's birth, his enlightenment and his attainment of Nirvana, and sees a great procession of saffron-robed monks walking 3km from Mendut to Pawon then Borobudur. At Borobudur crowds gather and, as the full moon rises, candles are lit and flowers strewn about as offerings, followed by praying. You won't be walking far but it will be slow in a crowd this size. Allow extra time to explore Borobudur. — *www.borobudurpark.co.id*

LEFT: **Helping hikers along the Tiger Leaping Gorge**

BELOW: **Serpent seers in Abruzzo, Italy**

Search for snow leopards

BHUTAN

WHY NOW The weather is great and there are absolutely stunning displays of flowers
WHERE Countrywide
DATES April and May

04 MAY Ruled in accordance with Buddhist values, the Bhutanese have a real respect for life. The country has banned hunting and logging, and has vowed to maintain at least 60% of its land under forest cover for all time, in accordance with the belief that a healthy environment is essential spiritual happiness. This makes it a natural wonderland.

Bhutan is home to an incredible cross-section of habitats and wildlife, including rare species. For instance, tackling the three-week Tashitang trek is probably the best way to see snow leopard, as well as red panda and the bizarre takin. Also, from March to May, the country's rhododendrons are in full bloom. — *www.tourism.gov.bt*

Brave the Snake Festival

ITALY

WHY NOW To see serpents predict the future
WHERE Cocullo, Abruzzo
DATES First Thursday in May (7 May 2015; 5 May 2016; 4 May 2017; 3 May 2018)

05 MAY The Processione dei Serpari sees a statue of St Domenic (protector against snake bites) paraded in tiny Cocullo, adorned with jewels, money and live snakes. Afterwards the squirmers are released back into the forest, leaving villagers immune from snake bites for another year. It's very *Raiders of the Lost Ark*, except these snakes have no bite: they are nonvenomous but their fangs are removed anyway.

Festivities start around 10am, with the parade commencing at noon. The actions of the snakes are read a little like tea leaves. If they writhe around the statue's head, it'll be a good harvest; if they slither towards the arms, woe is us.
— *www.abruzzoturismo.it*

Hike the Larapinta Trail
AUSTRALIA

WHY NOW May is about as comfy as it gets in this desert: averages of 23°C and little rain
WHERE Alice Springs to Mt Sonder
DATES May

06 MAY

The Larapinta Trail is one of the world's great desert treks, stretching 223km across the Australian outback from Alice Springs to shapely Mt Sonder. Covering virtually the whole length of the West MacDonnell Ranges, one of the oldest mountain chains in the world, the trail switches between quartzite ridges, spinifex plains and the plunging gorges of the West MacDonnells.

Allow between 12 and 16 days to complete the trail; it breaks down into 12 distinct sections, so shorter hikes are possible. Summers (November to March) are hot – much too toasty for long-distance walking, especially as the trail offers little shade. May to August is best, though nighttime temperatures are fairly chilly from June. — *www.larapintatrail.com.au*

RIGHT: **Giraffes are easy to spot in South Luangwa National Park, Zambia**

BELOW: **Pink roses are picked and dried in Morocco's High Atlas mountains**

Inhale the Rose Festival
MOROCCO

WHY NOW To party amid petals in the desert
WHERE El-Kelaâ M'Gouna
DATES Early May (exact dates vary depending on harvest time)

07 MAY

In the dry folds of the High Atlas, approaching the Sahara Desert, there's an unexpected place called the Vallée des Roses. And in spring, the entire area is awash with perfect-pink Persian roses. In the small town of El-Kelaâ M'Gouna, roses nestle among hedgerows: although they're not immediately visible, they're the town's lifeblood, used to produce rosewater.

The flowers are harvested in May, an event celebrated in the colourful and sweet-smelling Rose Festival, which draws around 20,000 people. The three-day do is a time of song and dance, feasting, souk-like markets and a chariot procession through a shower of rose petals. Prepare for a real seduction of the senses. — *www.visitmorocco.com*

See great gatherings of giraffes

ZAMBIA

WHY NOW The giraffes are concentrated here at the end of the wet season
WHERE South Luangwa National Park
DATES May

08 MAY Spanning an area 700km long by 100km wide, the Luangwa Valley is part of the Great Rift Valley; it's also an isolated haven for a unique giraffe: the Thornicroft's giraffe.

In South Luangwa, the Luangwa River carves a course south to the Zambezi River through a mosaic of mopane, miombo woodlands and grasslands that flood during the wet season (November to May). When the park floods, the sandy soils around Mfuwe remain above water, providing dry islands on which around 700 giraffes gather while waiting for other areas to drain. It's a sanctuary for them, and a bonus for visitors, as the giraffes become easier to spot.

Thornicroft's giraffes are recognised by their dark brown neck spots and the lack of blotches below the knees, but they share with all giraffes the long necks and 45cm-long tongues that give them access to foods few other herbivores can reach. Look for mothers with calves, a fairly rare sight because up to 75% of the calves are killed by predators in their first year. Also watch for males engaged in 'necking' battles that involve pushing and swinging their heads at each other; necks and jaws can be broken.

May is also the month when the rarely visited North Luangwa National Park becomes accessible. — *www.zambiatourism.com*

Appreciate contemporary art in Venice

ITALY

WHY NOW View the groundbreaking Biennale

WHERE Venice

DATES May to November (9 May-22 Nov 2015);
odd years: Art Biennale; even years: Architecture

09 MAY Venice may be a city of history, a city of canals winding betwixt 15th-century palaces and merchant houses, where time often seems to stand still. But its big bi-annual cultural event is anything but stuck in the *doge* ages. The Venice Biennale is a celebration of contemporary art; since its inauguration in 1895, it has focused on showcasing the out-there, the avant-garde, the artists breaking new boundaries. The Biennale welcomed abstract expressionism in the 1950s, pop art in the 1960s, postmodern works in the 1970s. It has always been on, or ahead of, the trend.

The event lasts from spring to autumn. It includes a range of exhibitions, centred on the giardini, an area of parkland on the Bacino di San Marco. Here, there are tens of national pavilions, representing the arts of that country – participants come from places as diverse as Australia and Azerbaijan, Iceland and Iraq.

These days, it's not all about art. An eclectic programme of dance, music, architecture and theatre accompanies the exhibitions, while the Venice Film Festival (held every year, August/September) is part of Biennale too.
— *www.labiennale.org*

Horse ride in Andalucía

SPAIN

WHY NOW To gallop on thoroughbred horses through spring-fresh landscapes

WHERE Andalucía

DATES May (Feria del Caballo: early/mid May)

10 MAY Andalucía is steeped in equestrian tradition. The horse has long been part of rural life and the region is the chief breeding ground of the elegant Spanish thoroughbred, also known as the Cartujano or Andalusian. Also, countless good riding tracks crisscross Andalucía, and *picaderos* (stables) can take you on a guided ride. Many of the mounts are Andalusians or Andalusian–Arab crosses – medium-sized, intelligent, good in traffic, easy to handle and sure-footed.

One of Andalucía's biggest festivals, the Feria del Caballo (Horse Fair) in Jerez, is a celebration of all things equine. Colourful parades of horses pass through the Parque González Hontoria fairgrounds. Male riders wear flat-topped hats and frilly shirts; their female pillion partners wear long, spotted dresses. It makes a fine add-on to a few days of riding in the Andalucían mountains.
— *www.andalucia.org*

Ogle a whole lot of oilbirds

VENEZUELA

WHY NOW You'll be blown away by hordes of screaming nocturnal birds
WHERE Cueva del Guácharo National Park
DATES April to June

11 MAY You're staring into a cave that sounds like a portal into the underworld. From deep within rises a deafening roar, then suddenly thousands of birds with 1m wingspans erupt like a river of dark demons: the nightly exodus of *guacharos* ('those who wail'), the only nocturnal fruit-eating birds.

By day, the 15,000 oilbirds nest on ledges in their namesake cave. At sunset they fly into the night to eat, echo-locating by emitting clicks in the manner of bats. Although they migrate seasonally to follow fruiting crops, they predictably occur at Cueva del Guácharo, near Caripe; numbers peak from April to June, nesting season. — *www.venezuelaturismo.gob.ve*

Sail the Bermuda Triangle

BERMUDA

WHY NOW A time of smooth seas, barring an occurrence of the paranormal kind...
WHERE Atlantic Ocean, near Bermuda
DATES April and May

12 MAY Throw caution to the Atlantic Ocean wind and tack into the Bermuda Triangle, the notorious section of the Atlantic that's bound by Bermuda to the north, Florida to the west and Puerto Rico to the south. It's thought as many as 100 ships and planes have vanished here, with mysterious disappearances dating back to the mid-19th century.

Still game? If you can sail, rent a boat in Bermuda or Florida; the non-qualified could join a cruise. Either way, ideally you want to make your crossing by the end of May – Bermuda's hurricane season starts on 1 June, after which seas can be even more treacherous. — *www.gotobermuda.com; www.visitflorida.com*

RIGHT: **An illusion of impalas in Kruger National Park**

BELOW: **It's a sailor's life at St David's Island, Bermuda**

Appreciate the prairie

USA

WHY NOW You'll see the prairie in full splendour and – maybe – baby bison
WHERE Tallgrass Prairie Preserve, Oklahoma
DATES Late April to mid-June

13 MAY The first European explorers who tried to cross the Great Plains called this the 'Great American Desert'. Yet it was home to 30 million bison and staggering numbers of pronghorn antelope, elk, bears and wolves. Today, the chunk known as the Tallgrass Prairie Preserve is home to 2500 bison.

May, the best time to look for newborn bison, it incredibly vibrant. There is a profusion of wildflowers and birdsong. You may hear the booming calls of greater prairie chickens or see armadillos. In all, more than 300 bird and 80 mammal species make this their home. — *www.nature.org/ourinitiatives/regions/northamerica/unitedstates/oklahoma*

Hike Kruger's wild trails

SOUTH AFRICA

WHY NOW Kruger averages around 25°C with almost negligible rainfall
WHERE Kruger National Park
DATES May

14 MAY With its vast savannahs and abundant wildlife, Kruger National Park is one of the world's best safari spots. It's reputed to have the greatest variety of animals of any African park, with 147 recorded mammal species and 507 bird species.

The best way to get personal with this impressive roll-call of critters is on one of Kruger's wilderness walking trails. These experiences are done in small groups, led by knowledgeable armed guides. They offer a superb opportunity to get a more intimate sense of the bush than is possible in a vehicle.

There are seven wilderness trails in the park, each with its unique attractions. For example, the Napi Trail is known for its opportunities to see the Big Five; the Bushmans Trail features treks to San rock paintings.

The walks are not particularly strenuous, covering about 20km a day at a modest pace, for two days/three nights. The itinerary of each is determined by the group's interests, the time of year and the disposition of the wildlife.
— *www.sanparks.org/parks/kruger*

Watch saints race at the Corsa dei Ceri

ITALY

WHY NOW Race up a steep hill to honour the local saint

WHERE Gubbio, Umbria

DATES 15 May (St Ubaldo's Day)

15 MAY Few Italian festivals can hold a candle to Gubbio's centuries-old Corsa dei Ceri ceremony, which is held to commemorate the city's patron saint, St Ubaldo. Contested since the 12th century, it's a strongman competition of unusual proportions.

Three teams race through the city's streets and up the steep slopes of Monte Ingino to the Basilica of St Ubaldo, where the saint's body lies. Each team carries a so-called 'candle' (*ceri*), which is actually a 4m-long wooden pillar bearing a statue of one of three 'rival' saints (Ubaldo, George and Anthony). Each pillar weighs around 400kg.

The race begins at 6pm with a blessing by the bishop, then there's a sprint around the city and the climb to the basilica, 300m above. It's a colourful affair: each *ceraiole* (candle holder) wears the colours of the saint they carry: yellow for Ubaldo, blue for George, black for Anthony. It's not a fair fight: St Ubaldo always wins – it's his day, after all. — *www.ceri.it*

Be starstruck at Cannes

FRANCE

WHY NOW Join the world's silver-screen superstars on the French Riviera
WHERE Palais des Festivals, Cannes
DATES Mid-May

16 MAY

For 12 days in May, Cannes – on the glitzy Côte d'Azur – is centre of the cinematic universe. Producers, distributors, directors, stars and hangers-on descend to buy, sell or promote more than 2000 films.

The festival is split into 'in competition' and 'out of competition' sections; the former aim to win the prestigious Palme d'Or, awarded to the film that best 'serves the evolution of cinematic art'. Most films are 'out of competition'.

Official screenings are in the Palais des Festivals, but you won't get into these. Free tickets are often available to films after their first screening. Or go celeb-spotting by the red-carpet entrance to the Palais. — *www.festival-cannes.org*

Take a cycle safari

BOTSWANA

WHY NOW The best weather and the best wildlife coincide for great viewing by bike
WHERE Mashatu Game Reserve
DATES May to September

17 MAY

Pinched between Zimbabwe and South Africa, Mashatu Game Reserve is one of the largest private wildlife reserves in Southern Africa, and an excellent place to view big cats and elephants (over 1000 elephants have been counted here).

The reserve is only open to prebooked guests staying at one of two accommodation options, among the most luxurious in Botswana. Once here, however, you have the chance to add a unique twist to the traditional safari by touring the 250 sq km park on a bicycle. Morning and afternoon mountain bike safaris range out from the lodges, following elephant paths in the company of reserve rangers. — *www.mashatu.com*

Find Komodo dragons

INDONESIA

WHY NOW See these giant lizards fighting and mating, and see newly hatched little'uns
WHERE Komodo National Park
DATES May

18 MAY

Komodo dragons weigh upwards of 166kg, can take down and kill a full-grown water buffalo and loom large in the imagination of locals, who revere them as mythical ancestors. Reaching lengths of 3m, these prehistoric lizards are the top predator on the few islands where they live, and everything is potential prey – including humans.

Visitors to the islands will almost certainly see dragons. During courting season, you may spot big males on their hind legs, struggling to pin each other down. During mating, females fight back so ferociously that an amorous male must fully restrain her in order to avoid being seriously hurt. — *www.indonesia.travel*

LEFT: **Watch the Race of the Saints in Umbria, Italy**

BELOW: **Komodo dragons have a mildly venomous bite but a bad reputation**

Raft the Tara River

MONTENEGRO

WHY NOW Take to the Tara when the water is in full flow

WHERE Durmitor National Park

DATES May to October

19 MAY The Tara River slices through the mountains of Durmitor National Park, in the northwest of Montenegro. It's a powerful waterway, and has carved out a canyon that drops to 1300m at its deepest point – the Grand Canyon is only 200m deeper. Rafting the river has become popular, with trips operating from May to October – though it's in the month of May that the melting snow causes the river to be at its fullest, fastest and most thrilling.

The 82km raftable section starts from Splavište, south of the 150m-high Tara Bridge, and ends at Šcepan Polje on the Bosnian border. The classic two-day trip heads through the deepest part of the canyon on the first day, stopping overnight at Radovan Luka. Most of the day tours from the coast traverse only the last 18km; you miss the canyon's depths, but it's still a beautiful stretch. — *www.visit-montenegro.com*

RIGHT: **TIM BARKER – GETTY IMAGES**

Explore Wadi Rum

JORDAN

WHY NOW Avoid summer heat and winter chill
WHERE Wadi Rum
DATES April to May

20 MAY Made famous by TE Lawrence and the Arab Revolt of 1917–18, Wadi Rum offers extraordinary desert scenery. Its myriad moods and dramatic colours make for a memorable scene. Blazing in summer, and with cold winds howling down from Central Asia in winter, now is the month to discover this desert.

Wadi Rum is a series of valleys about 2km wide, stretching north to south for about 130km. The desert landscape is punctuated by towering *jebels* (hills) that have eroded into soft sandstone over 50 million years. These *jebels* offer some challenging rock climbing. One good climb for amateurs is up Jebel Rum (1754m), Jordan's highest peak.

Excursions into the desert can be made by camel or 4WD. You can ride out and back from Rum village, cross to the archaeological site at Petra (about five nights), or follow in Lawrence of Arabia's camel prints to Aqaba on the Red Sea (three to six nights).
— *www.visitjordan.com*

Revel in reading

WALES

WHY NOW Be in 'Book Town' as it welcomes the big-wigs of the literary world
WHERE Hay-on-Wye, Powys, Wales
DATES Late May/early June (21–31 May 2015)

21 MAY For ten late-spring days, the tiny hub of Hay-on-Wye becomes the centre of intellectual thought and theories. Around 85,000 people descend on this small market town on the Wales–England border to hear talks by the great and the good; speakers range from politicians to poets, writers to scientists, philosophers to musicians. Hay is alive with ideas. Indeed, Bill Clinton once called it 'the Woodstock of the mind'.

Come and spend your days at the tented festival village, sharing thoughts and listening to new ones. In the evening, a party vibe takes over, with bands and comedians taking to the stage. — *www.hayfestival.com*

Gawp at garter snakes

CANADA

WHY NOW It's the largest concentration of snakes in the world
WHERE Narcisse Snake Dens, Manitoba
DATES May

23 MAY If snakes make you nervous, approach the Narcisse Snake Dens with caution: the ground will be covered with thousands of red-sided garter snakes.

There are about 70 hibernacula (hibernation dens) in Manitoba, some with more than 10,000 snakes. Awakened from hibernation by the warming air, males emerge from deep cracks where they've been sleeping in wriggling masses. Once peak numbers are on the surface in early May, females emerge over the course of several weeks, triggering frantic 'mating balls' where 100 males furiously weave around any female they find. — *www.gov.mb.ca/conservation/wildlife/ spmon/narsnakes*

Be blown in Tornado Alley

USA

WHY NOW The spring months see the greatest number of storms and twisters
WHERE Central USA
DATES April to June

22 MAY Tornado Alley stretches between the Rocky and Appalachian Mountains, covering central US states, such as Oklahoma, Colorado, Arkansas, Texas and Nebraska. Spring here is the time of tornadoes, which spin with winds up to 500km/h. In May it's not uncommon for the Alley to experience more than 400 twisters.

Join a tornado-chasing tour and you'll likely locate a storm. Typically, tours run for six days, beginning in twister-central Oklahoma City. Using satellite radar imaging, your guides will trace and chase the big blowy events, hopefully delivering you to a safe box-seat view. — *www.nssl.noaa.gov*

RIGHT: **Numbers of hikers on the Inca Trail are limited; book ahead for the best slots**

BELOW: **A twister touches down in Oklahoma**

Hike the Inca Trail

PERU

WHY NOW The landscape is beautifully green but the June crowds have yet to arrive

WHERE Cusco region, southern Peru

DATES May

24 MAY The El Camino Inca is not the only route to the archaeological site of Machu Picchu, but it is the only one that winds its way past three major Inca sites in good repair. Any one of Sayacmarca, Phuyupatamarca or Huiñay Huayna would be considered a great day trip out of Cusco if they were accessible by road, but none can be reached without hiking all or part of the Inca Trail.

The trail is only 43km long but has steep ascents, especially to 4198m Dead Woman's Pass, followed by swooping descents into the cloudforests bordering the Amazon Basin. The trail's end goal – Machu Picchu – remains a mystery: the accounts of Spanish conquistadores don't mention it, and archaeologists can only speculate on its function. It is beautifully located and expertly built, and despite its remoteness, attracts thousands of visitors – the site is accessible by train as well as by foot. However, savvy trekkers know to time their visit to Machu Picchu for the early morning and late afternoon, when it is relatively empty. — *www.incatrailperu.com*

Run down a hill after a cheese

ENGLAND

WHY NOW Take a cheesy tumble

WHERE Cooper's Hill, Brockworth, Gloucestershire

DATES Spring Bank Holiday (25 May 2015; 30 May 2016; 29 May 2017; 28 May 2018)

25 MAY Think the most dangerous thing about cheese is the mould? Then you've never stood atop Cooper's Hill on this mad Monday. The premise is simple: a handmade, 7-pound circle of Double Gloucester cheese is rolled down the hill and a gaggle of people chase down behind it. The first to the bottom of the hill (or to grab the cheese) wins, and gets to keep it. Which does nothing to explain the mud, the slippery grass, the slope and the injury toll.

The course for the event is a swathe of grass cut through the forest on Copper's Hill. The slope is at times vertical and at some lesser moments has a 50% grade. The idea may be to run after the cheese but for most it means tumbling down the hill; even if you catch up to the bloody thing it's a whole other matter to grab it. Each year competitors are injured – sprains, strains, broken bones. And yet runners return, competing year after year, suggesting this particular cheese is fiendishly addictive.

The first cheese is rolled at midday and there are five downhill races. At a count of 'three' the cheese is rolled; competitors lurch off the plateau at 'four'. It's then like a spin-dry cycle to the bottom. Between each of the downhill races there's also an uphill race for those who prefer fit to fast. — *www.cheese-rolling.co.uk*

RIGHT: **CHRISTIAN KOBER – GETTY IMAGES**

Walk the Camino

SPAIN

WHY NOW Make the most of the long days to complete the ultimate European pilgrimage
WHERE Roncesvalles to Santiago de Compostela
DATES May and June

26 MAY For more than 1000 years pilgrims have taken to the Camino de Santiago – the Way of St James – setting off on foot to reach the apostle's tomb in the Iberian Peninsula's far northwest.

Today, this magnificent long-distance walk is a mix of pilgrimage and adventure. It runs for around 780km from Roncesvalles, on the border with France, to Santiago de Compostela in Galicia. Expect to take a month; en route you can stay in *albergues* (pilgrims' hostels).

Starting in May avoids the peak summer season but makes the most of lengthening daylight hours. Also, the countryside is a delight – rivers are full, and hillsides are bursting with wildflowers and swaying green crops. — *www.csj.org.uk*

RIGHT: **Snorkelling the sardine run off Port St Johns**

BELOW: **End of the road – the cathedral of Santiago de Compostela**

Horse-trek the steppes

KAZAKHSTAN

WHY NOW To tiptoe and horseshoe through the tulips
WHERE Aksu-Dzhabagly Nature Reserve
DATES April and May

27 MAY The Aksu-Dzhabagly Nature Reserve is a beautiful 1319-sq-km patch of valleys and mountains climbing to the Kyrgyz and Uzbek borders east of Shymkent. At the west end of the Talassky Alatau range, stretching from the edge of the steppe at about 1200m up to 4239m at Pik Sayram, it's a region best explored on horseback. One of the best rides spends three days climbing to 900-year-old petroglyphs. More demanding treks go over 3500m passes with nights spent in caves.

Aksu-Dzhabagly is home of the tulip, and in April and May its meadows are dotted with bright-red Greig's tulip. Wildlife you might spot includes bears, ibex, argali sheep and golden eagles; the park is even home to snow leopards. — *www.wildnature-kz.narod.rus*

Snorkel the sardine run

SOUTH AFRICA

WHY NOW To observe a seasonal ocean wonder, involving many millions of fish

WHERE Coastal Eastern Cape and KwaZulu-Natal

DATES Late May to early July

28 MAY Between late May and early July millions upon millions of sardines gather along South Africa's east coast in a seething, silvery mass up to 15km in length, 3.5km wide and nearly 40m deep – so big it's said to be visible even by satellite.

From their spawning grounds off Cape Agulhas, the sardines thread a 1600km path, riding a countercurrent north along the coast, making their way up along the northern Eastern Cape and the southern shore of KwaZulu-Natal. In turn, each and every predator in the oceanic food chain follows this moving feast. Dolphins, seabirds, game fish and orcas all join the fracas; there are also many shark species, from bronze whalers to hammerheads and great whites. The sardine run also happens to coincide with the annual migration of humpbacks, which are on the move north into warmer waters to mate and calve.

Visitors who witness the feeding frenzy will long remember the adrenaline rush as huge whales breach metres away from the boat and dolphin pods ride the bow-wave. You can watch from on deck, though snorkellers score ringside views of the spectacular action. Diving should only be attempted by very experienced divers, in the right conditions – hungry predators could pose a risk. — *www.southafrica.net*

Make an Everest attempt

NEPAL

WHY NOW This week is the most likely opening of the so-called 'Everest window'

WHERE Himalaya

DATES Late May

29 MAY

Late May is key in the Everest climbing calendar. Not only is 29 May the anniversary of the first ascent (in 1953) by Edmund Hillary and Tenzing Norgay, but this time is also the most likely opening of the 'Everest window' – a pause in winds on Everest's summit, brought about by monsoons further south, that allows in a draft of climbers.

If you want to join the few to have stood atop Everest, check your bank account: it costs about US$35,000. If you lack the skills or money, you can still share part of the mountaineering experience by trekking to Nepal's Everest base camp, on the Khumbu Glacier. Most treks begin at Lukla, passing through the Sherpa village of Namche Bazaar, and on to base camp, at 5340m, about 11 days later. — *www.welcomenepal.com*

RIGHT: **Hell-Bourg village in the Cirque de Salazie, Réunion**

BELOW: **Camp 1 on Mt Everest in Sagarmatha National Park, Nepal**

Listen to howler monkeys

BELIZE

WHY NOW To explore this compact wildlife wonderland before the rains descend

WHERE Community Baboon Sanctuary

DATES December to May

30 MAY

In Belize black howler monkeys are known as baboons, and the Community Baboon Sanctuary, 40km outside capital Belize City, is the only area established entirely for their conservation. It's a community-based initiative, located in the village of Bermudian Landing. Landowners pledge to voluntarily manage their land in a monkey-friendly fashion, creating corridors for howlers. The scheme has spread to surrounding villages, resulting in the densest concentration of howlers found anywhere: up to 250 individuals per hectare.

This density of monkeys makes for a particularly vocal population. When you hear their deafening calls resonating through the forest, you'll quickly understand how they got their name. — *www.howlermonkeys.org*

Find France in the Indian Ocean

RÉUNION

WHY NOW It's dry season until October, and May and June are the best times to trek

WHERE Réunion, Indian Ocean

DATES May and June

31 MAY With its cafes serving croissants and its beret-clad boules players, the island of Réunion is like a slice of France relocated to the Indian Ocean. And what an island! Sheer and lush, it appears to have risen dripping wet from the deep blue sea. Like Hawaii, Réunion has breathtaking natural landscapes, a live volcano and a subtly tropical climate – just with added baguettes.

The island boasts more than 1000km of hiking trails, which criss-cross an utterly awe-inspiring landscape of jagged mountains, lushly forested valleys, tumbling waterfalls and volcanic tuff. Vast swathes of this incredible interior are accessible only on foot, so it's remarkably intact. There are two major hiking trails that you can follow. The GR R1 does a tour of Piton des Neiges, passing through Cilaos, the Forêt de Bélouve, Hell-Bourg and the Cirque de Mafate. The GR R2 makes an epic traverse across the island from St-Denis to St-Philippe via the three cirques.

Réunion also has more than 1400km of special biking trails, winding through forests and down mountainsides. They are graded like ski runs, according to level of difficulty. — *www.reunion.fr*

Sail the Blue Voyage

TURKEY

WHY NOW For an idyllic summer sail on the
Mediterranean and Aegean Seas
WHERE Southwest Turkey
DATES May to early July

01 JUN Between the wars, writer and painter Cevat Şakir Kabaağaç wrote an account of his idyllic sailing excursions along Turkey's southern Aegean and western Mediterranean coasts, an area then untouched by tourism. Kabaağaç called his book *Mavi Yolculuk* (Blue Voyage), a name that has come to represent all sailing journeys along these shores.

Gülets (wooden yachts) now sail two routes here with great frequency. Most popular is a four-day, three-night cruise between Fethiye and Kale (Demre); the route between Marmaris and Fethiye, also four days, is said to be prettier. Either way, you'll pass some cracking coastline.

Experienced sailors can opt for a bareboat charter and crew themselves. Bareboats sleep six to 11 passengers. Marmaris and Fethiye are good places to ask around about charters.

Visit before school holidays start to avoid the influx of tourists and the highest temperatures. Winds tend to pick up a little in July and August too. In May/June average highs reach 28-30°C, but you can always jump overboard if you need to cool down. — *www.goturkey.com*

June

Climb the 100 Mountains

JAPAN

WHY NOW If you want to summit all 100, it's best to start at the beginning of summer

WHERE Countrywide

DATES Early June

02 JUN In 1964 noted alpinist and author Fukada Kyūya released his book, *Hyakumeizan*, in which he chose his 100 Famous Mountains of Japan, selecting them for a variety of reasons – height, history, shape, character and individuality. It was his wish that keen Japanese hikers would choose their own 100 and set out to climb them in their lifetimes.

It didn't quite work out that way. Thanks in part to being popularised by Crown Prince Naruhito, Kyūya's 100 Famous Mountains are now the accepted 100. They have become almost every Japanese hiker's target trek-list – whether they can manage to conquer them all in one year or whether it takes three decades.

The mountains are fairly well spread, stretching from Yaku-shima, an island off the southern tip of Kyūshū, to Japan's far north, with plenty in the Kita Alps, Minami Alps, on Shikoku and beyond.

Don't have time for them all? Aside from obvious and iconic Mt Fuji, consider Mt Tsukuba, only 877m, but steeped in legend – it has two peaks (one male, one female) and many devotees visit its shrines to seek marital blessings; on clear days, the skyscrapers of Tokyo are visible from its summit.

Or how about 1721m Mount Rishiri? This extinct stratovolcano to the north of Hokkaido rises up from the ocean and offers fabulous views over a scatter of other isles that dot the Sea of Japan. — *www.jnto.go.jp*

Listen to world music

MOROCCO

WHY NOW Wrap your listening chops around
Mawazine, a celebration of global tunes
WHERE Rabat
DATES Early June (30 May–7 Jun 2015)

03 JUN Mawazine is a meze-platter of a music festival. The offering is varied and delicious, ranging from spiritual choirs, Berber rock, Touareg blues, Congolese soul, Colombian cumbia, Indian sitar, Middle Eastern rap and Uzbek folk to the more mainstream-pleasing likes of Stevie Wonder and Kylie Minogue.

Mawazine was created in 2001 as a cultural initiative to push a more liberal image of Morocco; it's grown into an internationally acclaimed if sometimes controversial event, with some Muslims believing its Western leanings are a threat to their culture. But as a showcase of big-name stars, homegrown talent and lesser-known genres, it is utterly unsurpassed. — *www.festivalmawazine.ma*

Track tigers

INDIA

WHY NOW Though hot, the tail end of the dry
season offers the most likely tiger sightings
WHERE Corbett National Park, Uttarakhand
DATES June

04 JUN Corbett was India's first national park, and is now home to around 10% of the country's tigers. Its high forests and dense understorey make tiger sightings unreliable, but by visiting now you stand the best chance: the forest has died back, waterholes are scarce and grass cover is minimal after winter burn-offs.

In Corbett, safaris take two forms: jeep and elephant-back. The jeeps range further, heading across to pools in which tigers may be seen cooling themselves from the 40°C heat. Elephant travel is more atmospheric.

Corbett is also home to around 50 species of mammals and 600 species of birds. To get to the park, take the overnight Ranikhet Express from Delhi to Ramnagar.
— *projecttiger.nic.in/corbett.htm*

LEFT: **Two down, 98 to go – Mt Rishiri and Mt Himenuma, Japan**

BELOW: **Double trouble – two tigers in the Jim Corbett National Park, Uttarakhand**

Hike & raft around Bovec

SLOVENIA

WHY NOW Come as summer shrugs the Alps free of snow and pumps water into the Soča River

WHERE Bovec

DATES June to September

05 JUN

The small Slovenian town of Bovec has a great deal to offer adventure-sports enthusiasts. With the Julian Alps above, the Soča River below and Triglav National Park at the back door, you could spend a week propelling yourself through the outdoors without ever doing the same thing twice. Try ice- and rock climbing, skydiving, paragliding, potholing, bungee jumping and, in winter, sleighing and skiing. But best of all is the rafting and hiking.

The rafting season on the 96km-long Soča River runs from April to October; June is particularly good, as snowmelt keeps water levels high. Rapids range from easy to extreme, and rafting trips usually cover about 10km.

Hikes out of Bovec range from a 2-hour stroll south to Čezsoča and the protected gravel deposits in the Soča, to an ascent of Rombon (2208m), 5 hours away. The most popular walk is to Boka Waterfall, 5.5km southwest of Bovec. The waterfall drops 106m from the Kanin Mountains into the valley and is almost 30m wide – it's an impressive sight, especially now with the last of the snowmelt. — *www.bovec.si*

Spot game & climb dunes

NAMIBIA

WHY NOW You'll find wildlife beginning to cluster around drying waterholes
WHERE Countrywide
DATES June to September

06 JUN Vast Namibia is a place unlike any other – and is ideal in June. Stretching more than 2000km along Namibia's Atlantic coast is the Namib Desert. Here, dunes rise to 300m, and are best climbed during the cooler southern-hemisphere winter months. In the south is Fish River Canyon, where an 85km hiking trail follows the sandy riverbed – though in June you'll likely see the river in flow. Due to floods and heat, the route is only open mid-April to mid-September. In the north is Etosha National Park. Its name means 'Great White Place of Dry Water'; come now and you'll find wildlife beginning to cluster around drying waterholes.
— *www.namibiatourism.com.na*

LEFT: **Kayaking the Soca River gorge in Triglav National Park**

BELOW: **Ancient acacia trees in the Namib Desert, Namibia**

Join the Baby-Jumping Fest

SPAIN

WHY NOW See devilish men hurdle newborns
WHERE Castrillo de Murcia, near Burgos
DATES Sunday following Corpus Christi (7 Jun 2015; 29 May 2016; 18 Jun 2017; 3 Jun 2018)

07 JUN A bizarre one, this. At El Colacho – the Baby-Jumping Festival – grown men dress up in red and yellow costumes and leap over babies. The ritual has taken place in Castilla y León since 1620. It's how the villagers of Castrillo de Murcia celebrate the Catholic feast of Corpus Christi each year.

The idea is that the jumpers, with their devil costumes and truncheons, are personifications of diabolical evil. The babies (who must have been born in the previous 12 months) are laid out on mattresses on a procession route and, when the 'devils' leap over them, evil follows the leaper, and the babies' souls are cleansed.
— *www.turismocastillayleon.com*

Attend the Bounty Ball

AUSTRALIA

WHY NOW Fly to a remote Pacific isle to commemorate its mutinous past
WHERE Kingston, Norfolk Island
DATES 8 June

08 JUN In 1789, Fletcher Christian rebelled against his captain, William Bligh, as they sailed around the South Pacific. It became known as the Mutiny on the Bounty. The mutineers settled on Pitcairn Island, but before long had outgrown it; with permission from the British government, their descendants set off for then-uninhabited Norfolk Island (now a 3-hour flight from Sydney), and arrived on 8 June 1856 to set up a new home.

Bounty Day celebrates this arrival. There's a first landing reenactment at Kingston Pier, then processions, hill-rolling, games, a feast. Finally, everyone dons their glad rags for the evening's Bounty Ball. — *www.norfolkisland.com.au*

Surf Bali

INDONESIA

WHY NOW This month sees the very best waves
on the paradise isle

WHERE Bukit Peninsula, Bali

DATES June

09 JUN

Like a Native American dream-catcher, Bali's southern Bukit Peninsula droops into the Indian Ocean, picking up swells that have journeyed across the globe just to tumble onto its superb sandy tropical beaches. From Ulu Watu, near the peninsula's southwestern point, to the coastal village of Canggu, north of Seminyak, the mid-year brings trade winds from the southeast for warm water and epic waves.

And you won't have to run the gauntlet of territorial hard-heads: there's something here for everyone, from surf learners to surf legends. Kuta is Bali's surfing nursery, with gentle beach breaks and tubes. Canggu has a good right-hander at high tide, while a 2.5m swell at Balangan can be a classic wave.

Kuta, the former fishing village turned overdeveloped tourist hub, is also the place to broaden your Indonesian surf experience; from here you can arrange one-week 'surfaris' to other parts of Indonesia, including to the legendary Grajagan (G-Land) on eastern Java. You'll find surfboards and boogie boards for rent at Kuta, with variable quality and prices.

Kuta is also the main entry point for travellers flying into Bali – Denpasar Airport is nearby. — *www.balitourismboard.org*

Yomp around Yosemite

USA

WHY NOW Snowmelt is gushing down the waterfalls and Half Dome is hikeable
WHERE Yosemite National Park, California
DATES June

Yosemite might not have been the world's very first national park – that honour goes to Yellowstone, further east – but it was it was where John Muir, godfather of the conservation movement, was first inspired; Yosemite became the world's second national park in 1890 and has figured in most fresh-air fiends' 'top ten parks' ever since.

No surprise either: it is 3100 sq km of granite gloriousness, a happy valley of alpine summits, enormous and abundant trees, profuse wildlife, roaring cascades and 1300km of hiking trails.

June is a great month to go. The snowmelt from those lofty Sierra Nevada peaks see the numerous waterfalls – including Bridal Veil Falls (see *above*) and 739m Yosemite Falls, North America's highest – at their fullest and most impressive. Also, the snow has usually cleared from all the roads by this time.

Finally, the iconic hump of Half Dome is now climbable – the cables that are installed annually, to ease passage to the steep peak's summit, should be in place from late May (until mid-October). — *www.nps.gov/yose*

Celebrate Lajkonik

POLAND

WHY NOW Partake in a part of Polish legend
WHERE Rynek Główny, Krakow
DATES Thursday after Corpus Christi (11 Jun 2015; 2 Jun 2016; 22 Jun 2017; 7 Jun 2018)

11 JUN

When the head of Krakow's raftsmen defeated a Tatar marauder in the 13th century, he slipped into the Mongolian's robes and triumphantly rode into the city. The folkloric myth has been celebrated for more than 200 years with the procession of Lajkonik.

Clad in Mongol robes, the figure rides a hobbyhorse topped with peacock feathers, accompanied by the Mlaskoty musical troupe. The pageant proceeds from Zwierzyniec to the main square, where the mayor greets and honours Lajkonik. En route, the energetic larrikin dances, jumps, greets passers-by and strikes people with his mace, which is said to bring good luck. — *www.krakow.pl/en*

Gorge with St Anthony

PORTUGAL

WHY NOW To eat sardines and find true love with a bit of help from the matchmaker saint
WHERE Alfama, Lisbon
DATES 13 June

13 JUN

On the feast day of St Anthony, patron saint of Lisbon, the Portuguese capital goes sardine crazy. This is a nod to when the 13th-century Catholic saint was in Rimini, Italy. Depressed that the locals wouldn't listen to his sermons, he wandered to the shore to confide in the fish. Suddenly, rows of fish raised their heads above the waves and bowed to show their reverence.

Today, in Lisbon, there's a parade on Avenida de Liberdade and balconies are draped with streamers and paper lanterns. Also, single girls carry out rituals to implore Anthony – the matchmaker saint – to help them find a worthy husband. — *www.visitportugal.com*

Climb Mt Damavand

IRAN

WHY NOW It's the start of the trekking season, when conditions are best on this 5671m peak
WHERE Mt Damavand, Alborz Range
DATES Mid-June to September

12 JUN

Mt Damavand (5671m) is the highest mountain in the Middle East and one of the most recognisable icons in Iran – it appears on the IR10,000 note.

Damavand is a walk-up; summiting doesn't require technical gear, just good fitness. Climbing too quickly is the most dangerous aspect of this route, given the lung-squeezing altitude. Ascents start in Reyneh. You spend the first day walking to Camp 2, then on to Camp 3 (around 4250m) the next day, before heading for the summit.

June to mid September is the best climbing season: paths are usually snow-free, the weather is milder and basecamp can be easily accessed by public transport. — *www.damawand.de*

RIGHT: **Hiking the West Coast Trail in Pacific Rim National Park Reserve, British Columbia, Canada**

BELOW: **Women in Lisbon wearing traditional clothes on St Anthony's Day**

Hike the West Coast Trail

CANADA

WHY NOW Start one of the world's great hikes just before peak season begins
WHERE Vancouver Island, British Columbia
DATES 14 June (or May–Sep)

14 JUN

The 75km West Coast Trail on Vancouver Island was originally constructed as an escape route for shipwreck survivors, following a century of horrific maritime accidents. It's a stunning hike that takes between five and seven days, passing through virgin spruce, cedar and hemlock forests, across cliff tops and over suspension bridges, along stretches of deserted beaches punctuated by clear tidal pools, and up and down steep gullies and waterways.

Every kilometre must be earned, and a good level of fitness is required. You'll climb hundreds of rocky steps, cross streams on slippery logs, scale cliffs on rock-face ladders, and plough through knee-deep mud. Heavy fog and torrential rain are de rigueur (as are chance encounters with bears and even cougars).

The trail is open from May to September, and permits are required. Between 15 June and 15 September (peak hiking season) additional reservations are also required – so starting on 14 June means optimal weather conditions without having to reserve. — *www.pc.gc.ca*

Wonder at the White Nights

RUSSIA

WHY NOW Enjoy after-hours action in the fine Russian city, when the sun barely sets
WHERE St Petersburg
DATES Mid-June to early July

15 JUN Forget about sleeping in Russian high summer. Instead, embrace the Beliye Nochi – White Nights. Due to its northerly latitude (roughly the same as southern Greenland), the city of St Petersburg enjoys wonderfully long days from around late May to early July; the very brightest period is during the second half of June, when it doesn't get dark at all. Instead, a magical twilight accompanies the witching hours; streetlights stay off and locals don't bother with bed.

St Petersburg makes the most of this extra illumination. A cultural festival takes over town, with a wealth of world-class opera, ballet and orchestral performances, many held at the grand Mariinsky Theatre.

But you don't have to go high-brow to revel in the White Nights. Spend a day sun-soaking in the Letnii Sad (Summer Garden) or by the Neva River, then hop on an evening cruise or take a late-night river promenade to see the mighty bridges parting (a local tradition). Finally, party at an oh-so-hip nightclub and watch the sun *not* set on the regal city. — *www.visitrussia.org.uk*

Go bookish on Bloomsday

IRELAND

WHY NOW Live like a literary great, by spending the day as a James Joyce character
WHERE Dublin
DATES 16 June

This celebration of great Irish scribe, James Joyce, takes place on the day he chose to set his masterpiece, *Ulysses*. Bloomsday's literary pilgrims make life reflect art by descending on the locations visited by the novel's protagonist, Leopold Bloom. The tradition began in 1954, when some local writers in horse-drawn cabs attempted to visit all the locations in the modernist yarn.

Dressed as Edwardians, Joyce fans start with an Irish breakfast – a reference to the kidney-scoffing Bloom. The day includes readings, guided walks and stops at landmarks such as Davy Byrne's pub, where, like Bloom, they eat a gorgonzola sandwich. — *www.visitdublin.com*

LEFT: **The Church of our Saviour on the Spilled Blood in St Petersburg's summer**

BELOW: **Make a heroic effort to celebrate Bloomsday in Dublin**

Cheer at the regatta

ITALY

WHY NOW Watch a 13th-century boat race – and enjoy jeering the losers
WHERE Palazzo Medici, Pisa
DATES 17 June (St Ranieri's Day)

Pisa's 1500m dash up the River Arno dates back to the 1290s. Four narrow rowboats, representing the city's four districts, race; each contains a steersman, a climber and eight oarsmen struggling against the current. The finishing line is a boat anchored at Palazzo Medici, a location decided in 1737 upon the request of the Duke of Montelimar, who was staying in one of the palaces there.

The climbers must scale the boat's 10m mast and grab a *paliotto* (silk banner). The blue banner indicates first place, white is second, red is third. The winners receive an ox or rooster; the losers a pair of goslings – and torrents of abuse. — *www.pisaunicaterra.it*

Sail to see walruses

USA

WHY NOW You'll see thousands of jostling, galumphing, mock-fighting male walruses
WHERE Walrus Islands Sanctuary, Alaska
DATES June to August

When female and immature walruses head north each summer to follow the receding ice pack through the Bering Strait, the males stay behind and whoop it up with 'the guys'. Actually they spend their time sleeping and sunbathing on beaches around Alaska's Bristol Bay, making occasional forays to catch dinner. They also do quite a bit of mock fighting as they pack together on wave-swept beaches and argue over sleeping spots. And the action gets pretty exciting on Round Island, where 2000 to 14,000 males jostle on a single beach. Charter a boat in Dillingham and visit Round Island on a day trip or be dropped off for a wild camping experience. — *wildlife.alaska.gov*

Raise a dram to the Ridings

SCOTLAND

WHY NOW Hail horses and ancient traditions
WHERE Scottish Borders
DATES Selkirk Riding is held on the second Friday after the first Monday in June

19 JUN

The Riding of the Marches, or Common Riding, takes place throughout the summer in major Scottish Borders towns. Its roots date back to the Middle Ages, when riders would be sent to the town boundary to check on the common lands. In those dark days of brigands, rogues and highwaymen, the young riders faced many perils, including clashes with incursive neighbouring settlements.

Today's colourful event involves extravagant convoys of horse riders following the town flag as it's taken on a well-worn route. Festivities vary from town to town but all usually involve lots of singing, sport, pageants, concerts and, of course, 70 Shillings, 80 Shillings and other tartan ales. No Scottish shindig is complete without mythical quantities of alcohol, and tipples like Curds and Cream (a mix of rum and milk) are as important as the procession.

Selkirk's event is one of Europe's largest equestrian gatherings and one of the oldest Common Ridings. It remembers the Battle of Flodden Field (1513), when the English annihilated James IV's invading Scottish army and just one of Selkirk's soldiers returned.

While you're in the area, visit antique-packed Abbotsford House (a few kilometres away from Selkirk), the 19th-century residence of the Scottish literary colossus Sir Walter Scott. — *www.visitscotland.com/library/commonriding*

LEFT: **DAVID FERNIE – ALAMY**

Watch awesome opera

ITALY

WHY NOW Enter a 2000-year-old amphitheatre to watch unbeatable operatics
WHERE Verona
DATES Mid-June to September

20 JUN Built by the Romans in AD 30, the Arena in Verona could hold 30,000 spectators in its day. And it continues to put on quite a performance each summer, once the opera season starts.

From June to early September, productions are put on here. And there's nothing quite like hearing world-class divas belt out a bit of *Aida* in such a historic setting. Even if you have no clue what the singers are saying, spending a balmy evening amid a 'Bravo!'-shouting audience, watching candles light up as the sun goes down, is magical indeed. Just remember: take a cushion – Roman stone terraces don't come with padding. — *www.arena.it*

Dive around Bazaruto

MOZAMBIQUE

WHY NOW For great weather and underwater conditions, and the chance to see passing whales
WHERE Bazaruto Archipelago
DATES June to September

22 JUN The Bazaruto Archipelago, off southern Mozambique, is a quintessential tropical paradise, with clear waters that offer excellent diving and snorkelling.

Since 1971 much of the archipelago has sat within a national park; thanks to this protected status, nature is in rude health. Dolphins swim alongside 2000 types of fish, loggerhead, leatherback and green turtles, and elusive dugongs, which forage among the sea-grass.

June to October is dry season: clear blue skies, abundant sunshine and almost no rain. Diving conditions are good all year, but migrating humpback whales pass by from June to September. — *www.divebazaruto.com*

See solstice at Stonehenge

ENGLAND

WHY NOW Watch the sun rise over Neolithic stones, along with druids and dawn-seekers
WHERE Stonehenge, Wiltshire
DATES Summer solstice, usually 21 June

21 JUN The celebrations to mark the longest day of the northern year date back to pre-Christian times and inspire various rituals, from fertility rites to invocations of future agricultural success.

One of the most famous summer solstice celebrations is at England's Stonehenge. From 1972 to 1984 neo-druids and other alternative communities converged on the Neolithic stone circle for the Stonehenge Free Festival, but in 1985 a clash between riot police and travellers setting up the festival lead to the site being off limits for solstice. Thankfully, it reopened in 1999, and the spiritual dawn now attracts more than 20,000 people. — *www.stonehenge.co.uk*

LEFT: **Wildebeest cross the Mara River**

BELOW: **Sunrise at Stonehenge**

Marvel at the Migration

KENYA & TANZANIA

WHY NOW Things get pretty exciting when over a million wildebeest cross croc-infested rivers
WHERE Masai Mara & Serengeti
DATES June to August

23 JUN Although Africa's wildebeests are sometimes called 'clowns of the plains', they are deadly serious when they set out on their annual trek from their calving grounds in Tanzania's Serengeti to fresh grazing in Kenya's Masai Mara.

The result is the most famous mammal migration on earth, as over a million wildebeest are joined by 500,000 gazelles and 200,000 zebras on a sweeping journey in search of food. Predators are in close attendance, including 6m-long Nile crocodiles that lie in wait at each river crossing. These crossings – first the Grumeti River in Tanzania, then the Talek and Mara Rivers in Kenya – are terrifying for the wildebeest, which line up on the bank, pushing each other towards the water below.

The wildebeest migration is an ongoing event: wildebeest are constantly on the move, making one complete circumnavigation of the Serengeti each year. In late June the wildebeest turn north and head towards the Mara, so this is a good time to catch them as they cross the northern Serengeti. — *www.serengeti.org*

Attend Inti Raymi

PERU

WHY NOW The most important Inca ceremony is re-enacted – but without the llama sacrifice

WHERE Sacsayhuamán, Cuzco

DATES 24 June

24 JUN This paean to the sun god, Inti, used to involve mass sacrifice. Llamas got the chop in the gory ritual, which was also dedicated to Pachamama, Inti's wife and the goddess of fertility. Thankfully, no blood is shed these days, and there are even comfy chairs for the tourists.

The annual Inti Raymi festival reenacts traditions dating back 500 years to the Incan empire's heyday – back then it was the biggest ceremony in then capital, Cuzco. It celebrated the Incan New Year and winter solstice, when the sun was furthest from this side of the earth and Inti needed to be buttered up.

Today's action takes place at the mysterious stone ruin of Sacsayhuamán, on the outskirts of Cuzco. The lucky actor who is selected to portray Sapa Inca, the emperor, is borne to the hilltop edifice in a golden chariot. Fortunately for his pallbearers, it's a replica of the original, 60kg beauty.

Starting from Qorikancha, the sun temple, the procession winds through the city streets, which are filled with music, prayers and flowers; ladies with brooms sweep away evil spirits.

Upon arriving at Sacsayhuamán, speeches are delivered in Quechua, the Incan language, and the faux sacrifice is performed. The high priest holds a heart up to Pachamama and reads the future in the bloodstains. As Inti's orb slides below the horizon, bonfires spark and the procession returns to Cuzco. — *www.peru.travel*

See surfing hippos

GABON

WHY NOW It's the beginning of the dry season
and the whale season in wild West Africa

WHERE Loango National Park

DATES June to September

25 JUN Dubbed 'Africa's Last Eden', 1550 sq km Loango National Park was one of Gabon's first protected areas. Unspoilt, and rich in a diverse wealth of wildlife, it is also nicknamed 'the land of surfing hippos' for the discovery that hippos come out of the forest to swim in the ocean surf here. Nowhere else can you watch hippos, elephants, leopards and forest buffalo walking on a white sand beach by the ocean.

Only recently did scientists realise that the 100km of uninhabited coastline is also home to the second greatest concentration and diversity of whales and dolphins in the world. Among the 14 species found here are 1500 to 3000 humpback whales that arrive in June to calve and spend the winter. — *www.africas-eden.com*

Climb Svolværgeita

NORWAY

WHY NOW If you're climbing this far north do it
in summer, maybe under the midnight sun

WHERE Lofoten Islands

DATES June and July

26 JUN The small but modern port town of Svolvær is as busy as it gets on Norway's Lofoten Islands, and much of the activity centres on a pinnacle of rock. Svolværgeita (the Svolvær Goat) is one of the symbols of Lofoten, a distinctive two-pronged peak that towers above the town. Climbing it is claimed as one of Norway's great adrenaline rushes, not so much for the climb but for the challenge once you reach its top. Having scaled the Goat, it's almost compulsory that you then jump from one 'horn' to the other.

Most people can easily access the base of Svolværgeita, but reaching the horns, Storhornet and Lillehornet, requires a 40m technical climb before you make the 1.5m jump between them. — *www.lofoten.info*

LEFT: **Inti Raymi, Peru's Festival of the Sun**

BELOW: **Rock climbers overlooking Svolvaer in the Lofoten Islands**

Cycle end to end

GREAT BRITAIN

WHY NOW The weather favours a summer ride, with June the best month for quiet roads

WHERE Land's End to John O'Groats

DATES June to early July

27 JUN Travelling from Land's End to John O'Groats – from the extreme southwest tip to the northeast corner of the British mainland – is a route cycled by around 3000 people every year. It can be ridden along numerous routes, most totalling around 1600km in length. The Cyclists' Touring Club produces an info pack for end-to-enders.

Most cyclists do the trip in two to three weeks, though if you're short on time the record stands at a smidge over 41 hours. If you're not hurried, make provisions to stretch it out a little – Land's End to John O'Groats may be the UK's epic ride but there's plenty to enjoy by lingering in places such as Dartmoor, the Lake District, Loch Ness and the Grampians.

Summer, just before school holidays, is the best time, with long daylight hours. For the best conditions, begin in Land's End and ride to John O'Groats (even if heading south to north feels psychologically uphill). Riding in this direction, the winds are more likely to be favourable and there'll be no riding into the midday sun. — *www.ctc.org.uk*

Groove at Glastonbury

ENGLAND

WHY NOW Bring your wellies for the biggest mud-n-music festival around
WHERE Worthy Farm, Somerset
DATES Last weekend in June (24–28 Jun 2015)

28 JUN Welcome to Glasto. The colossal summer knees-up is the world's biggest and best music festival. It's like Woodstock, except it takes place (almost) every year. The list of performers who have rocked the venue's muddy fields reads like a who's who of popular music: Dylan, Bowie, Oasis, Blur, Björk.

More than 175,000 revellers descend on 900 acres of farmland, bringing tents, cider and, if it's one of the 'muddy years', Wellington boots. Much of the entertainment has nothing to do with the headline acts on the Pyramid Stage, but rather the quirky outer tents, surreal glades and spiritual sunsets that make this a gathering like no other. — *www.glastonburyfestivals.co.uk*

LEFT: **Not quite halfway; cycling through Wales**

BELOW: **Rioja's Batalla del Vino – a riotous good time or a scandalous waste of wine?**

Wage a Wine War

SPAIN

WHY NOW Partake in the Batalla del Vino, a chance to soak and be soaked by Spanish plonk
WHERE Haro, La Rioja
DATES 29 June (St Pedro's Day)

29 JUN On St Pedro's Day in Haro, capital of Spain's Rioja-producing region, thousands take to the streets with vino-loaded water pistols, supersoakers, gourds, buckets, bottles and even old boots to wage a Wine War. The 3-hour drenching commemorates a medieval dispute with neighbouring Miranda de Ebro and dates back 300 years; the local council even provides the ammunition. The result: tens of thousands of litres of cheap red sprayed around Biliblio, the clifftop battlefield.

To take part, you must wear a white shirt (it's compulsory). And arming yourself with some sort of water weapon is highly recommended. — *www.haro.org*

Scale Mt Elbrus

RUSSIA

WHY NOW It's the best season for tackling Europe's highest peak
WHERE Caucasus, Russia–Georgia border
DATES June to September

30 JUN Welcome to Europe's highest mountain: volcanic Elbrus, on the Russia–Georgia border, bulges 5642m up from the Caucasus Ridge, the geographical divide between Europe and Asia.

The climb to the summit is not technically difficult, and is made easier by a cable car and chairlift that take you up to 3800m. It's then a fairly easy, though crevasse-sliced, walk up to Camp 11 – which needs to be booked in advance in high season (the more clement summer months). The final assault from here is made in a day – about 8 hours up and 8 hours down. A long slog, but the reward is to stand atop a continent. — *www.elbrus.su*

See the Land of Fire & Ice

RUSSIA

WHY NOW Come in midsummer for endless days and the finest weather

WHERE Kamchatka Peninsula

DATES July and August

01 JUL Closer to LA than Moscow, and dubbed the 'land of fire and ice', Kamchatka is one of Russia's least-explored but most spectacular regions. A 1000km-long peninsula separated from the mainland by the Sea of Okhotsk, this hyperactive volcanic land bubbles, spurts and spews in a manner that suggests Creation hasn't yet finished. The region claims more than 200 volcanoes; 20 or more rank among the world's most volatile.

The thermal activity also produces hot springs, heated rivers and geysers. The most spectacular examples are found in the Valley of the Geysers, where around 200 fumaroles blast steam and mud from the canyon floor.

In addition, Kamchatka's large areas of forest and grassland are home to an array of wildlife, including 10,000 to 20,000 brown bears. — *www.visitkamchatka.com*

July

Ride a summer bobsled

AUSTRIA

WHY NOW The Olympic bobsled run opens for summer fun now

WHERE Igls, Innsbruck

DATES July and August

02 JUL In 1976 the Olympic Winter Games journeyed to the Austrian city of Innsbruck, the capital of the Tyrol region. Here, high above the city in the ski resort of Igls, a bobsled track snaked like plumbing across the Alpine slopes. A few days of competition and the world moved on, leaving Igls and its track to slide into history. Or not. Igls decided to throw its track open to the public. Bobsled runs behind professional drivers quickly became a winter favourite; more recently, summer visitors have been able to climb aboard, with wheels replacing runners for two months of the year.

The summer bob might be modified, but the thrill is not. In a bobsled driven by a world-class pilot, you whizz down the 1270m-long run, likely screaming as you negotiate the run's 14 curves at speeds of up to 100 km/h. You'll feel the full G-force thrill of banking and bending through a blur of Alpine countryside.

Early July is also the ideal time to hit the many hiking trails in the region; these are brightened by Alpine rose, which blooms from mid-June. — *www.olympiaworld.at; www.knauseder-event.at*

Yee-haw! at Stampede

CANADA

WHY NOW It's the world's biggest cowboy party
WHERE Stampede Park, Calgary, Alberta
DATES Starts on the first Friday after Canada Day
(1 July), for two weeks

03 JUL More mild west than wild west, Calgary – known colloquially as 'Cowtown' – dons its spurs for the self-proclaimed 'greatest outdoor show on earth'. Bringing together an invitation-only list of the world's best cowboys, the 10-day equine-influenced party is headlined by one of the richest rodeos on earth.

Evenings at Stampede Park belong to the chuckwagon racing: four wagons and outriders hurtle around a race track at 60km/h (think *Ben Hur* meets Ascot). Outside the main arena, the Stampede goes from mares to fairs, with rides, deep-fried food and the Indian Village, which offers a glimpse into First Nation traditions. — *calgarystampede.com*

LEFT: **Innbruck and the Alps, setting for summer bobsledding**

BELOW: **Celebrate Independence Day in the USA with fireworks in New York**

Party for Independence

USA

WHY NOW Feel all-American amid a firework spectacular on Independence Day
WHERE New York City
DATES 4 July

04 JUL You could be anywhere in the US of A today. It is Independence Day, when every American small town, big city and hub in between commemorates the adoption of the Declaration of Independence on 4 July 1776 with fireworks, barbecues and parades.

So yes, you could be anywhere – but New York is best. The Big Apple celebrates biggest, with Macy's department store launching the mother of all pyrotechnic displays: more than 40,000 firework shells, launched from barges on the Hudson River, explode over the skyscrapers. For something different, head to Nathan's in Coney Island at noon, to watch the annual hot-dog-eating contest. — *www.nycgo.com*

Watch wife-carrying

FINLAND

WHY NOW See macho men race with the missus
WHERE Market Sq, Sonkajärvi
DATES First weekend in July (4–5 Jul 2015; 2–3 Jul 2016; 1–2 Jul 2017; 7–8 Jul 2018)

05 JUL This bizarre festival has its roots in the custom of pillaging neighbouring villages for womenfolk. Today's unreconstructed men may be disappointed to discover they're not allowed to keep their partner at the end – unless she is actually their wife.

Over a distance of 253.5m, contestants must tackle sand, grass and gravel surfaces, two dry obstacles and a 1m-deep water section. All this while carrying a 'wife' – who must be aged over 17 and weigh more than 49kg. The only equipment the wife-carriers are allowed is a belt. The winning couple receives the woman's weight in beer. — *www.sonkajarvi.fi*

Swim the English Channel

ENGLAND & FRANCE

WHY NOW Be first out of the blocks in Channel-swimming season
WHERE Dover to Cap Gris Nez
DATES Late June to September

06 JUL

Want a challenge? Then why not swim the English Channel!

There are official regulations for this 32km-long crossing. No wetsuits are allowed – only grease, goggles and an armless and legless costume. All the more reason to do this in summer, when the water temperature is a little higher (15°C in late June, up to 18°C in September), and there are more hours of sunshine.

The route runs across the open water from Shakespeare's Cliff near Dover to Cap Gris Nez in Pas-de-Calais, northern France. Oh, and if you think you're quick, know this: the record time is just under 7 hours.
— *www.channelswimmingassociation.com*

Summer in the Arctic

GREENLAND

WHY NOW In this Arctic land, spring begins now: watch flowers burst through melting snows
WHERE Island-wide
DATES July

07 JUL

The world's largest island has vast swathes of beautiful, unfenced wilderness, and now is the time to explore it under near permanent daylight, and at its warmest.

Greenland's dominant feature is its ice cap, the world's second-largest, covering around 80% of the land; experienced cross-country skiers can spend three exhausting weeks traversing it. However, the island offers marvellous trekking for those seeking a less arduous total-wilderness experience. Almost all walking is on unmarked routes. Views are magnificent and the purity of light is magical, with the silence broken only by ravens, streams or the reverberating thuds of exploding icebergs. — *www.greenland.com*

RIGHT: **Runners brave the bulls in Pamplona**

BELOW: **Summer sees Nuuk's red cathedral surrounded by green in Greenland's capital**

Get close to humpbacks

CANADA

WHY NOW Humpbacks come near shore to feed, resulting in wonderfully up-close whale-watching
WHERE Avalon Peninsula, Newfoundland
DATES June to September

08 JUL

Humpback whales prefer to feed near shore, so this species suffered terribly at the hand of hunters. Now that their population is recovering, it's once again possible to watch their feeding techniques.

Several thousand humpbacks arrive on the Avalon Peninsula in June to feed on billions of spawning capelin, a small fish that lays eggs in wet sand. It's the largest gathering of hungry humpback whales in the world.

One of the best viewing spots is St Vincent's Beach, where the sand drops off so steeply into deep water that the whales practically swim onto the beach to feed. A truly special sight.
— *www.atlanticwhales.com*

Run with the bulls

SPAIN

WHY NOW To watch the drunken gore-fest that is the Fiesta de San Fermin

WHERE Plaza de Toros, Pamplona, Navarra

DATES 6–14 July

09 JUL Pamplona's Running of the Bulls is an unbridled outpouring of Spanish passion. As part of the festivities dedicated to the town's patron saint, San Fermin, hundreds of 'runners' sprint in front of a six-pack of raging bulls. Every year there are injuries and even the odd fatality.

The *encierro* (bull run) begins at Corrales del Gas. The dash through central Pamplona is swift, taking about three minutes. With the bulls charging at up to 55km/h, it's impossible to outrun them for the whole course, so runners tackle sections before jumping out of the way. The two scariest bits are Estafeta, the stone alley with only doorways to take refuge in, and the narrow entrance to Plaza del Toros. It's a regular bottleneck for fear-crazed runners and their snorting pursuers. Pile-ups, where runners fall over and create a human barrier for the poor sods behind them, are a big danger.

Before the rocket is fired, signalling the bulls' release, stewards circulate to persuade the inebriated not to run – the fiesta's other big aspect is the primal all-out partying.
— *www.sanfermin.com*

Watch fishing bears

USA

WHY NOW You can see the bears catching salmon amid waterfalls
WHERE Katmai National Park, Alaska
DATES July and September

10 JUL

If you've ever seen photos of brown bears standing on the lip of a waterfall and catching leaping salmon with their gaping mouths, you are looking at Brooks Falls in Alaska's Katmai National Park. This immense park is home to one of the densest populations of brown bears in the world (estimated at 2200), as well as some of the world's largest salmon runs, so when the salmon are running the rivers in July and September this is absolute paradise for the resident bears.

The 700kg bears here are so huge because they have access to abundant high-quality food. They generally don't bother humans, but they are still extremely dangerous and unpredictable – backcountry hikers should exercise caution here. Most visitors are content to watch bears from the viewing platform at Brook Falls near the main visitor centre, which leads to crowding during the July peak season, but many of the park's vast wilderness areas are rarely visited.

Katmai's diverse landscapes range from the volcanic Valley of Ten Thousand Smokes to endless alpine peaks, fertile coastal plains and complex coastlines of fiords and headlands. This is a great place to observe moose, caribou, wolves, lynxes, wolverines, sea otters, bald eagles and killer whales. — *www.nps.gov/katm*

LEFT: **PAUL SOUDERS– GETTY IMAGES**

Gamble on the Camel Cup

AUSTRALIA

WHY NOW Watch a clutch of cantankerous camels compete in the Red Centre

WHERE Alice Springs, Northern Territory

DATES Middle Saturday of July (11 Jul 2015)

11 JUL Come July, the dusty Outback outpost of Alice explodes with bellydancing, bands, rickshaw rallies and, most importantly, camel races. Camel racing's appeal lies in the beasts' unpredictability and irascibility. They snarl, gurn, bite, and can spit more than 3m. At the start of a race, they might stay right where they are or even reverse; when they get going at full tilt, jockeys have to do their utmost to stay astride.

Held at Blatherskite Park, part of the Central Australian Show Society grounds, the desert extravaganza offers all sorts of trophies in addition to the main Imparja gong. The Afghanistan Cup is presented by the country's ambassador to Australia, commemorating the Afghans who brought camels to the Outback and constructed telegraph lines and railways. In the Honeymoon Handicap, 'grooms' race halfway around the arena before lowering the camels, and handing the reins to their 'brides'. Tykes and ungulates can compete in the hobby camel capers and the Prettiest Camel contest.

— *www.camelcup.com.au*

Dive with great white sharks

SOUTH AFRICA

WHY NOW Get in the water with fearsome predators and watch them hunt young seals
WHERE Dyer Island, near Cape Town
DATES June to August

12 JUL

There are so many great white sharks around South Africa's False Bay, Mossel Bay and Dyer Island that the area is considered the Great White Shark Capital of the World. These toothy predators patrol the deep around the Cape-fur-seal colonies, often launching ferocious attacks by accelerating vertically with such explosive force that they erupt completely out of the water.

Watch the sharks up-close from small boats or descend into a cage for heart-racing views. Peak season is June to mid-August. June is better for seeing sharks near the boats (so, good for cage diving); July and August are best for the breaching behaviour. — *www.whiteshark.co.za*

Feel manly at Naadam

MONGOLIA

WHY NOW Watch the festival of the manly arts, Mongolia's own mini Olympics
WHERE Ulaanbaatar
DATES 11–13 July

13 JUL

Mongolia's major festival is a celebration of 'manly sports': archery, wrestling, horse racing and, unofficially, drinking *airag* (fermented mares' milk). Perhaps most quintessentially Mongolian is the horse racing, a tribute to the animals used by nomads on the Steppe.

Proceedings begin with the jockeys singing to calm the horses. After a gallop across the plains, the winner is commended with a song. Music is also key in the archery; contestants sing to their arrows to implore them to travel straight.

Wrestling is the only game women don't do: the wrestlers' open-front jackets are designed to out female infiltrators. — *www.mongoliatourism.org*

LEFT: **Riders at the Alice Springs Camel Cup compete for the prestigious Gold Lions Camel Cup**

BELOW: **Wrestling is one of the three 'manly' sports of Mongolia's Naadam**

Cycle the French Alps

FRANCE

WHY NOW Be inspired as the Tour de France rolls through the mountains
WHERE French Alps
DATES Mid July

14 JUL

When the Tour de France rolls into the French Alps, everything else is forgotten. Pelotons of world-class cyclists grind out enormous climbs, then plummet like bobsledders in a whizz of thighs, Lycra and cheering crowds. In the hours before they arrive you can ride the climbs yourself (or just wait to watch the pros).

Alpe d'Huez defines the Tour's Alpine stages. This 13.8km climb has an average grade of 8.5%, and 21 hairpin bends. It also becomes a grand celebration of people, colour and sounds.

The days that the Tour passes through the Alps varies a little, but 14 July is a good bet – and it's also Bastille Day: *vive la France*! — *www.letour.com*

Traverse a glacier

PAKISTAN

WHY NOW It's peak trekking season, and the only time you'll be able to cross the glaciers
WHERE Karakoram Mountains
DATES Mid-June to September

 15 JUL Northern Pakistan is heaven for mountain lovers, a place where you can walk for days on even the most popular routes without seeing another trekker. Foremost among the trekking regions is Baltistan, the centre of the Karakoram's glaciers, peaks and rock towers. Five of the biggest glaciers – Biafo, Baltoro, Chogo Lungma, Panmah, and Kaberi and Kondus – offer the longest glacier traverses outside the sub-polar zones.

The ultimate is to traverse the length of one of these glaciers. Two treks epitomise this experience: the Hispar La trek to Snow Lake, and the Baltoro Glacier trek to K2 Base Camp. Both lead up massive ice highways lined with magnificent peaks into the heart of the Karakoram. — *www.tourism.gov.pk*

RIGHT: **The dress code says kimono at Gion Matsuri Festival in Kyoto. Japan**

BELOW: **Pakistan's Karakoram range is one of the world's least explored mountain regions**

Join the 300 Club

ANTARCTICA

WHY NOW Be one of the few mad souls to have ice-run naked at the South Pole
WHERE Amundsen-Scott South Pole Station
DATES July

 16 JUL If you're ever at the Amundsen-Scott South Pole Station in July (a time when no normal tourist would brave the dark Antarctic winter), keep an eye on the thermometer. Because when it hits -73°C (-100°F) you'll have the chance to tick off an outdoor experience that few others ever have, and one that ensures entry to a rather exclusive (eccentric?) club.

First, crank up the sauna and steam in it until it reaches 93°C (200°F). Once heated, run naked (but for shoes) out into the snow; the brave may push on further, and do a circuit around the Ceremonial South Pole. If you can secure photographic proof of your cool runnings, you can join the 300 Club – so named for the 300°F drop in temperature between the sauna and the polar air. — *www.antarctica.ac.uk*

Gaze at Gion Matsuri

JAPAN

WHY NOW Visit the old imperial capital at its kimono-wearing best

WHERE Kyoto

DATES 17 July

17 JUL

Japanese culture often mystifies outsiders, and Kyoto's multifaceted parade-cum-kimono display is no exception. The procession of *yamaboko* floats on 17 July remembers the occasion in AD 869 when 66 dignitaries, each representing a Japanese province, trooped through Kyoto to beseech Gozu Tenno, god of plague, to give the city a break.

It takes up to 40 people to move the teetering temples on wheels. For three mornings from 10 July, you can watch them being built out of huge, carved blocks, some weighing more than 10 tonnes. Once the construction is over, along with the purification of the portable shrines in the river, Kyoto gets down to the serious business of celebration.

Devotional performances take place, including one by dancers in heron costumes. Gaggles of white-faced teenage girls click through the streets in wooden clogs and *yukata* (summer kimonos). Residences in the merchant quarter play 'open house', offering the chance to see Japanese heirlooms in their original setting.

A star of the parade itself is *chigo*, a local boy who rides the main yamaboko wearing Shinto robes and a golden phoenix crown. The poor lad has to undergo weeks of purification to prepare.

Gion Matsuri lasts throughout July but is most colourful in the middle of the month. There's plenty more to do here though – the imperial capital until 1868, Kyoto has hundreds of temples and gardens. — *www.jnto.go.jp*

Join the Festa del Redentore

ITALY

WHY NOW For fantastic fireworks over the canals
WHERE Venice Somerset Island, Nunavut
DATES Third weekend in July (18–19 Jul 2015; 16–17 Jul 2016; 15–16 Jul 2017; 21–22 Jul 2018)

18 JUL Between 1575 and 1577, a plague swept through Venice, claiming 50,000 lives – a third of the population. When the epidemic abated, the Senate, thanking the Redeemer (Jesus) for answering its prayers, built Il Redentore church and started a festival.

Today, the event is an excuse for a lot of fireworks. The whole city loads into gondolas during the day. At sunset St Mark's Basin fills with thousands of illuminated boats decorated with flowers and balloons. At 11.30pm those celebrants who have run out of vino and focaccia are consoled by the fabulous display.

On Sunday, Venetians have until the afternoon to recover before a gondola regatta. Remembering the festival's religious roots, mass is held before the Patriarch of Venice in Il Redentore, on the island of Giudecca. Reluctant churchgoers are lured by a 330m-long temporary bridge across Giudecca Canal, formed of gondolas. — *turismovenezia.it*

Behold Hundreds of Beluga

CANADA

WHY NOW Beluga whales concentrate in great numbers to moult and rear calves
WHERE Venice Somerset Island, Nunavut
DATES July and August

19 JUL

Beluga whales – 5m-long, and as white as Carrara marble – strike such expressive poses that you'd swear they're making faces at you. So watching hundreds of thousands of them in their summer moulting grounds is quite a moving sight.

In summer, belugas migrate to traditional moulting and calving sites, nearly always by river mouths where the slightly warmer water is ideal for newborn calves. Adults also take advantage of shallow gravel bars to rub old skin layers off. This is a very active time for belugas, who make shrill ringing calls heard for miles as they splash in the water.

These gatherings can be seen at the mouth of Québec's St Lawrence River or Manitoba's Churchill River. To see belugas in an Arctic setting, head to the north edge of Somerset Island in Nunavut. Fly from Ottawa to Iqaluit, then by private plane to Cunningham River.
— *www.nunavuttourism.com*

LEFT: **GUILLEM LOPEZ**

Feel pure at Mwaka Kogwa

TANZANIA

WHY NOW Cleanse yourself for the Persian New Year in Zanzibari style
WHERE Kae Kuu, Makunduchi, Zanzibar
DATES Usually 4 days in the third week of July

20 JUL

Walloping your neighbour with the stalk of a banana plant doesn't sound like a healthy pursuit, but in Zanzibar it's seen as a purification ritual. The theory is that by taking out aggression and settling scores, participants will start the coming year in harmony.

In practice, it's a gleeful scuff. Two brothers from Makunduchi take on two southern siblings and their friends soon pile in. On the perimeter of the battlefield, women show off their best outfits and sing in the local Kikae dialect. The ceremony ends when the *mganga* (healer) torches a coconut-thatch hut; a ritual designed to ensure that any house fires that occur in the new year do not cause fatalities. — *www.tanzaniatouristboard.com*

Have fun at Heiva

TAHITI

WHY NOW Join Polynesia's biggest party – wear flowers, bang drums and dance like crazy
WHERE To'ata Sq, Pape'ete
DATES Late June to late July

22 JUL

Traditionally a celebration of life or a preparation for war, and now a gala of French Polynesia's indigenous culture, Heiva sees the islands of Tahiti explode with drum-cracks, feathered costumes and vibrant parades. Visitors might find themselves adorned with hibiscus garlands and Tiare flowers as they are dragged into the party.

As well as dances (a little reminiscent of the Maori haka) and traditional sports, a more modern addition is a the Mr and Miss Tahiti showdown: contenders must scale palm trees, crack open coconuts and lift stones to prove their romantic worth.
— *www.tahiti-tourisme.com*

Windsurf at Vasiliki Bay

GREECE

WHY NOW To make the most of 'Eric', a summer afternoon creature
WHERE Vasiliki Bay, Lefkada
DATES July and August

21 JUL

Windsurfing is the most popular water sport in Greece, and little wonder when Vasiliki Bay, on the south coast of the Ionian island of Lefkada, is considered the best place to windsurf in Europe. Nor are conditions here elitist, with many reckoning that Vasiliki Bay is one of the best places to learn the sport.

You'll find a wide, sheltered bay just waiting for the afternoon winds – known locally as 'Eric' – to blow in. Along the beach, numerous windsurfing companies have staked prominent claims; they offer all-inclusive tuition and accommodation packages. If they've got spare gear, some will rent it to the independent enthusiast. — *www.lefkada-greece.biz*

RIGHT: **Don't let the name put you off the Badwater Ultramarathon**

BELOW: **Windsurfers in Vasiliki Bay, Greece**

Run the Badwater Ultra

USA

WHY NOW To discover that madness is a hot, hot, hot foot race

WHERE Death Valley, California

DATES Mid July

23 JUL Billed as the world's toughest foot race, the Badwater Ultramarathon puts the 'deathly' back into Death Valley. Beginning at Badwater, the lowest point in the Western Hemisphere (85m below sea level) in Death Valley's navel, the race crosses three mountain ranges to the Mt Whitney Portals, the trailhead to the summit of the highest peak in the contiguous United States. Not content to inflict 217km of running and 4000m of ascent on its competitors, the race is held in midsummer, a time when Death Valley once suffered the second-highest temperature on record: 56.7°C.

If you're still keen (seriously?!), you must pass a rigorous selection process. All applicants are ranked on a scale of zero to 10, according to their previous ultramarathon achievements, with the 90 highest-ranked runners accepted into the race. If you make the grade, you must behave in the spirit of the event. According to the rules, 'all racers must display courtesy, good taste, decorum, and sportsmanship at all times. Nudity is specifically not allowed'.

— *www.badwater.com*

Try the most dangerous trek

CHINA

WHY NOW Come in summer for the safest and best conditions
WHERE Huá Shān, Shaanxi province
DATES May to September

24 JUL

Treks around the globe jostle for the title of world's best, but few aspire to be known as the most dangerous. By design or fluke, that 'honour' seems to have fallen squarely on China's sacred mountain Huá Shān in Shaanxi province, near to the city of Xī'ān (home to the Terracotta Warriors). This hike is a high-wire act without a net, requiring trekkers to scale a massive cliff-face on chains.

Huá Shān has five peaks: East Peak is the best place to watch sunrise; West Peak is thought to be the most elegant; North Peak is known as the Cloud Terrace Peak; Middle Peak is also called Jade Lady Peak; South Peak is Huá Shān's highest (2160m), as well as the highest peak among the Five Sacred Mountains of China.

It is the route up the South Peak that some suggest claims dozens of lives every year. The most dangerous point on the route is Plank Rd, a narrow ledge about 30cm-wide built along the side of a vertical cliff; rusting hand chains are the only thing holding you to the rock and away from a massive drop from the cliff. This is not the time to get vertigo.

If that all sounds a little too precarious or energetic, there's always the option of ascending the peak by cable car – a 20-minute ride.
— *www.travelchinaguide.com*

LEFT: **DIANA MAYFIELD – GETTY IMAGES**

See cinema outside

FRANCE

WHY NOW Watch movies under the stars at the Cinéma en Plein Air

WHERE Parc de la Villette, Paris

DATES Late July to late August

25 JUL

The Parc de la Villette, on the northeast edge of the 19th arrondissement, doesn't sound that promising – this 55 hectare area was formerly the city abattoir. But since a revamp in 1979 it's been one of Paris's key outdoor and cultural spaces, home to 10 themed gardens, three major concert venues, Europe's biggest science museum and the highly distinguished Conservatoire de Paris music college.

The best time to visit, however, is during Cinéma en Plein Air month. A large screen is erected amid the trees and sculptures and an eclectic selection of films is shown – everything from arthouse gems to all-time classics. Entrance is free; deckchair hire costs a few euros.

Movies are played in their original languages, with French subtitles. But even if you don't understand everything on screen, you can still enjoy the atmosphere: balmy Paris evenings; picnic blankets, baguettes and a bottle of Bordeaux; a convivial atmosphere with your fellow alfresco cinema-goers, underneath the stars. — *www.villette.com*

Hike Croagh Patrick

IRELAND

WHY NOW Make a St Paddy pilgrimage
WHERE Croagh Patrick, County Mayo
DATES Reek Sunday, the last Sunday in July
(26 Jul 2015; 31 Jul 2016; 30 Jul 2017; 29 Jul 2018)

Overlooking Clew Bay, Croagh Patrick (764m) is Ireland's most hallowed place of pilgrimage, and has been since at least the 12th century. And the last Sunday in July – Reek Sunday – is a national day of pilgrimage, when around 25,000 devotees choose to make the 2- to 3-hour climb to the chapel at its summit.

It's the mountain's association with Patrick, the best known of Ireland's patron saints, that is Croagh Patrick's glory. It's believed that, in AD 441, the saint fasted for 40 days and 40 nights on the mountain. Legend also has it that Patrick famously evicted Ireland's snakes while he was here. — *www.croagh-patrick.com*

LEFT: **Arthouse cinema under the stars in Paris, France**

BELOW: **Take the scenic route to Shey monastery, south of Leh in Ladakh**

View basking sharks

ENGLAND

WHY NOW It's the prime time to see really big fish off a small isle
WHERE Isle of Man, Irish Sea
DATES June to August

There was a time when huge summer gatherings of basking sharks were welcomed by local fishermen because these giant 2000kg fish yielded a lot of meat and oil. Today, they're not hunted and fortunately they still gather from June to August to feed among plankton swarms on productive sea coasts such as the Isle of Man. Here, most of the shark sightings are reported within 1km of land along a 40km stretch of coast on the south and southwestern shores of the island.

It's obvious when these sharks show up – high dorsal fins signal their presence. In ideal conditions, over 100 basking sharks can be seen at a time. — *www.manxbaskingsharkwatch.com*

Motorbike the Himalaya

INDIA

WHY NOW Make the most of the short snow-free season to motorbike at 5600m
WHERE Ladakh, Himalaya
DATES Late June to August

Winding into the Himalaya from the Ladakhi city of Leh, the road to Khardung La (5602m) is the highest motorable road in the world. The pass itself is nondescript, occupied by a grubby military camp. But none of this detracts from the distant vistas and the thrill of biking there. Nor will it influence the altitude-induced dizziness.

It's worth braving the breathlessness to ride here, though. This is the 'roof of the world', a land of awesome scenery, secluded monasteries and a rich diversity of people.

Roads can be poor and weather changeable so make sure that you can handle a motorbike well. — *www.ladakh-tourism.net*

Climb into a coffin

SPAIN

WHY NOW Join in with the Fiesta de Santa
Marta de Ribarteme

WHERE Las Nieves, Pontevedra, Galicia

DATES 29 July

29 JUL The Fiesta de Santa Marta de
Ribarteme is an unlikely group
therapy session. Those who've
had near-death experiences climb
into coffins; the boxes are carried
into Santa Marta de Ribarteme, the church
dedicated to Mary Magdalene's sister, with the
coffins' inhabitants playing dead.

Afterwards, the procession heads up to the
cemetery, then back to the church, where a
Saint Martha statue is produced; financial
tokens are offered by participants, in gratitude
for having survived their scary experiences.

The festival combines Christianity with
paganism and a large dose of profanity. There
are brass bands and fireworks, and stalls
flogging plastic tat and octopus cooked in
copper cauldrons. — *www.galicia.es/en*

RIGHT: **Arctic fox cubs
at play on Wrangel
Island, Russia**

BELOW: **A male Lesser
Bird of Paradise
performs in the
highlands of Papua
New Guinea**

Spot birds of paradise

PAPUA NEW GUINEA

WHY NOW There are male courtship displays
during the cooler, drier season

WHERE Tari Valley, Southern Highlands

DATES June to September

30 JUL Papua New Guinea's birds of
paradise are so gorgeous and
bizarre that early scientists could
not believe they were for real.
Unfortunately, seeing them in their
native habitat can be difficult – PNG is tough
to travel in. But if you're game, and keen to see
the birds' incredible courtship displays, head
for Tari Valley, home to more types of birds of
paradise than anywhere on earth.

Tari's 15 species include the blue bird of
paradise, which hangs upside-down with its
electric blue feathers spread like a tutu, and the
Lawe's parotia, which wears a bonnet of wiry
plumes and dances with strange high steps. Also
look for King-of-Saxony and superb birds of
paradise and Princess Stephanie's astrapias.
— *www.papuabirdclub.com*

Sail to Wrangel Island

RUSSIA

WHY NOW Wrangel Island is ice-free for only a short window of time
WHERE Wrangel Island Reserve
DATES July and August

31 JUL

Wrangel Island is located in the Chukchi Sea, far above the Arctic Circle and 140km north of Siberia – it is properly wild and remote. It is also basically off-limits to the outside world – except for a few icebreakers that may or may not make it through Wrangel's extensive pack ice and fierce storms during the brief summer season. However, the rewards of a visit are off the charts, and provide just enough incentive that each summer a handful of tour companies book space on the couple of icebreakers powerful enough to make this arduous journey.

Wrangel, which measures 7600 sq km, is the only land mass in the productive Chukchi Sea, and virtually every animal in the region comes here to breed or feed in its shallow waters. Wrangel boasts the greatest population of Pacific walruses in the world, with up to 100,000 animals on a single beach. It's also home to some of the planet's highest concentrations of polar bear dens. Then there are the 200,000 nesting snow geese, snowy owls, Arctic foxes, musk ox and reindeer.

Another fact makes Wrangel unique: it was the only significant part of the Arctic region not covered in glaciers during the Pleistocene epoch, meaning that soils, plants and animals have survived unscathed here for millions of years, resulting in the highest biodiversity of any site in the entire Arctic region.
— *www.wild-russia.org*

Celebrate at Crop Over

BARBADOS

WHY NOW Raise a rum or two to the Caribbean sugar harvest

WHERE National Stadium, Bridgetown

DATES Late May to August

During Crop Over, Barbados dissolves into three months of rum-soaked fun. The tradition began in 1780, when plantation workers celebrated the end of the cane harvest. The festival declined with the sugar industry, but was revived in 1974.

The main events in late May and June are the Cavalcade, a parade of Calypso and costumes that moves around the island. In July, the pace picks up with heats of competitions such as Pic-O-De-Crop, a fusion of Calypso and social commentary.

In the first week of August, the capital fills with the scent of Bajan cuisine and the sound of steel drums. The Calypso rhythms climax at Cahobblopot on the first Sunday in August, when the Tune of the Crop is announced and everyone has a huge party.

— *cropoverbarbados.com*

August

Watch a mass bat exodus

USA

WHY NOW You'll see 20 million bats – the largest gathering of mammals in the world
WHERE Bracken Cave, Texas
DATES June and August (when public tours run)

02 AUG

Long feared and misunderstood, bats are gaining new-found admiration. And even the unsure will be awestruck by the bats of Bracken Cave.

The Mexican free-tailed bats at Bracken Cave form the largest gathering of mammals in the world – an astounding 20 million bats. The cave itself is off-limits because it is a maternity colony. But each evening at sunset the adult bats issue forth in a mighty torrent.

The bats then spend 8 hours eating their weight in insects, with the entire colony eating an estimated 200 metric tonnes of bugs each evening. Amazingly, when the females return to the cave at dawn they manage to find their own pup amid babies packed up to 2000 per sq metre. — *www.batcon.org*

RIGHT: **Pack water and fuel for the Canning Stock Route**

BELOW: **A super-sized bat cave in Texas**

Hike the Valley of Flowers

INDIA

WHY NOW To see and smell the valley's full floral display
WHERE Bhyundar Valley, Uttarakhand
DATES August to October

03 AUG

In 1931 British mountaineer Frank Smythe wandered into the Himalayan Bhyundar Valley to find hundreds of species of wild flora carpeting the earth. He named it, quite simply, the Valley of Flowers.

To find the flora for yourself, begin trekking from near the Uttarakhand town of Joshimath, a long, uncomfy drive into the Himalaya from Rishikesh, and follow the crowded pilgrims' trail towards the holy lake of Hem Kund. Branching away from the trail 6km before the lake, you enter the valley, which is 10km long and 2km wide. From August, it's also a palette of kaleidoscopic colour.

Camping is not allowed, but accommodation is available in Ghangaria, which is only about 7km away. — *www.euttaranchal.com*

Drive the Canning Stock Route

AUSTRALIA

WHY NOW It's the coolest and best time to be on the Canning
WHERE Wiluna to Halls Creek, Western Australia
DATES May to September

04 AUG The world's longest and most remote stock route doubles as perhaps the most difficult road journey in Australia. Stretching more than 1700km across the arid heart of Western Australia, between Wiluna in the south and Halls Creek in the north, it crosses through uninhabited but vegetated desert country, pushing across more than 800 sand dunes and passing through five native title areas.

People have walked the Canning, including the eponymous Alfred Canning, and there have been rare crossings by bicycle, but it's predominantly a route for the hardiest of 4WDers – this is not for novices. Mechanical knowledge and offroad driving skills are vital.

Tackling the Canning in the Australian summer is absolute suicide. Not only can it be extremely hot and dangerously wet but travelling outside the main season means there are few other people around to help you, should you need it – not a good thing when you're attempting to cross such harsh terrain.

The route usually begins to see the first adventurers in late April or early May. By the middle of October the season is coming to a close. In August, days tend to be mild, though nights can get very chilly indeed.
— *www.canningstockroute.net.au*

Delve into the interior

ICELAND

WHY NOW The innards of this tumultuous isle are only really accessible in summer
WHERE Inland Iceland
DATES July and August

05 AUG Iceland's vast, barren interior is one of Europe's great wilderness areas. And it's so weirdly otherwordly that the Apollo astronauts held training exercises here before launching off on the 1969 lunar landings.

It is only really accessible in July and August; driving here at other times can be treacherous or impossible. There are practically no services, accommodation, bridges, mobile-phone signals, and no guarantees if things go wrong.

There are four main routes through the interior – the Kjölur, Sprengisandur, Öskjuleið and Kverkfjöll Routes; historically, they were places of terror to be traversed as quickly as possible. Today they attract hardy visitors to such sights as Herðubreið (1682m), Iceland's most distinctive mountain; and Askja, a 50-sq-km caldera created by a colossal explosion in 1875 and containing Iceland's deepest lake.

Also here is one of the world's finest trekking routes: the Laugavegurinn. Usually passable from mid-July to September, the trail runs from Landmannalaugar to Þórsmörk; it's around 53km long and can be completed in three to four days. The Laugavegurinn is a bewilderment of crazy landscapes: it crosses lava flows and a black pumice desert, traverses rocks and hillsides of every conceivable colour, passes steaming fumaroles, makes cold stream crossings and offers views of torrential waterfalls. There are huts en route, which should be booked well in advance. — *www.visiticeland.com*

Cycle into the Amazon

ECUADOR

WHY NOW The highlands' dry(ish) season offers the most comfortable cycling conditions
WHERE Baños to Puyo
DATES June to September

06 AUG

When it comes to views of the upper Amazon Basin, it doesn't get much better than the stretch of road from Baños to Puyo in the central highlands of Ecuador. The bus ride is great, but taking in the views from the seat of a mountain bike is even better.

For a start, it's mostly downhill – the road follows the Río Pastaza canyon as it drops from Baños, at 1800m, to Puyo, at 950m – but there are some definite climbs, so ready those legs for the 60km ride. Along the way you'll pass the waterfall of Agoyan, ride through road tunnels and see the Rio Verde cable car, which stretches dramatically across the gorge. You can also detour on foot to the waterfall of Pailon del Diablo (Cauldron of the Devil), one of the country's best cascades. — *www.ecuador.travel*

Bop at Oppikoppi

SOUTH AFRICA

WHY NOW The Rainbow Nation's biggest festival rocks the bushveld
WHERE Near Northam, Limpopo Province
DATES Second weekend in August

07 AUG

While Glastonbury has its mud, Oppikoppi has its dust. Out here, in the harsh-but-beautiful sunbaked savannah, the stuff gets everywhere. But on this raucous, tune-pounding, hippy-happy weekend, you likely won't give a jot.

First held in 1994, Oppikoppi now has seven main stages, welcomes around 150 acts and hosts about 20,000 fun-loving, beer-swilling attendees. The programme runs from South African rock acts to jazz, metal, soul, hip hop and *kwaito* – a South African take on house music that mixes in some tribal rhythms to create irresistibly dancey beats. Comedians, DJs, box car races, dust surfing and a Naked Dash (shoes obligatory, clothes not allowed) flesh out the fun. — *oppikoppi.co.za*

LEFT: **Kerlingarfjöll mountain range in Iceland is situated near the Kjölur highland road**

BELOW: **The cable car at the Rio Verde waterfall in the Pastaza River valley, Ecuador**

Kiteboard on Maui

USA

WHY NOW The wind is at its best – with August being Kite Beach's blowiest month

WHERE Kanaha, Maui, Hawaii

DATES June to September

08 AUG Kanaha Beach, on Maui's north shore, is a tranquil stretch of coast with wonderful views of the West Maui Mountains. But kiteboarding has become so popular here that they've renamed the place 'Kite Beach'. There are even areas set aside solely for kiteboarders.

It's an appropriate name-change: Kanaha is considered to be the birthplace of modern kitesurfing, dating from the mid 1990s when water-pioneers Laird Hamilton and Manu Bertin started riding surf-style boards with footstraps on Maui's north shore.

It's impressive to watch, and hard to master. Instruction is available at Kite Beach. First you learn how to fly the kite; then you practice body-dragging (letting the kite pull you across the water); finally you step on board. Anyone can try here, though: a reef keeps waters near shore flat for beginners, while the more experienced can head beyond the reef to tackle breaking waves. — *www.gohawaii.com*

Pig out at the Pig Festival

FRANCE

WHY NOW Eat, squeal and party like a pig!
WHERE Trie Sur Baïse, Hautes-Pyrénées
DATES Second Sunday in August (9 Aug 2015; 14 Aug 2016; 13 Aug 2017; 12 Aug 2018)

09 AUG The smell of roast pork fills the air at La Pourcailhade (the Pig Festival), a bash that gives everyone an excuse to eat like a porker at the swill trough.

Trie Sur Baïse, once home to France's largest pig market, fills with decorative piggy displays. In the old market, waiters flourish pigtail corkscrews and banqueters dig in until it's time for the sports. The Piglet Race pits the speediest runts against each other, but the strangest contests are purely human affairs. In the Black-Pudding-Eating Competition, men force down lengths of congealed blood stretching over 1m.

The event that challenges entrants to really make pigs of themselves is the Cri do Cochon (pig-squealing championships). Contestants have to imitate the animals, representing stages in their lives, from the squeals of newborn piglets to the wheeze of an old hog.

— *www.tourisme-hautes-pyrenees.com*

Dive with hammerheads

COSTA RICA

WHY NOW For the sharks, school is in
WHERE Isla del Coco, 600km southwest of the
Costa Rican mainland
DATES August

10 AUG

In the opening minutes of the film *Jurassic Park*, a helicopter swoops over a lushly forested island with dramatic tropical peaks. That island is Isla del Coco (Cocos Island), in the eastern Pacific Ocean. It's extremely wet, with about 7000mm of annual rainfall, and legend has it that a band of pirates buried a huge treasure here – despite more than 5000 treasure-hunting expeditions, it's never been found. For divers, however, there is a great treasure chest. The waters around Cocos offer probably the best shark diving in the world.

Though it's the Central American wet season in August, it's also the busiest time for sharks. You can't stay on the island, so book a 10- to 12-day live-aboard boat trip out of San Jose.

The submerged mountain at Alcyone is the great dive drawcard. Here the largest schools of hammerheads are found, white-tip reef sharks mill about and whale sharks cruise by. You'll wonder if Jacques Cousteau was looking above or below the ocean surface when he described Cocos as the 'most beautiful island in the world'.
— *www.aggressor.com; www.underseahunter.com*

See rare wild ass

INDIA

WHY NOW See the stallions fighting in the breeding season
WHERE Wild Ass Wildlife Sanctuary, Gujarat
DATES August to October

11 AUG Few tourists wander west to the clay deserts of Gujarat. Little grows here, and the earth is blinding white from the soil's salty crust. Known as the Rann of Kutch, this desert floods for about a month during the monsoon; the rest of the year, it's bone dry.

This is the site of India's largest wildlife sanctuary and the world's final refuge for Indian wild asses. In the 1960s there were just over 300 wild asses remaining but today, in the Wild Ass Wildlife Sanctuary, there are closer to 3000. Things get especially exciting here during mating season when males fight for fertile females, rearing up while kicking and biting savagely. — *www.gujarattourism.com*

Coasteer in Pembrokeshire

WALES

WHY NOW If you're going to jump in and out of the Irish Sea, do it in warmer weather
WHERE Pembrokeshire, south Wales
DATES July to September

167

12 AUG Coasteering is Wales' private piece of adventuring. The sport – which involves navigating along the intertidal zone of a craggy shore without boards or boats – was pioneered in the 1980s in Pembrokeshire.

It's a bit like canyoning, but practised along a rugged coast. Equipped with wetsuit, flotation jacket and helmet, you traverse along cliffs using a combo of climbing, scrambling, jumping and swimming. You might be dodging waves, sliding down water shoots or leaping off precipices. Try coasteering around its birthplace, St Davids – your only regret will be that it wasn't created in a place with warmer water. — *www.visitpembrokeshire.com*

Make merry with Mozart

AUSTRIA

WHY NOW Come over all classical in the awesome Alpine city
WHERE Salzburg
DATES Mid-July to end of August

13 AUG It's no surprise that the city that gave birth to Wolfgang Amadeus Mozart is so keen on classical music. And this passion is best expressed during the summer Salzburger Festspiele (Salzburg Festival).

Performances of chamber music, opera and orchestral brilliance – including plenty of Mozart, of course – resound throughout the city. And many of the venues are as impressive as the music: concerts are held in opulent baroque churches, glittering cathedrals and grand great halls. This is high art of the highest order – bring your glad-rags and give your ears the outing of their lives.
— *www.salzburgerfestspiele.at*

LEFT: **Diving with hammerhead sharks at Isla del Coco**

BELOW: **Haute couture on stilts, a performance group at the Salzburg Festival**

Hike the Kokoda Track

PAPUA NEW GUINEA

WHY NOW It's the coolest, driest time of year
WHERE Kokoda to Owers' Corner
DATES May to September; allow six to 11 days

14 AUG

Every steep, slippery step on the Kokoda Track's 96km rollercoaster requires concentration. Imagine how tough it must have been when carrying a pack and rifle, ill with dysentery and waiting to be ambushed by enemy troops. Such was the trail's origin: this was the route used by Japanese troops attempting a sneak attack on Port Moresby; they were repelled by Australian forces and Papua New Guineans, but from July 1942 to January 1943, this tract of jungle saw fierce battles. Today, the trail attracts hundreds of hikers. The route runs through the Owen Stanley Range's rainforest-cloaked mountains and traditional villages where you can meet local people, stock up on fruit and stay in simple huts. — *www.papuanewguinea.travel*

Hip swivel at Elvis Week

USA

WHY NOW Pay your respects to the King
WHERE Memphis, Tennessee
DATES One week around 16 August (the anniversary of Elvis's death)

15 AUG

On the anniversary of the King's death, Elvis impersonators converge on Memphis, where Presley ate his last peanut butter 'n' jelly sandwich in 1977.

Events taking place at Graceland, the King's kitsch-filled mansion, include an Elvis trivia treasure hunt, and music and film nights, featuring his gospel backing bands and screenings of classics such as *Viva Las Vegas*. There's a 100-booth memorabilia fair in the Memphis Cook Convention Center, an Elvis scrapbooking class and an Elvis art contest. Also, associates of the great man flock to the city to wow audiences with tribute concerts and Elvis anecdotes. — *www.elvis.com*

RIGHT: **Edinburgh's festival is a feast of live performances, some in the shadow of Castle Rock**

BELOW: **Watch the Palio for free from the centre of the Piazza del Campo**

Cheer on Il Palio

ITALY

WHY NOW See horses gallop through the ancient city, while the locals go loco
WHERE Il Campo, Siena, Tuscany
DATES 2 July and 16 August

16 AUG

The Italians' factional tendencies can be seen in all their glory at Il Palio, a bareback horse race that lasts for 90 seconds. During the short dash around Piazza Il Campo, jockeys can do almost anything to their opponents; the winning steed is often riderless.

This event strikes at the heart of Sienese civic pride. Each horse represents one of the city's 17 *contrade* (districts), all of which have their eye on the victorious palio banner. The horses are blessed in the *contrades'* churches, and medieval parades accompany the competitors when they register. Before the race, bright flags bearing the *contrades'* ancient symbols are waved.
— *www.ilpalio.org*

Applaud at the Edinburgh Festival

SCOTLAND

WHY NOW Be entertained by an abundance of opera, art, classical stars and wannabe comedians
WHERE Edinburgh
DATES Three weeks from mid-August

17 AUG

Is there any better location for the world's largest arts festival than the Scottish capital, where a castle looks down from its volcanic perch at Georgian streets and Gothic alleys?

The official reason for the three weeks of frenzy that turn Edinburgh into a citywide performance artwork is the highbrow festival of classical music, opera, theatre and dance. But it's far more hip to check out the fringe festival, which is always entertaining. Performers sink their savings into tiny venues and hand out flyers, waiting for a visit from all-powerful critics.

You have to be quick to interpret the programme and snap up tickets, or you may end up at a show that makes you snigger for all the wrong reasons. But there's plenty of free entertainment out on the streets. Buskers battle for possession of the Royal Mile with Special Brew-swigging tramps intent on reclaiming their town from the thespians. Oh, and there's a book festival, a film festival and a fireworks finale too.
— *www.edinburghfestivals.co.uk*

Snorkel with humpbacks

TONGA

WHY NOW You can swim in crystal-clear waters with mothers and calves
WHERE 350km north of Nuku'alofa
DATES July to September

18 AUG Southern hemisphere humpback whales suffered tremendous hunting pressure until the 1970s; only 500 remain in the once mighty Tongan calving grounds. Given this history, it is remarkable that these gentle 15m-long giants readily approach and trust snorkellers and swimmers in the breathtakingly clear waters off Tonga, making an already incredible experience even more moving.

Humpbacks migrate from Antarctica to Tonga's Vava'u Group to give birth from July to September, when the warm waters are most ideal for their vulnerable young calves. A handful of licensed whale-watch operators from Vava'u follow Tongan guidelines in approaching the whales, letting curious whales swim as close as they choose, but not approaching within 30m. Boat operators also bring along underwater microphones so you can hear one of the most complex and beautiful songs produced by any animal. If you'd rather watch from land, try the Toafa Lookout on west Vava'u island.

Amazingly, so few tourists visit Vava'u that you might feel like you're having this once-in-a-lifetime experience to yourself. The flip side is that the infrastructure is pretty basic – but if swimming with mighty whales in an unspoiled island paradise is your version of heaven, that won't worry you at all.

— *www.thekingdomoftonga.com*

Watch stacks of seabirds

IRELAND

WHY NOW You'll catch the peak movement of migrating birds

WHERE Cape Clear Island, southwest of Cork

DATES Mid July

19 AUG When the bird observatory at Cape Clear Island was established in 1959, this island off southwest Ireland already had a reputation as a spot for seeing rare birds that had strayed over from North America or Asia. But no-one realised it would soon become one of the top 'seawatching' sites in the world.

The spectacular seabird migration peaks in the third week of August as countless birds from North Atlantic colonies rush south. On peak days, counts of 20,000 Manx shearwaters per hour have been recorded, as well as 1600 Cory's shearwaters, 800 great shearwaters and a steady stream of razorbills, cormorants, skuas, puffins and fulmars. A daily ferry from Baltimore, southwest of Cork, provides access to the island.
— *www.capeclearisland.com*

Hike the Kalalau Trail

USA

WHY NOW Kauai is one of the world's wettest places, but August usually sees just 45mm of rain

WHERE Kauai, Hawaii

DATES August

20 AUG The Kalalau Trail is a heart-breaking path, both beautiful and brutal, following an ancient Hawaiian footpath along the valleys of Kauai's Na Pali Coast. It passes hidden waterfalls, wild beaches and visions of traditional Hawaii, ending below the steep fluted *pali* (cliffs) of Kalalau, where sheer green cliffs drop into brilliant turquoise waters. Many rare native plants grow on this coast, and wild goats are frequently seen along the trail.

The classic hike, the only way to access this coast by land, involves walking 18km into Kalalau Valley, camping at Kalalau Beach for two nights and then hiking back out the third day. Permits are required, and campgrounds are often booked up; apply for permits well in advance.
— *www.hawaiistateparks.org/hiking/kauai*

LEFT: **Sun-dappled humpback whales in Vava'u, Tongo**

BELOW: **Hiking the Kalalau Trail**

Kayak with killer whales

CANADA

WHY NOW The whales arrive to eat their fill of migrating salmon
WHERE Johnstone Strait, British Columbia
DATES July to September

21 AUG From the water-level seat of a sea kayak your first impression of a 7m-long killer whale might range from heart-beating fear to all-out awe, but it's an experience you will never forget. Sightings like this are virtually guaranteed in British Columbia's Johnstone Strait, on the northeast shore of Vancouver Island, where the world's greatest concentration of killer whales gather each summer to feed on migrating salmon. Indeed, whale-watching – not only for killer whales but also for minke and humpback whales – is now a major draw for the tiny seaside town of Telegraph Cove.

Fortunately for observers, the resident killer whales of Johnstone Strait live in large stable pods with fairly predictable seasonal patterns (as opposed to far-ranging transient pods). Even so, finding a pod might entail joining a tour group that is in radio contact with other groups, so you can get the latest location information. Most of these resident whales spend their entire lives in the same extended family groups and local naturalist guides will recognise many individual whales. — *www.killerwhalecentre.org*

Hike on Mt Olympus
GREECE
WHY NOW For the most favourable mountain conditions, when the peak is snow-free
WHERE Mt Olympus, Thessaly
DATES June to October

22 AUG Mt Olympus, chosen by the ancients as the abode of their gods, is Greece's highest and most awe-inspiring mountain. It takes two days to climb to Olympus' highest peak, Mytikas (2918m); however, it's worth spending more time here if you really want to explore the mountain.

Linger to walk among its 1700 species of plants; also look out for chamois, deer, wild pig, jackal and even wolf. There are also archaeological finds dating back to the Iron Age and an intriguing swirl of legends.

The village of Litohoro is the best base for Olympus; it has bus links to Athens and Thessaloniki. — *www.olympusfd.gr*

LEFT: **An orca comes for a closer look in Johnstone Strait, British Columbia**

BELOW: **Coral's spawning is a spectacle up close or from a distance**

Catch coral spawning
CARIBBEAN
WHY NOW The reefs might just erupt!
WHERE Any tropical island between Florida and South America
DATES August and September

23 AUG Coral reefs are among the most productive and diverse ecosystems on the planet. Yet it was only in the 1980s that scientists discovered how they spawn: they release all their eggs and sperm over a few hours on single nights around full moon. The water turns pink and the fish have a feeding frenzy.

Spawnings occur on different nights according to species and location, but fortunately scientists are piecing together site-specific tables that can help increase your chances of catching one of these spectacular and rarely observed events.
— *www.nova.edu/ncri/research/a21/caribbean_coral_spawning_table.pdf*

See dead people
MADAGASCAR
WHY NOW Look on as Madagascans exhume the bodies of their deceased ancestors
WHERE Hauts plateaux (highlands)
DATES June to September

24 AUG Traditional Malagasy culture is rooted in respect for its ancestors, as the Merina people's Famadihana (Turning of the Bones) exhumation ceremony bears testament. Living family members gather at the clan's tomb, which is prised open, and straw-wrapped ancestors are passed out. The family dances with the bodies, re-wraps them in special *lambas* (scarves), sprays them with perfume and sits in contemplation, with the bodies in their laps. The ancestors are then returned to their resting place, along with offerings of money and alcohol. The ceremony is practised during the dry winter months, when it's not so damaging to expose bodies to the elements. — *www.madagascar-tourisme.com*

Hike the Tian Shan

KYRGYZSTAN

WHY NOW Most high-altitude treks or climbs take place in high summer
WHERE Tian Shan Range
DATES July and August

25 AUG

This highest and mightiest part of Central Asia's Tian Shan mountain system is in eastern Kyrgyzstan. It's an immense knot of ranges, with dozens of summits above 5000m, which culminates in Pik Pobedy (Victory Peak, 7439m) and Khan Tengri (7010m), which is often likened to the Matterhorn.

The best selection of treks is out of the town of Karakol. The Terskey Alatau range that rises behind the town offers a fine taste of the Tian Shan. Of numerous possible routes that climb to passes below 4000m, the best of them take in the alpine lake Ala-Köl above Karakol, and the Altyn Arashan hot springs above Ak-Suu.

Of the Tian Shan's thousands of glaciers, the grandest is 60km-long Inylchek, rumbling westward from Khan Tengri. Across the glacier's northern arm, a huge, iceberg-filled lake (Lake Merzbacher) forms at 3300m every summer. In early August, the lake bursts its ice-banks and explodes into the Inylchek River below. The most common walking route to the Inylchek is a wild six-day trek from Jyrgalang.

Nearby Lake Issyk-Kul is Kyrgyzstan's biggest attraction. At 170km long, 70km across and up to 695m deep, it's the second-largest alpine lake after South America's Lake Titicaca.

Peak walking season is June to September; most high-altitude treks or climbs take place in July or August. — *www.kyrgyzstan-tourism.com*

LEFT: JAMES STRACHAN – GETTY IMAGES

Arm yourself at La Tomatina

SPAIN

WHY NOW Toss a load of tomatoes

WHERE Buñol, Valencia

DATES Last Wednesday in August (26 Aug 2015; 31 Aug 2016; 30 Aug 2017; 29 Aug 2018)

26 AUG Getting pelted with tomatoes may sound like a medieval punishment, but it's all in the name of fun at La Tomatina, a raucous red riot that began in 1945, possibly as an anti-Franco protest. For one morning a year, the small town of Buñol in eastern Spain dissolves into the world's greatest tomato fight. Some 140 tonnes of the squishy red beauties are trucked in for the running battle, which is concentrated around Plaza del Pueblo and attracts around 30,000 visitors.

Goggles are recommended, cameras should be left at home. Women must be aware that a wet T-shirt competition is an unofficial part of the day. Tomatoes are supplied, but ensure they are squashed or fruit might not be the only thing left bruised. — *latomatina.info/en*

Be a part of Burning Man

USA

WHY NOW Head to the desert commune carnival

WHERE Black Rock Desert, Gerlach, Nevada

DATES Week prior to and including US Labor Day weekend (first Monday in September)

27 AUG Burning Man is more than a festival; it's a Utopian society. Key principles such as radical self-expression and communal effort rule this 45,000-strong, 5-mile-wide temporary desert 'city', where inhibitions are left at the gates.

Creativity is key. Teams of entrepreneurial artists assemble sculptures in 40°C heat; the results range from a colossal sculpture made of lorries to the poignant Temple of Forgiveness – this plywood structure is torched on the last night. There are also all sorts of performers, from the theatrical to the surreal, and plenty of music. The drinks are all free too: at Burning Man, you 'pay' by doing your bit, whether it's picking up litter or simply spreading some smiles.
— *www.burningman.com*

RIGHT: **The Tombstone Range is ablaze with autumn colour in Canada**

BELOW: **A fruity fight at La Tomatina in Spain**

See fleeting Fall colours

CANADA

WHY NOW To catch the brief, golden blush of autumn in the remote mountains

WHERE Tombstone Range, Yukon

DATES Late August to early September

28 AUG Straddling the Arctic Circle, Canada's Yukon is historically a place of gold rushes – but it is in autumn that parts of the territory really shine. Right now the endless Arctic days are beginning to fade away into eternal night, but on the Tombstone Range, out of Dawson City, the colours are only getting brighter. Autumn here is almost subliminal, blowing in and out seemingly in a moment. But, though brief, it is spectacular, with the Arctic tundra turning a variety of reds and golds, the vivid colours offset by the black granite peaks of the range.

The hiking possibilities in the Tombstone Territorial Park are extensive. For those who prefer their adventure on wheels, the park is cut through by the Dempster Hwy, a gravel hell-raiser that begins 40km out of Dawson City and rolls 747km north to Inuvik on the shore of the Beaufort Sea. It was once a dog-sled track, and services are few and far between. There's a service station at the southern start of the highway, and from there it's 370km to the next. Ferries cross the Peel and Mackenzie Rivers or, if the freeze has already begun, they are crossed on ice bridges.

In Dawson City itself, the adventure of choice is a little more distasteful. Inside the Downtown Hotel, you can join the Sourtoe Club – to become a member you must drink a shot of whisky with an amputated toe in it, and the toe must touch your lips... — *travelyukon.com*

Surf at Puerto Escondido

MEXICO

WHY NOW The wet season brings rain – but also the best waves

WHERE Puerto Escondido, Oaxaca

DATES May to September

29 AUG Mexico's Pacific coast has some awesome waves. Among the best are the summer breaks at spots between San José del Cabo and Cabo San Lucas in Baja California, and the 'world's longest wave' on Bahía de Matanchén, near San Blas. However, most cherished are the barrelling waves at Puerto Escondido – the 'Mexican Pipeline'.

Escondido's barrels roll into long, straight Zicatela Beach, which doubles as the town's hip hang-out, with its enticing cafes, restaurants and accommodation. The heavy beach break here will test the mettle of most surfers – good board skills and experience are required to ride the waves. If you're no pro, you can try other water sports – snorkelling, diving, sportfishing or looking for turtles, dolphins and even whales. By night, enjoy the busy bar scene, with its live music and a freewheeling, unpretentious air. Development here has remained on a human scale, and part of Puerto Escondido's charm is that it remains a fishing port and market town as well as a tourist destination.

The centre of town rises above the small Bahía Principal. The Carretera Costera (Hwy 200) runs across the hill above it, dividing the upper town – where buses arrive and most locals live and work – from the lower, more touristic part.

Within easy day-trip distance are the coastal lagoons of Manialtepec and Chacahua, which teem with birdlife. — *www.visitmexico.com*

Catch the stork migration

BULGARIA

WHY NOW Watch the elegant passing of
hundreds of thousands of birds
WHERE Black Sea coast, 25km north of Varna
DATES Late August to late September

30 AUG In autumn, myriad pelicans, storks and raptors migrate down the coast between the Black Sea and the tip of the Balkan Mountains. These migrants congregate here from all over Europe because this is their best route for migrating south to the eastern Med.

Upwards of 200,000 white storks, along with 20,000 white pelicans, 10,000 lesser spotted eagles, 20,000 common buzzards and many other birds use this route, with flocks of hundreds or thousands of birds seen per day.

The sheer 100m-high limestone cliffs of Cape Kaliakra, just outside the town of Albena, provide a spectacular platform for viewing passing birds. Migration begins in late August, peaking in the third week in September, though timing varies each year. — *bspb.org/index.php*

Be a champion bog snokeller

WALES

WHY NOW Squelch through a peat bog
WHERE Llanwrtyd Wells, Powys
DATES Summer Bank Holiday (31 Aug 2015;
29 Aug 2016; 28 Aug 2017; 27 Aug 2018)

31 AUG Little Llanwrtyd Wells has supplemented the tourist magic of being Britain's smallest town with a series of bonkers events – the daftest of which is the World Bog Snorkelling Championships. Held in the Waen Rhydd Peat Bog, the mucky endurance test challenges intrepid, mud-loving contestants to swim two lengths of a 55m trench, with only flippers, a snorkel and a good dose of determination to help them through the quagmire. Conventional swimming strokes are not allowed. Wetsuits are optional but advisable.

Two variations on the event are the triathlon, which also includes a 30km cycle and a 20km fell run, and the mountain bike bog snorkelling, which is just silly. — *tourism.powys.gov.uk/ llanwrtyd-wells.php*

LEFT: **Surfing Puerto Escondido off Oaxaca**

BELOW: **Snorkel the Waen Rhydd peat bog outside Llanwrtyd Wells to become a World Champion**

Watch 120,000 elephants

BOTSWANA

WHY NOW At the peak of the dry season
elephants line up along the Chobe River to drink
WHERE Chobe National Park
DATES September and October

01 SEP At the waterholes and riversides of Chobe National Park, African elephants use their bulk to dominate access to precious water during the dry season. As Chobe has a population of 60,000 to 120,000 elephants, things get pretty exciting as the parched period reaches its peak in September and October and everything from bossy buffalo to irritated lions tries to crowd in for a drink.

Although Chobe is famous for its fantastic concentration of elephants, they are a big problem for the park's ecosystems because there are so many that they eat all the foliage and topple trees. However, this is still the best time to see thousands of elephants lining up along the river each morning and evening. They are exceptionally tolerant of vehicles; the close-up views are unsurpassed.

Another great sight at Chobe are the hungry lions preying on the vulnerable buffalo calves as they approach the brush-lined rivers. You might get to see a lion kill. While you're waiting you'll be entertained by a parade of red lechwe, zebras, sables and other antelope.
— *www.botswanatourism.co.bw*

September

Rise in the rainforest

BOLIVIA

WHY NOW Make the most of the dry season in this remote wildlife utopia
WHERE Madidi National Park
DATES April to October

02 SEP The Río Madidi watershed is one of South America's most intact ecosystems. Most of it is protected by the 18,000-sq-km Madidi National Park, which ranges from steaming lowland rainforests to 5500m Andean peaks. This little-trodden utopia is home to a mind-boggling variety of Amazonian wildlife, including 44% of all New World mammal species, 38% of tropical amphibian species, over 10% of the world's bird species and more protected species than any park in the world.

RIGHT: **Reed dancers in Swaziland**

BELOW: **Climbing Via Ferrata on Mt Cristallo in the Dolomites, Italy**

Stay at Chalalán Ecolodge, where it's the sounds more than sights that provide the magic: the incredible dawn chorus, the evening frog symphony, the roar of tropical rainstorms and, in the morning, the thunder-like chorus of hundreds of howler monkeys. — *www.chalalan.com*

Via ferrata in the Dolomites

ITALY

WHY NOW *Vie ferrate* are usually accessible from mid-summer to autumn
WHERE Dolomites
DATES July to October

03 SEP The spiky peaks of the Dolomites are, in fact, ancient coral reefs eroded by glaciers and weather into fantastic and spectacular peaks. Appropriately, such unique mountains have spawned a unique pastime.

Via ferrata (iron way) is neither hiking nor mountaineering; it uses ladders, brackets, chiselled footholds and bridges to allow progress on steep or vertical cliffs. Steel cable is bolted to the rock and acts as handhold and security, with walkers clipping on with a karabiner system.

The first *vie ferrate* were created as military tools to move troops quickly over difficult terrain. There are now dozens of routes through the Dolomites. Try Ivano Dibona, a spectacular but technically straightforward route to the summit of Monte Cristallo. — *www.dolomiti.org*

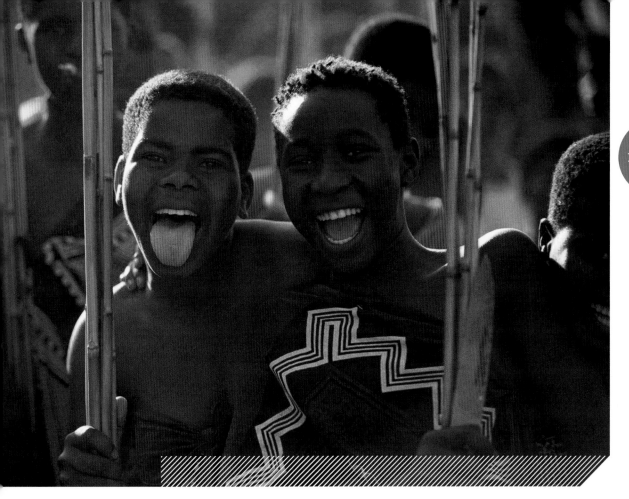

Relish the Reed Dance

SWAZILAND

WHY NOW Join Swazi royalty and watch the debutantes' ball in the bush

WHERE Lobamba

DATES Late August/early September

04 SEP Swaziland may be a pint-sized country, but Umhlanga (the Reed Dance) attracts up to 30,000 participants. They're all women, who shimmy with *umhlanga* (reeds) above their heads – the event is all about finding a partner.

The women converge on Lobamba to help repair the house of the queen mother, who rules alongside the king and is known as Indlovukaki (Great She-Elephant). They spend days and nights searching for reeds before handing their finds to the queen mum and performing the dance, watched by potential suitors. Clad in traditional beaded skirts and sashes denoting their tribes, the dancers must be careful not to drop or damage their reeds. Princesses wear red feathers in their hair, and hard-working participants who searched for reeds by night carry torches.

The women are fuelled by the presence of the monarch and the knowledge that the Swazi queen mother must not be of the royal clan. As at the Ncwala ceremony, held in late December or early January, there are signs that identify the unchaste – an incentive to avoid premarital sex. King Mswati III already has one Umhlanga dancer among his 13 wives.

Once the festival is over, explore further. Tiny Swaziland boasts some spectacular wilderness. Don't miss Mkhaya Game Reserve, one of the best places to spot rare black rhinos in the wild. — *www.thekingdomofswaziland.com*

Have a Highland fling

SCOTLAND

WHY NOW Down a dram at the Highland Games
WHERE Memorial Park, Braemar, Aberdeenshire
DATES First Saturday in September (5 Sep 2015;
3 Sep 2016; 2 Sep 2017; 1 Sep 2018)

05 SEP Caber-tossing can be seen across Scotland's north during summer, but the most famous Highland games take place in Braemar. More than 20,000 people, many sporting traditional kilts, converge on a 12-acre site for the Braemar Gathering.

Local lads and international athletes alike compete in events including tug-of-war, a hill race up the 860m Morrone, hammer-throwing, stone-putting and the long jump. Less rigorous entertainment includes Highland dancing, pipers and the children's sack race.

The royal family is among the spectators who toast the winners of the track (and heavy) events with a dram of single malt whisky. The tradition of royal patronage stretches back to Queen Victoria, who was a big fan. She first attended the gathering in 1848; in 1866 she granted a 'Royal' prefix to the society that organises the event.

The games date back 900 years. They took place informally for many centuries, but were formalised in 1820 due to the rise of Highland romanticism initiated by writer Sir Walter Scott.
— *www.braemargathering.org*

Watch the historic regatta

ITALY

WHY NOW Watch the Venetians row like it's 1489
WHERE Venice
DATES First Sunday in September (6 Sep 2015; 4 Sep 2016; 3 Sep 2017; 2 Sep 2018)

06 SEP The Regata Storica, a series of rowing races on the Grand Canal, commemorates the welcome given to Caterina Cornaro, wife of the King of Cyprus, in 1489 after she renounced her throne in favour of Venice. The most famous regatta out of 120-plus that take place here between April and September, the event begins with a parade of boats decorated in 16th-century style.

The main event is the men's *caorline* (broad lagoon vessels) contest. The races start in the Castello area and proceed up the canal to Santa Chiara, where the boats turn around to pound back to the finish at Ca' Foscari, to whoops and cheers. — *www.regatastoricavenezia.it*

LEFT: **Matching kilts and marching pipers at the Highland Games in Braemar**

BELOW: **A manta ray in the Maldives**

Swim with manta rays

MALDIVES

WHY NOW The water is a bit murky but it's the best time of year for manta rays
WHERE Lankanfinolhu Faru, North Male' Atoll
DATES May to November

07 SEP Lankanfinolhu Faru – Manta Point – just north of the Maldive Islands' capital of Male' is an excellent and predictable place to see mantas. Divers descend about 18m, hold onto rocks and wait; you may be treated to a half-hour session of incredible close-up views.

The Maldives are an expensive and rather limited destination – you are largely required to stay at the private resorts that own many islands. However, you can escape the resorts by booking a liveaboard trip: join a specialist dive boat to sail around the archipelago, taking in the best sub-aqua locations as well as remote sandy beaches and local culture, well away from other tourists. — *www.visitmaldives.com*

Focus on fashion

USA, ENGLAND, ITALY & FRANCE

WHY NOW Mix with the beautiful people in the world's four fashion hotspots
WHERE New York, London, Milan & Paris
DATES From early September to early October

08 SEP Want to know what to wear next season? Then you need to be at Fashion Week, dahling. From early September a cavalcade-in-couture of designers – along with models, hipsters, Hollywood stars and hangers-on – do the rounds of the world's most important fashion cities. The aim: to showcase their collections for the coming spring.

The first week is held in New York, before the whole kit and caboodle moves to London, then Milan, then Paris. While getting into the A-list shows is practically impossible, other events for mere mortals who like clothes are held around the main event in each city. Just be sure to dress the part. – *www.fashionweekonline.com*

Get wet at Angel Falls

VENEZUELA

WHY NOW The wettest months are best for seeing the world's highest waterfall in full flow
WHERE Angel Falls, Canaima National Park
DATES August and September

09 SEP

Angel Falls, the world's highest waterfall, has a total height of 979m and an uninterrupted drop of 807m – that's some 16 times the height of Niagara Falls.

It's a lot harder to reach than the US–Canadian cascade though, as it is located in a distant wilderness without any road access. The village of Canaima, about 50km northwest of the waterfall, is the major gateway but it also doesn't have any overland link to the rest of the country.

A visit to the falls is normally undertaken in two stages; flying into Canaima and then taking a light plane or boat to the falls. River trips can only run when the water is deep enough to be navigated by Pemon guides in wooden *curiara* boats; this is usually from June to December. The falls tend to be most voluminous in the wet months of August and September, though they are often covered by cloud.

The original indigenous Pemon name for the cascade is Kerepakupai Vená – 'waterfall of the deepest place'. It received its better-known moniker after US aviator Jimmie Angel became the first person to fly over the falls in 1933 and introduced the wonder to the wider world.
— *www.venezuelaturismo.gob.ve*

See flowers and dugongs

AUSTRALIA

WHY NOW Dugongs move into near-shore seagrass beds where seeing them is a certainty
WHERE Shark Bay, Western Australia
DATES September

10 SEP

Located 800km north of Perth, Shark Bay is a shallow 13,500 sq km lagoon fabulously rich in marine resources, including the world's most extensive seagrass beds and countless sea turtles, dolphins and whales. The placid 300kg dugong, a sea creature that gave rise to mermaid tales, occurs in huge numbers, with 10,000 congregating along the shore to give birth in September.

On dry land, be prepared for a thrill if you travel north to Francois Peron National Park, a paradise for wild camping and encounters with rare wildlife. Between August and October many of the region's 700 wildflower species will also be in bloom. — *www.sharkbay.org*

Tackle the Gauley River

USA

WHY NOW It's Gauley Season!
WHERE Gauley River, West Virginia
DATES 22 days (Fridays, Saturdays, Sundays, some Mondays) from Friday after Labor Day to mid-Oct

11 SEP

They call it Gauley Season: quite simply, it's one of the world's great white-water moments. Over six weekends each autumn, there are scheduled releases of water from the Summersville Dam in West Virginia to lower the Summersville Lake to its winter level. Up to 4 million L a minute pours from the dam, and waiting for it are a host of rafters to ride its sudden, gut-churning rapids.

The Upper Gauley drops around 200m in 45km and provides more than 100 rapids, including several Grade Vs. Grab a paddle and brace for deceptively named Sweet's Falls, a 5m plunge that helps make this the best white-water run in the US. – *www.nps.gov/gari*

RIGHT: **Maple leaves in Abisko National Park, Swedish Lapland**

BELOW: **Walk the circle of life around Mt Kailash, Tibet**

Circuit Mt Kailash

CHINA

WHY NOW Get here before the winter snows do, usually in October
WHERE Mt Kailash, Tibet
DATES September

12 SEP

The 52km *kora* (circuit) of Mt Kailash (6714m) is one of the most important pilgrimages in Asia, holy to Hindus, Buddhists, Bon-pos and Jains. Tibetan Buddhists believe that a single circuit cleanses the sins of one life, while 108 circuits brings nirvana in this life.

Darchen (4600m) is the gateway town for the kora. From here the route skirts the base of the Kailash massif and crosses a 5630m pass. The hike isn't easy – though some walk it in a day, four days is more comfortable. Very pious pilgrims circuit by prostrating themselves: they lie on the ground, stand, walk to where their hands were, lie down again and repeat. Ouch. — *www.freetibet.org/about/travel-guide*

Lap up Lapland in autumn

NORWAY, SWEDEN, FINLAND & NORTHWEST RUSSIA

WHY NOW You'll catch the spectacular autumn colours in Europe's wild north

WHERE Lapland

DATES September

13 SEP

Lapland covers the northern reaches of mainland Europe, stretching high above the Arctic Circle. The ethnic Sami and their reindeer call it home but otherwise its a little-trodden wilderness with few people.

However, there are large populations of boreal animals such as wolverines, elk, lynxes, Arctic foxes and brown bears living among the forests, lakes, bogs, glaciers, mountains and streams.

Travel here in September when the biting insects are gone and you can search for wildlife in a backdrop of autumn colour. The forests put on a dazzling show, and ground-hugging plants are equally colourful. In this season there is lots of activity, as resident animals scurry around fattening up for winter. Nights are cold but snow won't cover the ground until October.

Good spots include Lemmenjoki and Urho Kekkonen National Parks in Finland, Padjelanta and Sarek National Parks in Sweden and Øvre Pasvik National Park in Norway.

— *www.outdoors.fi; www.visitsweden.com; www.visitnorway.com*

Take to a mountain bike

WALES

WHY NOW It's before the worst downpours, so tracks are firm; holidaymakers have gone home

WHERE Countrywide

DATES September

14 SEP

Wales has become a mountain-biking mecca. Its trails were once dubbed the best in the world by the International Mountain Bicycling Association, and all-weather single-track radiates from seven excellent mountain-biking centres.

In North Wales head for the purpose-built tracks at Coed Y Brenin Forest Park, and epic rides at Gwydyr Forest Park at the edge of outdoors-central Betws-y-Coed. Here you'll find the 28km Marin Trail, with some enticing single-track and testing climbs.

Explore Mid-Wales on some excellent networks by basing yourself at Machynlleth or Llanwrtyd Wells. Other good facilities in this area include Nant-y-Arian near Aberystwyth and the Hafren Forest near Llanidloes.

In South Wales, Afan Forest Park, east of Swansea, is also in the world-class rankings. The White's Level Trail adds rocky outcrops to the cycling challenge. There's also a superb specialist downhill course – the 15km Trwch Trail – at Cwmcarn, northeast of Caerphilly. — *www.mbwales.com*

Close the party in style

SPAIN

WHY NOW Hit end-of-season Ibiza, when the clubs go out with a bang
WHERE Ibiza
DATES Last three weeks of September

15 SEP Nowhere does partying quite like Ibiza. And after another hedonistic summer of sun-soaked drinking, drugging, dancing and debauchery, the Balearic island's nightclubs like to give the past season a right good send-off by hosting their biggest, best bashes of all.

The Ibiza Closing Parties are legendary. Clubs such as Es Paradis, Pacha, DC10 and Space vie to be coolest. They tend to attract a slightly older clubbing crowd, now the teens are back at college; these are hardcore clubbers and Ibiza old-hands, back for one last fix of dance delirium. Expect big-name DJs, high production values and outdoor arenas. Don't expect to get much sleep. — *www.ibiza.travel*

LEFT: **Riding Anglesey's off-road trails in Wales**

BELOW: **Rafters at Tapeats Creek on the Colorado River**

Raft the Grand Canyon

USA

WHY NOW Travel outside peak season to stand more chance of securing a trip
WHERE Colorado River, Arizona
DATES Mid-September

16 SEP If standing on South Rim peering down at the Colorado River has you twitching for a more intimate canyon experience, join the 22,000-plus people who raft it in inflatable boats each year. A run down the Colorado is an epic adventure. 'Normal' rapids are rated I to V, but the 160-plus rapids on the Colorado are rated one to 10, with many V or higher.

There's a lottery system for permits for independent rafting. Commercial trips also fill up well in advance and take three forms: oar, paddle or motorised; paddle trips are the most adventurous. Note, motorboats can't run after 15 September, so the river gets quieter from then. — *www.nps.gov/grca*

Spot wild dogs

BOTSWANA

WHY NOW The emergence of pups is timed to coincide with the dry season
WHERE Moremi Game Reserve
DATES September and October

17 SEP The Moremi Game Reserve encompasses the most productive portions of the massive Okavango Delta. And it's here that abundant red lechwe and high densities of impalas contribute to making this the ideal habitat for the African wild dog, southern Africa's most endangered large carnivore.

Not only does Moremi have a large population of these charismatic dogs, but the canids are inured to vehicles, permitting rare encounters. Pups are born midwinter to take advantage of peak prey concentrations around waterholes; by September you may see them making their first forays outside the den.
— *www.botswanatourism.co.bw*

Fall for the Fall colours

JAPAN

WHY NOW Witness the beginning of the wave of autumn colours
WHERE Daisetsuzan National Park, Hokkaido
DATES September

18 SEP

The northernmost of Japan's islands, Hokkaidō accounts for more than 20% of the country's land area yet contains just 5% of the population. The real beauty of the island lies in its wilderness regions, where there is superb scope for outdoor activities – not least around its 10 active volcanoes. Also, being so far north, Hokkaidō is the first place in the country to see the astonishing autumn colours, which usually explode at this latitude from mid-September.

Daisetsuzan National Park – Japan's largest national park – covers Hokkaidō's highest peaks and includes Hagoromo waterfall (see *left*). Most visitors, however, only travel around its boundaries, riding the gondolas and taking little more than a glance at its beauty. To really appreciate this landscape you must walk – a five-day traverse can take you across the summits of more than a dozen alpine peaks, including Hokkaidō's highest, the active volcano Asahi-dake (2290m).

A welcome by-product of all this thermal indigestion is the presence of so many onsen (natural hot springs). Soaking in one is an activity as Japanese as sumo. You'll even find a spring at the end of your Daisetsuzan traverse.
— *www.visit-hokkaido.jp*

Pull a face at Crab Fair

ENGLAND

WHY NOW Head to this 13th-century festival to have a go at gurning

WHERE Egremont, Cumbria

DATES Third Saturday in September

19 SEP This Cumbrian fest is one of the world's oldest fairs, created in a charter signed by King Henry II in 1267. Over the centuries, the event has featured a variety of once-popular pursuits, such as cockfighting and bull baiting. But none have been stranger than the gurning competition. Held in the Market Hall, the World Gurning Championship challenges contestants to contort their face into strange and unnatural shapes, with their head poking through an unwieldy horse's braffin (collar).

Originally a harvest festival, the fair kicks off with the Parade of the Apple Cart, a tradition derived from the serfs who paid their dues at the manor in wild fruit. The lord would give crab apples to the children, and today men throw apples from the cart and have a costumed wheelbarrow race. Other activities include a greasy pole climb, Cumberland wrestling and a sprint across the moors. The biskey (teacake) and treacle contest, in which participants race to gobble up enough treacle-soaked biskey to be able to whistle, has sadly died out.

— *www.egremontcrabfair.com*

Hike & dive Corsica

FRANCE

WHY NOW High tourist season is over but it's still warm and the sea is a pleasant 23°C
WHERE Corsica, Mediterranean Sea
DATES September and October

20 SEP For a small isle, Corsica offers adventure in large doses. The lush peaks and varied trails are ideal for hiking, while 1000km of coast and warm waters provide top diving.

Corsica's famed hike is the GR20, which stretches 168km through the granite ridges of the island's interior. To walk its entirety you'll need at least two weeks. For something shorter, try the Mare e Monti (Sea to Mountains) and Mare e Mare (Sea to Sea) trails that crisscross the island.

The diving is some of the Med's best. The rugged landscape continues underwater, with a carpet of yellow anemone and red coral. Try Golfe de Porto, where granite walls plunge to abysses 800m below. — *www.visit-corsica.fr*

LEFT: **Gurning at the Crab Festival**

BELOW: **You can spot whales from the coast of Hermanus in South Africa**

Visit Borneo's bat cave

MALAYSIA

WHY NOW You'll get to see 3 million bats on the move each evening
WHERE Gunung Mulu National Park, Sarawak
DATES July to September

21 SEP Scientists were stunned in 1977 when they began exploring the massifs around Gunung Mulu and found one record-shattering cave after another. Deer Cave, they discovered, had the world's largest cave passage and an immense population of bats, which make a nightly exodus. The cave's 12 bat species (the largest variety for a single cave) are estimated to number in the millions. This colossal mass of critters begins pouring from the cave at around 5pm, while day-flying swiftlets pour back in.

Access to Gunung Mulu is from Miri via a 30-minute flight or 12-hour boat ride. July to September are the driest months to visit. — *www.mulupark.com*

Watch whales

SOUTH AFRICA

WHY NOW Watch southern right whales
WHERE Hermanus, Western Cape
DATES September to November for peak of whale migration; festival late September/early October

22 SEP Near Africa's southernmost tip, Hermanus has a front-row view of the Cape Whale Route. During migrating season, you can glimpse endangered southern right whales from the shore. In an attempt to formalise the clifftop viewing, Hermanus started its festival and introduced the Whale Crier, who blasts a kelp horn to direct eager cetacean-spotters.

The festival is a great place to learn all about whales. There is also a range of activities on offer such as the Welcome Whale Wave Walk, where some 5000 people create a 5km human chain to say howdy to the seafarers, as well as music, arts and family entertainment. — *www.whalefestival.co.za*

Canoe Pagsanjan's rapids

PHILIPPINES

WHY NOW The wet season creates the very best rapids

WHERE Pagsanjan River, Luzon island

DATES August to September

23 SEP

Canoe rides through the rapids of the Pagsanjan River, near Manila, are one of Luzon's best thrills. The ride begins with skilled *banceros* (boatmen) paddling you against the flow of the river to Magdapio Falls, through an awesome gorge; some of the final scenes of Coppola's epic Vietnam War movie *Apocalypse Now* were shot here, which tells you a lot about its wildness.

At the top, the *banceros* will paddle you into the natural pool at the bottom of the 10m-high, three-drop falls. Then it's time to turn around and shoot the 14 rapids back downstream. You can just let the water do the work if you like – it's a fast and exhilarating ride, best when the water's nice and high.

— *www.itsmorefuninthephilippines.com*

RIGHT: **The Parthenon, starting point of the gruelling Spartathlon**

BELOW: **Dodge devils and firecrackers at Barcelona's Festival of the Virgin of Mercy**

Join Barca's biggest fiesta

SPAIN

WHY NOW Join the Catalan party as Barcelona is overrun with giants, devils and human pyramids

WHERE Barcelona, Catalonia

DATES Four days around 24 September

24 SEP

Les Festes de la Mercè (Festival of the Virgin of Mercy) is the Catalan capital's festa major and a final burst of prewinter madness.

Some 600 events take place. There's a swimming race across the harbour, a fun run and a series of free concerts. The Barcelona Acció Musical (Barcelona Musical Action) showcases new sounds, while the Festival of the Sky is an acrobatic assembly of jets and balloons. One of the most impressive sights is the *castell* competition – brave combatants compete to form the highest human pyramid; the towers rise up to eight storeys high. The *correfoc* (fire run) sees crowds hurl themselves along Via Laietana before 'devils', fire-spurting beasts and kids armed with firecrackers. — *www.bcn.es/merce*

Run the Spartathlon

GREECE

WHY NOW To run like Pheidippides and feel like a Greek god or goddess

WHERE Athens to Sparta

DATES Usually the last Friday in September

25 SEP

Marathons the world over celebrate the run of the ancient Greek Pheidippides from Marathon to Athens to announce a war victory over the Persians. But how many marathons honour his original run, from Athens to Sparta, to rustle up help for the same fight against the Persians? Only this one.

Runners in this annual ultramarathon begin in the Greek capital, Athens, and follow a 245km course believed to mirror Pheidippides' route as closely as possible. It starts at the foot of the Acropolis at 7am, usually on the last Friday of September. It then leaves the Greek capital, heading out toward the coast and towards Corinth.

At its highest point, the route rises to a thigh-bursting 1200m as it heads across Mt Parthenio. This is where, according to legend, Pheidippides met up with Pan, the ancient god of shepherds, flocks and mountain wilds. In the lingering summer heat, it's more likely now that runners will meet up with extreme fatigue.

To keep runners in check, there are 75 race control points along the punishing route, each with a cut-off time for any stragglers. The final cut-off is 36 hours, though the course record, held by Yiannis Kouros, is an astonishing 20:25:00. It's a tough, tough, tough run, but the people of Sparta flock to the finish, in front of the statue of King Leonidas, to welcome every exhausted athlete as a hero.

— *www.spartathlon.gr*

Slurp at the Oyster Festival

IRELAND

WHY NOW Munch on many molluscs

WHERE Galway, County Galway

DATES Last weekend in September (26–27 Sep 2015; 24–25 Sep 2016; 23–24 Sep 2017; 29–30 Sep 2018)

26 SEP The Galway Oyster Festival is dedicated to *Ostrea edulis*, the European flat oyster. The local molluscs are left to grow for three years in the clean waters of Brandon Bay and Clarenbridge, blooming into a juicy delicacy.

Tens of thousands of the slippery critters are consumed on the Guinness Oyster Trail, on which 30 pubs give out free trays of the seafood with pints of the dark stuff. Each establishment has a dedicated oyster-opener, and there's more nimble-fingered action on display at the World Oyster Opening Championship. International contestants vie to break the world record for prising open the tight-lipped urchins. If, at the end of the man-versus-mollusc showdown, they present the judges with a tray resembling a battleground, they lose points.

The city fills with craic such as the opening ceremony, where the Oyster Pearl (festival queen) presents the season's first oyster to the mayor. There's plenty of cheap stuff, but tickets for the more-exclusive Mardi Gras, gala ball and Saturday afternoon at the marquee, including the opening championship, can be pricey indeed. — *www.galwayoysterfest.com*

RIGHT: **GETTY IMAGES**

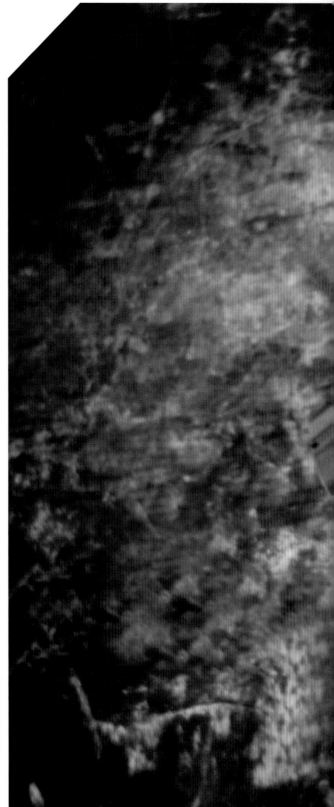

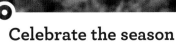

Celebrate the season

CHINA

WHY NOW Eat cake at the Mid-Autumn Festival
WHERE Countrywide
DATES 15th day of eighth month of Chinese lunar calendar (27 Sep 2015; 15 Sep 2016; 4 Oct 2017)

27 SEP Dating back to around 1000 BC, and formerly held on the autumn equinox, the Mid-Autumn Festival is mostly about worshiping the moon. The ancient Chinese realised that lunar movement correlated closely with changes in the seasons and therefore agricultural production. So, to say thanks for their harvest, they offered sacrifices to the moon around this time.

Today, the festival is a family-embracing affair, celebrated with plenty of dancing, feasting and stargazing; ideally you want to be near water, to better see the moon's glow reflected back.

Proceedings would be incomplete without the eating of moon cakes. These brill baked goods are said to have been key in outfoxing 13th-century Mongol invaders, when the Chinese hid plans for a rebellion inside the cunning buns. Now they're given as gifts and consumed with gusto. – *www.cnto.org*

Skydive over Mt Everest

NEPAL

WHY NOW The parachuting season over the world's tallest mountain is brief
WHERE Himalaya
DATES September to October

28 SEP In 2008 three skydivers became the first to jump from a plane above Mt Everest, leaping at 8992m, using supplementary oxygen and special suits. A year later Everest skydiving went commercial.

Experienced skydivers can make solo jumps; novices do tandem jumps strapped to an instructor. Apart from being the world's highest skydives, they are also the longest: training and preparation programmes last a fortnight, including four days of trekking to help with acclimatisation. Several days at the end of the trip are set aside for jump attempts in case bad weather descends, though this is the best time to be in the Himalaya – skies are usually clear and dry. The drop zone is on the slopes of Everest itself. — *www.everest-skydive.com*

RIGHT: **See Vermont when autumn leaves start to fall**

BELOW: **Looking towards Maletsunyane Falls in Lesotho**

See a kingdom by horse

LESOTHO

WHY NOW Cool and comfortable trekking ahead of the wet season
WHERE Malealea
DATES September to November

29 SEP Pony trekking is one of Lesotho's top drawcards. It's done on sure-footed Basotho ponies, the result of crossbreeding short Javanese horses and European full mounts. Lesotho's revered King Moshoeshoe the Great is recorded as having ridden a Basotho pony in 1830, and since that time these animals have become the preferred mode of transport for many villagers.

Malealea is the best pony trekking centre; popular routes include to Ribaneng Waterfall (two days) and Semonkong (five to six days). The Basotho Pony Trekking Centre, atop the delightfully named God Help Me Pass, is more no-frills, and the place to come if you want to ride away from the crowds for up to a week. — *www.visitlesotho.travel*

Partake in leaf-peeping

USA

WHY NOW Marvel at the colourful Northeast Kingdom Fall Foliage Festival

WHERE Vermont

DATES Six days, late September (from 28 Sep 2015)

30 SEP Strangely, the countryside of New England never looks better than when it starts to die. This US region is renowned for its fabulous autumn colours, when the forest-cloaked hillsides of maple, beech and birch seem to blaze a billion shades of yellow, orange and red.

The state of Vermont doesn't let the spectacle pass without fanfare. The Northeast Kingdom Foliage Festival is six consecutive days of arboreal admiration in six different towns in the state's remote and pretty-as-a-picture northeast corner. The towns – Walden, Cabot, Plainfield, Peacham, Barnet and Groton – each host their own events, which celebrate 'old Vermont': this is rural America how it used to be, with a heartwarming community feel, and surrounded by the awesomeness of autumn's hues.

Events veer to the traditional. You can attend a Great Pumpkin weigh-in, shop at traditional craft stalls, see glass blowers at work, join in folk dances, tour dairies, wander amid farm animals and take a hayride. There are also lots of guided walks around the towns' various historic sites and up to panoramic viewpoints, for excellent views of all those tremendous colour-turning trees.

Food features strongly during proceedings too. Brace your belly for lumberjack breakfasts, corn chowder and chilli lunches and barbecue beef suppers. It's scenery with scoff, and both are delicious. — *www.nekchamber.com*

Raise a stein at Oktoberfest

GERMANY

WHY NOW Join 6 million other beer imbibers

WHERE Theresienwiese, Munich

DATES Runs for 16 days, from late September to early October

01 OCT In 1810, a horse race was held to celebrate Bavarian Crown Prince Ludwig's wedding. The jamboree was such a rip-roaring success that it became an annual event and morphed into today's ribald party: Oktoberfest.

The amber nectar is quaffed by more than 6 million Lowenbräu-lovers. Sitting at long tables in huge tents, beer monsters work through more than 6.5 million L. The festival's diet also includes some 500,000 chicken, 104 oxen and more than 50,000 pork knuckle servings. The only beer available is the specially brewed Oktoberfest-Bier; you pay using tokens and must be seated to be served. Rules get trickier as drinkers become *Bierleichen* (beer corpses).

There's also a carnival and a few nostalgic faves: Germany's last remaining flea circus has been a fixture here since the 19th century. — *www.oktoberfest.de*

October

Behold courting albatross

FALKLAND ISLANDS

WHY NOW It's the beginning of the albatross mating season

WHERE Falklands Islands, South Atlantic Ocean

DATES October to March

02 OCT These remarkable islands 645km off the coast of South America were visited by Charles Darwin in the 19th century. Only 2500 people live here, 80% of them in the capital city, Stanley, leaving a lot of open space for wildlife.

The islands, at the confluence of Antarctic and sub-Antarctic waters, are rich in endemic birds and large seal and seabird colonies. This is the most important breeding site in the world for rockhopper penguins, the second most important for gentoo penguins, and the easiest place in the world to see king penguins. But the islands are most famous for their black-browed albatross colonies, a total of 800,000 birds – 80% of the world's population.

The albatross arrive in October, with mated pairs from the year before greeting each other after a year-long absence. Their subsequent courtship displays are loud and elaborate, as they face each other, spread their 2.5m-wide wings, point their bills skyward and moo and bray. The largest of the 12 albatross colonies is on uninhabited Steeple Jason Island, but they can be observed on other islands too.

October is also an excellent month for seeing new-born southern elephant seals; over 5000 pups are born on the islands each year. Two other seal species and a dozen species of whale are regularly observed in these waters.

— *www.falklandislands.com*

Have a balloon ball

USA

WHY NOW Take flight at the Balloon Fiesta
WHERE Albuquerque, New Mexico
DATES Early October (3–11 Oct 2015, 1–9 Oct 2016, 7–15 Oct 2017, 6–14 Oct 2018)

03 OCT

The Albuquerque International Balloon Fiesta is *a lot* of hot air. Simply, it's the biggest hot-air balloon event on the planet, which sees around 600 of the fantastic flying machines amass on a vast launch field in New Mexico, forming the centrepiece of a great, family-friendly fiesta.

It's a magical sight: balloons of myriad shapes and sizes, a rainbow of colour, billowing silk and roaring flames, plus food stalls and entertainment. There are various launch events too. Dawn Patrols see selected balloons rise up before sunrise; at Night Glows, grounded balloons fire their burners after dark to create magical illuminations; at Mass Ascensions, you can witness all 600-odd baskets taking off at once. – *www.balloonfiesta.com*

Find your match

IRELAND

WHY NOW Find the man/woman of your dreams
WHERE Lisdoonvarna, County Clare
DATES From the last Friday in August to first Sunday in October

04 OCT

With its population of about 1000, tiny Lisdoonvarna was famed for two things: its spas, which made it a popular Victorian resort, and its *basadóiri* (matchmakers). For a fee, these Guinness-swilling Cupids would help singletons find a partner.

Most of the hopefuls (mostly men) would bumble into town in September, when the crops were in and they had made enough hay to buy a lady a glass of porter. The Matchmaking Festival provided social events for these lonely-hearted pilgrims, and allowed local personages to keep undesirables away from their daughters.

The festival still features a *basadóiri*, local horse dealer Willie Daly, as well as amateur horse racing and traditional Irish craic by the pub-load. — *www.matchmakerireland.com*

LEFT: **Romance, Wandering Albatross style, on South Georgia island**

BELOW: **Like hot-air balloons... a lot? Albuquerque in October is the place for you**

Trek the Snowman

BHUTAN

WHY NOW There's only a narrow window of opportunity to attempt the Snowman Trek

WHERE Bhutan

DATES Late September to mid-October

05 OCT Bhutan is a country of rolling hills, towering crags and abundant forest. Virtually the entire place is mountainous, and to see the best of it you should spend a week or more on foot, trekking through the great forested wilderness that covers most of the country. A trek provides the best opportunity to experience the real heart of Bhutan and to get an insight into the rural culture of the kingdom.

The mother of all treks here is the Snowman. Fewer than half the people who attempt it actually finish it, either because of problems with altitude (it reaches over 5300m) or heavy snowfall. Its season is short – late September to mid-October – and its commitment is long: it takes around 25 days. But it is utterly spectacular. — *www.tourism.gov.bt*

See 200,000 turtles

COSTA RICA

WHY NOW The rainy season is your best bet for seeing *la arribada*

WHERE Fauna Silvestre Ostional Refuge

DATES September to October

06 OCT There is no predicting *la arribada*, 'the arrival' of mass numbers of olive ridley turtles on the Pacific coast beaches of Mexico and Central America. After a year at sea, these sea turtles lumber ashore over the course of several days to lay their eggs.

It starts slowly, a few skittish turtles coming ashore one night; on successive nights dozens show up, then hundreds of thousands suddenly arrive. The peak period is around September and October, and is most likely to occur around the first and the last quarter of the moon.

The best turtle beach may be Costa Rica's Ostional, where as many as 500,000 turtles have been counted. It's hard to know why so many come ashore at once, but they've been doing it for 190 million years. — *www.visitcostarica.com*

RIGHT: **Explore Vietnam's Halong Bay by boat**

BELOW: **Female Olive Ridley turtles laying eggs on Ostional beach, Costa Rica**

Visit Vietnam's perfect season

VIETNAM

WHY NOW October offers the best balance between heat, cold, dry and wet
WHERE Countrywide
DATES October

07 OCT
Vietnam has 3451km of coast and is 75% covered by mountains. It sounds custom-made for exploration and adventure, though Vietnam is only just beginning to realise its potential.

The first issue is picking the best time to begin a Vietnamese adventure. There are two monsoons: the winter monsoon comes from the northeast between October and March, bringing damp and chilly winters to all areas north of Nha Trang, and dry and warm temperatures to the south. From April to October, the summer monsoon brings hot, humid weather to the whole country except for those areas sheltered by mountains. October offers one of the best balances between heat and cold, dry and wet.

So what do when you're there? The Mekong Delta is cycling heaven, with barely a bump in its silted surface. The Hwy 1 coastal route is alluring, though the insane traffic makes it tough; better is the quieter inland trunk road, Hwy 14, which offers stunning scenery.

Halong Bay is Vietnam's big natural wonder: 3000 incredible islands rising from emerald waters, it's been likened to Guìlín and Krabi. Paddling among the karsts is popular.

The main diving area is Nha Trang, where there are around 25 dive sites. There are good drop-offs, underwater caves, a variety of corals and lots of reef fish. Surfing is also popular – Mui Ne Beach is one of the best spots.
— *www.vietnamtourism.com*

Hike the Kopra Ridge

NEPAL

WHY NOW Come for the best trekking weather in the Himalaya

WHERE Kopra Ridge, Annapurnas

DATES October and November

08 OCT

It used to be that most trekkers came to Nepal to hike the Annapurna Circuit, but in recent years roads have begun to devour the track, dulling the experience a touch. In response, trekkers are being pushed out to the Everest region or in quest of new routes in the Annapurnas. In 2008 signs began appearing among the teahouses of Deurali, spruiking a new route up to Kopra Ridge, draping down from 7219m Annapurna South.

The route branches off from the Annapurna Circuit at Deurali, just west of Tatapani, climbing to the alpine top of Kopra Ridge. The ridge is now home to a trekkers' lodge, which peers deep down into the Kali Gandaki, the world's deepest gorge, bottoming out almost 7000m below the summit of Dhaulagiri. Views also take in Annapurna South, Fang, Poon Hill and Dhaulagiri across the gorge.

The lodge is part of a community initiative, with trekkers' funds going towards village projects. Even the ridge's air of untouched isolation comes with a twist: the lodge serves as one of two solar-powered relay stations that transmit internet signals to surrounding villages, so you can check your emails 3500m up Annapurna South. — *www.welcomenepal.com*

LEFT: **MARK DAFFEY – GETTY IMAGES**

Kayak the Yasawa Islands

FIJI

WHY NOW The Fijian winter is warming up but cyclone season is still a few weeks away
WHERE Yasawa Islands, off Viti Levu
DATES May to October

09 OCT

After the mutiny on the Bounty in 1789, Captain William Bligh paddled through Fiji's Yasawa Islands on his way to Timor. However, given that he was being chased by Fijian canoes, he may not have enjoyed the experience as much as you will – in less life-threatening circumstances, the paddle along this 90km-long chain of 20 ancient volcanic islands off the northwest of Viti Levu is quite idyllic.

Famed for lovely white-sand beaches, crystal-blue lagoons and rugged volcanic landscapes, the Yasawa Islands forms a roughly straight line within the Great Sea Reef. Islands. Each island is no more than 10km apart, making for short paddles.

You'll find the best paddling along the western side of the islands, where you'll be sheltered from the prevailing southeast winds and can kayak at a more relaxed pace.
— *www.fiji.travel*

Safari in Tibet

CHINA

WHY NOW Travel is easiest now as the ground starts to freeze again, but it's not too cold
WHERE Chang Tang Nature Reserve, Tibet
DATES September and October

10 OCT Perched 4000m to 5000m above sea level in the rain shadow to the north of the Himalayas, the 700,000 sq km Tibetan Plateau is one of the harshest places on earth. Its northern region barely receives 20cm of rain a year and experiences below-freezing temperatures for 10 months out of 12.

Given these conditions, it's surprising that the Plateau is inhabited by a unique community of large mammals. Chang Tang, the largest of five major reserves on the Plateau, is home to Tibetan wild asses, Tibetan gazelles, Tibetan brown bears, dwarf blue sheep, snow leopards, wolves and lynxes. To the south there are 500 lakes where thousands of birds nest. — *www.tew.org*

Come see Círio de Nazaré

BRAZIL

WHY NOW It's the Amazon's biggest bash
WHERE Praça Justo Chermont, Belém
DATES Second weekend in October (10–11 Oct 2015; 8–9 Oct 2016; 7–8 Oct 2017; 13–14 Oct 2018)

11 OCT The largest festival on the River Amazon, the Círio de Nazaré revolves around a small statue of Nossa Senhora de Nazaré (Our Lady of Nazareth). Supposedly sculpted in Nazareth, the image is believed to have performed miracles in Portugal before getting lost in Brazil. A cattleman rediscovered it in 1700 on the site of Belém's Basílica.

During the festival, the sacred statue is carried in a river procession, then on a carriage through the streets. Supplicants grope to get a hand on the rope pulling the vehicle, which is thought to represent the link between the Saint and her dedicated followers.
— *www.ciriodenazare.com.br*

RIGHT: **Boats docked at Trogir, a historic town on Croatia's Dalmatian coast**

BELOW: **Roman Catholic pilgrims attempt to touch the Our Lady of Nazareth's image during the Círio de Nazaré in Belem, northern Brazil**

Safari in Ngorongoro

TANZANIA

WHY NOW Wildlife is concentrated around waterholes at the end of the dry season
WHERE Ngorongoro Crater, 165km west of Arusha
DATES June to October

12 OCT Located on the Serengeti Plain, Ngorongoro Crater is the world's largest unbroken caldera, its circular crater rim perched 600m over a wildlife-rich wonderland.

Only one major road descends into the crater and one climbs out. Access can be impossible in the wet season, but in the dry (July to October) there are 120km of roads to explore, offering fabulous wildlife-watching.

The crater is believed to have the highest density of predators in Africa. Lions and spotted hyenas are abundant; cheetahs are occasionally seen; leopards are present, although they stick to the forested rim. The shrubby areas are ideal for black rhinos. — *www.tanzaniaparks.com*

Island-hop by sailboat

CROATIA

WHY NOW The sting of summer has gone but the Adriatic remains warm

WHERE Split to Dubrovnik

DATES October

13 OCT With almost 6000km of coastline and 1185 islands (of which only 66 are inhabited), Croatia is ideal for water fun. The long, rugged islands off the mountainous coast stretch all the way from Istria to Dubrovnik, making this a yachting paradise. Fine, deep channels with abundant anchorage and steady winds attract sailors from around the world, and throughout the region yachts can tie up right in the middle of all of the island action.

A good place to charter a yacht is Split, from where you can sail out past bucolic islands such as Hvar and Korčula before continuing south to Dubrovnik. Some sailing knowledge and experience is handy, though if you want a hands-off experience you can join a skippered boat.

Autumn is a lovely time. It's after the heat and tourist rush of July to August but the temperatures are still pleasant. The sea's had all summer to warm up – it'll be a little chill, but jumping overboard for a swim is still possible. On land, the grape and olive harvest are in flow, and markets are full of seasonal produce such as mushrooms and chestnuts. — *www.croatia.hr*

Cycle the most dangerous road

BOLIVIA

WHY NOW Come at the end of the dry season to avoid a muddy run
WHERE La Paz to Coroico
DATES May to October

14 OCT The Yungas Hwy between the Bolivian capital La Paz and the town of Coroico is officially the world's most dangerous road, at least according to a 1995 Inter-American Development Bank report. Given that an average of 26 vehicles disappear over its edge each year, the title is well deserved.

It's a gravel track only 3.2m wide – just enough for one vehicle – with sheer 1000m drops, hulking rock overhangs, waterfalls that spill across and erode the highway, and a growing reputation among cyclists keen for an adrenaline rush. Bike hire is available in La Paz. Now all you need do is watch those edges, drunk drivers and marauding trucks.

Summer (November to April) is rainy season in Bolivia, when overland transportation becomes difficult in some areas – and certainly makes the Yungas Hwy even more perilous. The most popular, and most comfortable, time to explore is during winter (May to October) with its dry, clear days. Even so, good bike control – and a sense of derring-do – are recommended.
— *www.boliviatravelsite.com*

Glide the Morning Glories

AUSTRALIA

WHY NOW These awesome atmospheric creations usually occur at this time
WHERE Gulf of Carpentaria, north Queensland
DATES September to October

15 OCT

In Outback Queensland they say: if a sea breeze has blown through Burketown, and if the fridges in the pub have frosted over, there's a good chance the next day will bring a Morning Glory. Scientific? Maybe not. But the Gulf of Carpentaria is the only place where these enormous roll clouds – often 1,000km long, 1–2km high, hovering just 100m above the ground and travelling at up to 60km/h – can be predictably seen. Head here September to October for your best chance. They also offer one of the world's great gliding and hang-gliding adventures – Morning Glories have carried gliders for more than 700km and for up to 6 hours. — *www.tq.com.au*

LEFT: **Check your brake pads before descending the Yungas Hwy**

BELOW: **Put a smile on your face at MassKara in the Philippines**

Get arty in autumn

HUNGARY

WHY NOW Come over all cultural at the Café Budapest Contemporary Arts Festival
WHERE Budapest
DATES Nine days, mid-October

16 OCT

Formerly known as the Autumn Festival, Café Budapest is an excuse for the Hungarian capital to indulge in an wide programme of music, theatre and dance as the nights start to draw in. Expect everything from unknown musos to household names; highlights include the Jazz Marathon and the Night of Contemporary Galleries, when these exciting art spaces stay open until the wee hours.

Performances pop up across the city – everywhere from galleries, cinemas and the National Theatre to cool cafes and pubs (such as A38 and Café Jedermann). The festival is a super way to welcome the season.
— *www.cafebudapestfest.hu*

Smile at MassKara

PHILIPPINES

WHY NOW Wear a really big grin at this tropical masked ball
WHERE Bacolod, Negros Occidental
DATES Weekend nearest 19 October

17 OCT

MassKara's name is a fusion of the English word for 'many' and *cara*, Spanish for face. It's a perfect description of this Philippino fiesta, in which Bacolod's residents take to the streets wearing masks with radiant smiles.

The masked ball began in the early 1980s in response to two crises: a drop in sugar-cane prices and a tragic ship crash. The festival reminds Bacolod of its nickname: 'city of smiles'.

The beaming masks on show resemble everything from sea creatures to vegetable men. Plumes explode out of temples, and groups gather in clay or papier-mâché masks and glittering jumpsuits, grinning from ear to ear.
— *www.itsmorefuninthephilippines.com*

See Bridge Day BASE jumpers

USA

WHY NOW Watch daredevils leap
WHERE New River Gorge, West Virginia
DATES Third Sunday in October (18 Oct 2015; 16 Oct 2016; 15 Oct 2017; 21 Oct 2018)

18 OCT

It's the world's largest extreme-sports event. More than 450 BASE jumpers hurl themselves off a 265m-high bridge, watched by up to 200,000 spectators.

BASE stands for 'building, antennae, span, earth', the fixed points from which the adrenaline-seeking jumpers leap. Every year since 1980, the steel structure high above the New River has proven to be a perfect launching pad. It may be one of America's highest bridges, but jumpers still have just eight seconds to freefall and open their parachutes. They can land in the rapids below, nicknamed the 'River of Death', or on a patch of shoreline that's free of trees, boulders and spectators.

The 6 hours it takes the 450 thrillseekers to deploy is the only time pedestrians are allowed on the 900m-long bridge, which gives breathtaking views down the forested gorge. Some daredevils leap from trampolines and diving boards, others parachute from the bridge rails, and climbing teams rappel into the canyon. One couple even tied the knot here and celebrated by leaping into the void.

This is not an event for beginners: first-time participants must have made 100 previous parachute jumps and must take part in a training course; the danger level is high. However, anyone can take a tour of the gorge, wander across the impressive bridge and watch the jumping from below.

— *www.officialbridgeday.com*

Watch the deer rut

SCOTLAND

WHY NOW The boisterous and majestic males are in full rut
WHERE Isle of Rum, Inner Hebrides
DATES Mid-September to mid-November

19 OCT

The 104 sq km Isle of Rum has a sizable population of red deer. Much of the year, the deer roam in large, single-sex groups, but this changes in mid-September when the males develop shaggy ruffs and prepare for battle. There are few sights as majestic as a bull red deer silhouetted against the ocean, roaring with the unbridled lust of the breeding season.

The rutting season is a noisy, energised time. Males rarely eat during the two-month rut, and expend tremendous amounts of energy bellowing, copulating and battling any males that challenge their authority. Only males in their prime are up for the effort.

This beautiful island is owned by Scottish Natural Heritage, which operates a hostel at Kinloch Castle. — *www.isleofrum.com*

Dive the perfect Pacific

NEW CALEDONIA

WHY NOW The days are not too hot and sticky, and there's less likelihood of rain
WHERE New Caledonia
DATES September to December

20 OCT

A très French island in the middle of the Pacific, New Caledonia is surrounded by the world's largest coral lagoon – diving here is king.

There's around 1600km of reef, with the enclosed turquoise lagoon around the main island of Grande Terre covering around 23,500 sq km. In addition, near-shore fringing reefs surround all the smaller outlying islands.

From the capital, Noumea, it's a short trip to Amédée Islet, a marine reserve with plenty of underwater life. On Île des Pins there are dives to caves. On Ouvéa you can walk to natural shark nurseries. Late each year, large sharks give birth in the shallow waters. Their hormones make them placid (so they don't eat their offspring) and so not dangerous to visitors.
— *www.newcaledoniatourism-south.com*

LEFT: **Bridge Day BASE jumpers in West Virginia, USA**

BELOW: **A Hebridean stag bides his time**

Observe huge herds of buffalo

KENYA

WHY NOW The beginning of the rains brings the buffalo together

WHERE Masai Mara

DATES Mid-October to November

21 OCT Perhaps no other large animal has the African buffalo's reputation: an 850kg bull stands 1.7m tall at the shoulder and can reputedly push around a 4WD. Lone bulls can be extremely dangerous; even if blind or injured, buffalo might survive for years because of their size and bellicosity. Fortunately, with the arrival of the rains after mid-October, buffalo on the Masai Mara begin gathering in large herds among abundantly growing grasses. During this time they are pretty inactive and move in docile, grazing herds like their domestic counterparts.

Highly social, buffalo form large non-territorial herds that can number 1500 if there is enough food. At this time, cows in oestrus attract the attention of bulls who posture for dominance, circling, pawing the dirt, thrashing bushes and sometimes charging each other head-on.

This greening of the plains after the first rains is a beautiful time to visit the Masai Mara. The massive herds of wildebeest, zebras and gazelles are now heading southward towards the Serengeti and there's a lot of excitement everywhere. — *www.maasaimara.com*

Dress up for Jidai Matsuri

JAPAN

WHY NOW Don a costume – or admire those of others – at the Festival of the Ages
WHERE Kyoto
DATES 22 October

22 OCT

Jidai Matsuri began in 1895 to raise the city's morale after the Imperial Court shifted to Tokyo. The main event is the historical parade, featuring period costumes from eras dating back to AD794, when the city began its 1000-year tenure as capital. The parade starts at the city's final imperial palace, Kyoto Gosho, which was built only 14 years before Tokyo grabbed the glory. The mikoshi (portable shrines) of the first and last Kyoto emperors are joined by more than 2000 people during the 4.6km procession to Heian-jingū, a Shintō shrine built to imitate earlier palaces. It takes more than an hour for all the participants to pass one point. — *www.kyotoguide.com*

LEFT: **Cape buffaloes on the move in Kenya's Masai Mara**

BELOW: **Getting an aerial view of the Turquoise Coast in Ölüdeniz**

Paraglide at Ölüdeniz

TURKEY

WHY NOW Leap from the Father Mountain to soar like a bird – after the tourists have left
WHERE Ölüdeniz, Turquoise Coast
DATES September to November

217

23 OCT

If you like the idea of plummeting off a cliff with another person strapped to your back, you won't find many better places to do so than the Turkish town of Ölüdeniz. The resort is set around a sheltered lagoon, on the country's Turquoise Coast. It's popular in high summer; by autumn it will have quietened down, but is still warm and open for business.

Many companies in Ölüdeniz offer tandem paragliding flights. The best is the descent from 1900m Baba Dağ (Father Mountain), which is surrounded by fantastic thermals. Strapped to a pilot, you'll leap to catch the air currents and soar with the wind; it can take as long as 45 minutes to drift down. — *www.babadag.com*

Shoot the breeze

FRANCE

WHY NOW Be swept away by the aerial awesomeness of the Festival du Vent
WHERE Calvi, Corsica
DATES Five days, late October

24 OCT

Things can get a bit blowy out in the middle of the Mediterranean. And comely Calvi, a coastal town on the wild isle of Corsica, makes the most of the gusts by hosting a festival of wind.

It's a celebration of air in all its forms: hundreds of artists and wind freaks bring out their kites, balloons, hang-gliders and sculptures to celebrate the freedom of the breeze. There are exhibitions of windmill art, windsurfing competitions, graceful kite-flying demonstrations and microlights zipping about above the sea, with an emphasis on all things eco. A fun outing for all the family.
— *www.lefestivalduvent.com*

Hike the Hoerikwaggo Trail

SOUTH AFRICA

WHY NOW For pleasant walking conditions amid wildflowers on Table Mountain
WHERE Cape Town to Cape of Good Hope
DATES Mid-September to November

25 OCT Discover one of the world's most appealing hiking experiences. This five-day, four-night hiking trail runs for 75km between Cape Town and the tip of the Cape of Good Hope, crossing Table Mountain en route.

Hoerikwaggo is what the nomadic hunter-gatherer Khoi people called Table Mountain. The Hoerikwaggo Trail nods to this ancestry, giving you a chance to turn nomad yourself, exploring on foot this landscape of fragrant *fynbos* (natural shrubland), blindingly white-sand beaches, Atlantic Ocean coast, great gorges and, of course, the iconic slopes of Table Mountain itself.

The trail is not signposted – an accredited trail guide and good maps are highly recommended. There are four tented camps along the route: Smitswinkel, Silvermine, Slangkop and Orangekloof. All camps offer self-catering accommodation complete with kitchen and bathroom facilities for a maximum of 12 people. Braai facilities are available too, so you can end each day's hike with a traditional South African meat-heavy barbecue.
— *www.sanparks.org/parks*

Get close to polar bears

CANADA

WHY NOW The polar bears gather while waiting for ice to form

WHERE Churchill, Manitoba

DATES October and November

26 OCT The snow-locked town of Churchill, Manitoba, calls itself the 'Polar Bear Capital of the World' – and for very good reason.

Each year, for about six weeks from mid-October, over 1000 polar bears gather on the frozen tundra outside this remote northern outpost on Hudson Bay while waiting for the sea to freeze up. And immediately southwest of town is the 11,475 sq km Wapusk National Park, site of the largest polar bear maternity denning area in the world. All told, there are more polar bears than humans here, so the residents of Churchill shape their lives around keeping an eye out for bears and practising 'bear safe' behaviour.

Polar bears spend the summer wandering along the forest edges and shorelines of Churchill, living off their fat reserves in what is called 'walking hibernation'. By the time late October comes around they are gaunt and lethargic, saving their energy until they can get onto the ice and start hunting for seals.

This is the season when tourists descend on Churchill for 'tundra buggy' tours. These tough trucks, built very high off the ground to keep those inside safe, take people out onto the frozen plains, into the midst of the waiting bears. At this time the bears are fearless and very curious, and easily approached by vehicles, which allows for fantastic close-up views of these truly majestic mammals.
— *www.travelmanitoba.com*

Mountain bike in Moab

USA

WHY NOW Miss the summer heat and winter chill, and catch Moab Ho-Down Bike Festival too
WHERE Moab, Utah
DATES October

27 OCT Moab would horrify its founding fathers. Established as a Mormon outpost, it's fallen to a cult of adrenaline-juiced mountain bikers.

Set amid striking desert, Moab's most famous feature is slickrock, the smooth sandstone named because horses found it so slippery. Beneath the tyres of a mountain bike it is, conversely, more like stickrock.

Foremost among the slickrock rides is the Slickrock Trail, a Holy Grail of mountain biking, that winds across the ridges above town, with glimpses of the Colorado River and Arches National Park. Around 100,000 cyclists follow it every year, but it's not for the timid: it has steep climbs and terrifying descents. However, come away without 'bacon' (scabs) and you've arrived as a mountain biker. — *www.discovermoab.com*

Meet the Lord of Miracles

PERU

WHY NOW The Peruvian capital turns purple to give thanks to Christ
WHERE Lima
DATES 18, 28 & 29 October

28 OCT This large procession celebrates a 350-year-old mural of the Lord of Miracles – Christ. Painted by a freed slave, the fresco has survived vindictive authorities, bumbling workers and three earthquakes. The first procession took place in 1687, when an earthquake obliterated the chapel that housed the portrait, leaving only the altar and the mural.

Processions take place on major feast days in October, a *mes morado* (purple month). A 2500-strong brotherhood carries the two-tonne artwork. Everyone wears purple, the colour worn by the Nazarene nuns charged with looking after the holy image, and fuels themselves with *turrón de Doña Pepa* (nougat). In the Acho bullring, toreadors compete for the Golden Cape of Our Lord of Miracles. — *www.peru.info*

LEFT: **Polar bear rough-and-tumble while waiting for the ice to freeze in Churchill, Canada**

BELOW: **Moab's sandstone – and its massive horizons – are a magnet for mountain bikers**

See Kakadu spring to life

AUSTRALIA

WHY NOW The first sprinkles of rain signal the end of the dry season

WHERE Kakadu, Northern Territory

DATES October and November

29 OCT The Aborigines call this time the Gunumeleng, the time to pack up floodplain camps and move to high ground because the wet season thunderstorms are on the way. It's still hot, but sprinkles of rain start to soften up the parched earth and the paperbark trees are heavy with scented blossoms. The land is turning green and trees are full to bursting with fruit bats.

Kakadu is a large, diverse park, ranging from rocky plateaus to mangrove salt marshes. As water returns after a seven-month drought, the land springs back to life and the waterfalls begin to flow once more. This is also a great time to see birds, both the courting residents as well as the passing migrants.
— *www.parksaustralia.gov.au/kakadu*

RIGHT: **Beware Halloween monsters on New York's streets**

BELOW: **Rain brings waterfalls and green leaves to Kakadu**

Watch madcap movies

CANADA

WHY NOW See the year's best adventures on screen at the Banff Mountain Film Festival

WHERE Banff, Alberta

DATES Nine days, late October/early November

30 OCT Think Hollywood hiked up to 11, or the Oscars with added derring-do: the Banff Mountain Film Festival is an international competition of short films and documentaries that focuses on mountain sports and lofty environments.

From a bulging long-list, around 60 films are selected to be shown at the Banff Centre, in the heart of the Rockies; themes range from climbing to kayaking, heli-biking to snowboarding, BASE jumping to meeting the remote cultures that live in the hills. Whatever the subject matter, these are films that will thrill, inspire and awe, and which bring the world's wildest places to even armchair adventurers. — *www.banffcentre.ca/mountainfestival*

Get spooked at Halloween

USA

WHY NOW Dress up for the Big Apple's biggest night-fright-fest
WHERE New York City, New York
DATES 31 October

31 OCT The shrill doorstep cry of 'trick or treat' from children who are dressed as blood-curdling zombies and garish ghouls is as synonymous with the United States as baseball and Big Macs. It's an important part of American family life. Excited nippers hang up jack-o'-lanterns (carved pumpkins with grisly faces and candles inside) before donning rubber masks and doorstepping the entire neighbourhood.

As well as filling small-town America with wholesome family fun, the night gives the cities – particularly New York and San Francisco – a good excuse to dress up for decidedly unwholesome parties. The former organises the nation's largest event, not to mention its only major night parade. More than 2 million people, resembling everything from Beelzebub and Beetlejuice to Batman, turn up to watch giant puppets sway through Manhattan. Some of the puppets tower alongside the buildings on Sixth Ave; controlling them takes the efforts of up to 1000 people.

The name Halloween is a corruption of All Hallows' Eve – the night before the Christian festival All Hallows' Day (All Saints' Day). This in turn grew out of Samhain, the Celtic end-of-harvest festival, which is the source of the once-popular custom of apple bobbing. Apt, then, that the best place for Halloween now is most definitely the Big Apple.
— *www.halloween-nyc.com*

Celebrate the dead

MEXICO

WHY NOW It's the Day of the Dead and everyone – alive and deceased – is invited

WHERE Oaxaca, Mexico

DATES 1 and 2 November

01 NOV

Mexico's remembrance of departed souls is an upbeat treatment of immortality. In a belief system inherited from the Aztecs, Mexicans believe their dead are lurking in Mictlan, a kind of spiritual waiting room, and they can return to their homes at this time.

Families begin preparations to help spirits find their way home, starting with an arch made of bright-yellow marigolds. An altar is piled high with offerings: flowers, candles, *tamales* (cornmeal dough). People also leave out *pan de muertos* (bread of the dead), made with egg yolks, fruits and tequila, and adorned with a symbol of death.

The event climaxes at the cemetery. Families devote a day to cleaning the graves, decorating them with candles and flowers, having picnics and dancing to mariachi bands. By now, the streets are full of papier-mâché skeletons in dresses and hats.

Celebrations take place countrywide, but their heartland is southern Mexico, where indigenous culture is strongest. Mixquic is known as 'City of the Dead' for its procession that calls at shrines to the deceased. In Oaxaca there are graveyard tours. — *www.visitmexico.com*

RIGHT: **TRAVEL IMAGES/UIG – GETTY IMAGES**

November

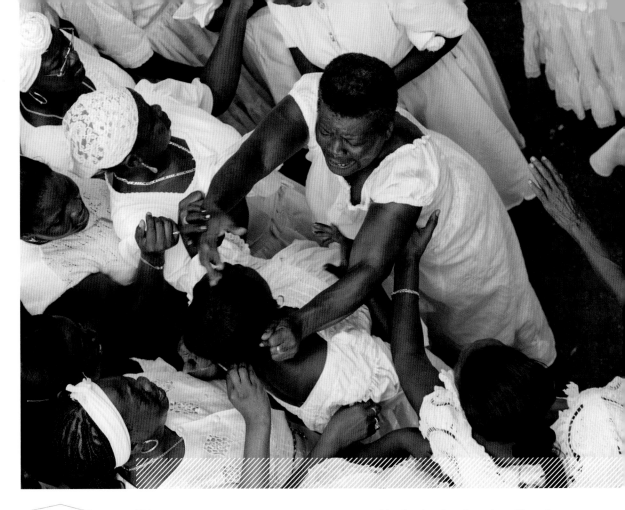

Dance at
Fete Gede

HAITI

WHY NOW The Caribbean isle puts on a
voodoo-style Day of the Dead

WHERE National Cemetery, Port-au-Prince

DATES 1 and 2 November

02 NOV If you don't make it to Mexico on
1 November, head to this offbeat
Caribbean isle for a different take
on the celebration. The festival of
Fete Gede is the voodoo religion's
version of the Day of the Dead, a major
difference being that the Haitian spirits are a
wee bit friskier. Indeed, there are stories of the
Gede (as the spirits are known) gatecrashing the
president and demanding money. He paid up,
of course.

Rituals take place throughout November
but the majority are at the beginning of the
month. Voodoo believers converge on the main
cemetery in Port-au-Prince, the Haitian capital,
to honour the Gede and the father of them
all, Baron Samedi. They lay out gifts such as
homemade beeswax candles, flowers and – to
warm the Gede's bones – bottles of rum stuffed
with chilli peppers.

Things get hotter than a habanero during
the dances in peristyle temples, in which the
dead are believed to participate. Because the
Gede are also associated with fertility, it pleases
them if children are present. Some participants,
believed to be possessed by the spirits, rub
peppered alcohol into their genitals.

This is all hot stuff in a pretty hot country:
be aware that a UN stabilisation force is in
operation in Haiti, and travel can be a bit on
the challenging side. Do seek advice on the
security situation before visiting.
— *www.haititourisme.org*

Bet on the Melbourne Cup

AUSTRALIA

WHY NOW Cheer Oz's biggest horse race
WHERE Melbourne, Victoria
DATES First Tuesday in November (3 Nov 2015; 1 Nov 2016; 7 Nov 2017; 6 Nov 2018)

03 NOV At 3pm Australian Eastern Standard Time, on the first Tuesday in November, virtually all Australians (and most New Zealanders too) down tools and tune in to a radio or TV – unless they're lucky enough to be at Flemington grandstand in the flesh. The Melbourne Cup is simply the mother of all horse races, a two mile flat race that induces even the most disinterested gamblers to have a flutter.

Of course, it's not all about the galloping. The event is an excuse to put on your finery and have a good old Aussie knees-up. At the track, the Fashions on the Field competition awards prizes to the best-dressed spectators (the bigger the hat the better), while the booze freely flows. — *www.melbournecup.com*

Watch La Diablada

PERU

WHY NOW Watch the devil himself dance through the lakeside town
WHERE Puno, Lake Titicaca
DATES Week leading up to 5 November

04 NOV There are various stories about the roots of La Diablada, the festival in which men dressed as demons parade through Puno. One version says the horned procession is in remembrance of the departure of the devilish conquistadors in the late 19th century. Another version reckons it's Puno's way of paying its respects to the spirits of Lake Titicaca.

Either way, a local incarnation of the Dark Lord himself leads the procession, accompanied by dancers shaking it like Peruvians possessed. A sure sign that there's nothing unholy afoot – and that La Diablada grew out of the mixture of Christianity and indigenous beliefs that characterises many Latin American festivities – is that the red monsters leave their crucifixes around their necks. — *www.peru.info*

227

LEFT: **Voodoo ceremonies take place in Port-au-Prince, Haiti**

BELOW: **It's all about the hats and the horses during the Melbourne Cup, the 'Race that Stops a Nation'**

Heat up on Bonfire Night

ENGLAND

WHY NOW Celebrate 17th-century treason with fireworks and pyromania
WHERE Lewes, East Sussex
DATES 5 November

05 NOV Bonfire Night is a remembrance of 17th-century skulduggery. In 1605, a group of Catholics, disgruntled at England's hardline Protestantism, decided to blow up the Houses of Parliament. But on 5 November, Guy Fawkes was rumbled in the vaults, and duly executed.

Now, on Guy Fawkes Night, a 'guy' is burnt on a pyre, to cheers from crowds, many of which know little and care less about the display's sectarian origins. Adults consume mulled wine, children wave sparklers. Everyone battles hypothermia and fireworks fill the sky.

Lewes, in southern England, has double the reason to bring out the rockets. In 1555, the Catholic queen Mary I had 17 Protestant rebels burned at the stake here. Up to 60,000 visitors flock to see effigies of the Pope get incinerated, in memory of the martyrs. The holy dummy is often joined by modern-day figures such as prime ministers, presidents and terrorists. Six Bonfire Societies parade the streets in medieval garb with flaming crosses, sending banger-filled barrels cracking and fizzling into the river.
— *www.visitengland.com*

Jump off the Sky Tower

NEW ZEALAND

WHY NOW It's spring – a great time to 'spring' from a lofty building!
WHERE Auckland
DATES November

06
NOV

Think bungee jumping, but with a very urban, very Auckland twist. New Zealand's largest city also presents one of the country's largest adrenaline rushes: Skyjump, a 192m, cable-controlled BASE jump from the tallest building in New Zealand.

Storeys above the restaurants and bars that fill the tower, you're fitted into a harness and a Superman-coloured suit and clipped to a cable. As you leap, a drum feeds out the cable, and you drop at a speed of around 85km/h by a fan descender. It's 20 seconds of superhero flight that almost impales jumpers on the city below. Instead, the descender slows the fall at the end, delivering you to earth on your feet. — *www.skyjump.co.nz*

LEFT: **Period costumes are worn for Bonfire Night in Lewes**

BELOW: **BASE-jumping from Auckland's landmark Sky Tower**

Kloof in Suicide Gorge

SOUTH AFRICA

WHY NOW The route is only open six months a year, and the gorges get cold, so come in summer
WHERE Suicide Gorge, Western Cape
DATES November to April

07
NOV

Kloofing is the South African term for canyoning. The object: to navigate your way through a dramatically narrow gorge by walking, scrambling, leaping into pools, sliding down rocks, swimming along streams, abseiling off high precipices – indeed, whatever means it takes – until you emerge at the bottom, hopefully wetter and better for it.

On the Western Cape, one of the most popular trips is through Suicide Gorge, a waterfall-splattered canyon in the Boland Mountains. At times the leaps here (some 15m high) make you feel the gorge is very aptly named. The trail is 18km and takes 8 hours to complete. — *www.capenature.org.za*

Kayak amid bioluminescence

PUERTO RICO

WHY NOW You'll pay off-season prices and get some respite from high temperatures
WHERE Vieques, 80km southeast of San Juan
DATES November and May (shoulder seasons)

08
NOV

What you see at Bioluminescent Bay are not the tiny dinoflagellates in the water but the incredible effect they create in vast numbers. This amazing place is a 'biobay', a lagoon with perfect conditions for cultivating bioluminescent microorganisms. The one on Vieques is considered the finest and brightest display left in the world; others have had their ecological balances destroyed by development.

The bay's water contains hundreds of thousands of dinoflagellates per litre, and when disturbed each one produces a blue-green flash. The effect when you swim or kayak in the water is dazzling. It's particularly fun to visit in the night or two after the full moon. — *www.biobay.com*

Dive into cenotes

MEXICO

WHY NOW The waters of these natural pools are at their clearest, plus the weather's divine
WHERE Yucatán Peninsula
DATES November to March

09 NOV In a cataclysmic collision 65 million years ago, a huge meteor struck the area that's now Mexico's Yucatán Peninsula, leaving a vast crater. Millions of years later cracks formed below the crater's limestone surface and rainwater began filling the cavities these fissures created. Eventually the surface layer around the underground chambers began to erode, revealing the intricate system of underground rivers and cenotes (sinkholes) that lay beneath.

The Yucatán is now pitted with around 3000 cenotes, including the Sacred Cenote at the Mayan site of Chichén Itzá. This awesome natural well is 60m in diameter and 35m deep, but sadly you cannot dive into it.

However, there are many cenotes that can be dived. In most accessible caverns, fixed lines guide divers through. Popular dives include Ponderosa, near Puerto Aventuras, and Cenote Azul, a 90m-deep natural pool on the shore of Laguna Bacalar. Cenote Dos Ojos is one of the most impressive, with stalactites and stalagmites in an eerie wonderland. You can swim 500m without leaving sunlight. — *www.visitmexico.com*

Say 'Arrrr!' like a pirate

CAYMAN ISLANDS

WHY NOW The financial capital of the Caribbean is overrun by salty brigands
WHERE George Town
DATES 10 days in early/mid-November

10 NOV The Pirate Festival is a 10-day menu of music, dance, games and controlled mayhem. It begins with a mock invasion: two replica 17th-century galleons, accompanied by other boats and even the odd submarine, carry out a 'surprise' attack on George Town Harbour.

However, most of the events on offer are safer than a censored sea shanty, and much is sponsored by the island's financial big-hitters (Deloitte 10km swim, anyone?). If you're an anticapitalist pirate, head for another port. The Cardboard Boat Regatta is fun (there's a prize for 'most spectacular sinking'); fireworks and street party bring the cutlass-waving to a close. — *www.piratesweekfestival.com*

LEFT: **Scuba diving a sun-lit cenote in Mexico**

BELOW: **Diwali takes its name from the lamps (*diyas*) lit by Hindus**

Celebrate Diwali

INDIA

WHY NOW See the light
WHERE Countrywide
DATES October or November (11 Nov 2015; 30 Oct 2016; 19 Oct 2017; 7 Nov 2018)

11 NOV According to the Hindu *Ramayana*, exiled Rama battled demons in dark forests before joining forces with Hanuman, the monkey god, to kill 10-headed demon-king Ravana and rescue his princess. So, to lead Rama home from exile, Hindus now burn butter and oil lamps: hence Diwali, the Festival of Lights.

The festival is a time for positivity and joy. Coming at the end of harvest season, it's a period of relative prosperity, and feels like India's version of Christmas. There are regional variations but Diwali generally includes ceremonies devoted to Lakshmi, goddess of wealth, not to mention firecrackers exploding in the streets. — *www.diwalifestival.org*

Hike out of the metropolis

HONG KONG

WHY NOW The weather's moderate, skies are clear, the sun shines – ideal for walking
WHERE Hong Kong
DATES October to December

12 NOV Über-urban Hong Kong is about more than downtown and dim sum. More than 7 million people live here, but they're squeezed onto just 10% of the available land, leaving around 1000 sq km open to exploration.

Walking trails in the territory are numerous, and include four long-distance paths. The 50km Hong Kong Trail cuts through five country parks on Hong Kong Island. The 70km Lantau Trail follows mountain tops from Mui Wo to Tai O and back. The 78km Wilson Trail begins on Hong Kong Island but carries on into the New Territories. The MacLehose Trail across the Kowloon Peninsula is 100km long. — *www.discoverhongkong.com*

Canoe the Everglades

USA

WHY NOW For the fewest mosquitoes
WHERE Everglades National Park, Florida
DATES November

13 NOV Covering Florida's southern tip, the 6070 sq km Everglades is the 3rd-largest national park in the USA. It's the country's largest subtropical wilderness. It's World Heritage listed. And it's a wetland of global importance. Simply, the Everglades are natural royalty.

Veined with channels and estuaries, this watery maze is best explored by canoe or kayak. The chief paddling route is the Wilderness Waterway, a 159km journey along the Everglades' western edge, gliding by mangroves and sawgrass prairies. It begins in Everglades City, and then winds through the Ten Thousand Islands and concludes at the Flamingo visitor centre. Allow seven to nine days for the journey, and expect to see a few of the Glades' most famous critters: alligators, dolphins, manatees and roseate spoonbills.

Campsites and chickees (platforms) are spread along the riverbanks. Backcountry camping permits are required – as is a keen sense of adventure. — *www.nps.gov/ever*

Join the Turnip Festival

SWITZERLAND

WHY NOW All hail the root vegetable!
WHERE Richterswil, Lake Zürich
DATES Second Saturday in November (14 Nov 2015; 12 Nov 2016; 11 Nov 2017; 10 Nov 2018)

14 NOV The turnip has never enjoyed much limelight. In an attempt to correct this, the good people of Richterswil, a small town on Lake Zürich, organise an annual celebration of the vegetable: the Räbechilbi Turnip Festival.

They've done this since 1905, organising a parade featuring 26 tonnes of carved root vegetables. It's terribly artistic: there are turnips resembling everything from elephants and roses to temples. Add in 50,000 candles and 10,000 hanging lanterns – which cover the houses, local church and even the funicular tramcar – and you have a veritable light-and-turnip spectacle.

All has not been in vain, either: the people of Richterswil were rewarded for their dedication to the humble *Brassica rapa* when the festival made it into the Guinness Book of Records in 1998. — *www.myswitzerland.com*

See rhino in Kaziranga

INDIA

WHY NOW The park typically opens in mid November as the floodwaters recede

WHERE Kaziranga National Park, Assam

DATES Mid-November to March

15 NOV Indian one-horned rhinos owe their existence to this expanse of riverside forest and grassland. It was first set aside in 1905 after the wife of the Viceroy of India visited the area and didn't see a single one of its famous rhinos. At the time there were only a dozen or so left. Today, Kaziranga is home to two-thirds of the world's Indian rhinos (about 2290) and the world's greatest density of tigers.

Kaziranga is a conservation success due in part to the staff, who are devoted to patrolling the park. Poachers still kill a few rhinos, but enforcement of local game laws is pretty strict.

Another problem for park animals are the high floodwaters when the Brahmaputra River breaks its banks from May to October. Wildlife survives by retreating to the Miri Hills or the Karbi Plateau. As the floodwaters retreat, the grasslands that cover over half the park green up and animals happily disperse.

Wildlife-watching is done from the backs of elephants or jeeps; there are also observation towers scattered around the park.

— *www.kaziranga-national-park.com*

Learn a language

ICELAND

WHY NOW It's Icelandic Language Day – plus you might see the Northern Lights
WHERE Reykjavík
DATES 16 November

16 NOV Happy Dagur Íslenskrar tungu! Sounds tongue-twisty, but it's exactly the phrase you'll need to master on Icelandic Language Day! Marked annually on 16 November, the birthday of 19th-century Icelandic poet and author Jónas Hallgrímsson, this semantic celebration is a reminder of the importance of protecting the Icelandic language.

It's not the simplest tongue to master – a day won't do it. But visit the near-Arctic isle in November anyway: it's off-season, so bargains can be found; temperatures don't dip below freezing; and it's peak Northern Lights time, with dark skies providing an ideal canvas on which the aurora might sparkle. – *www.iceland.is*

LEFT: **A pair of one-horned rhinoceroses (in Latin: rhinoceros unicornis) graze at Kaziranga National Park, India**

BELOW: **Yachts anchored off Tortola in the British Virgin Islands**

Sail the BVI

BRITISH VIRGIN ISLANDS

WHY NOW It's the very cusp of the high and dry season
WHERE Virgin Islands archipelago
DATES November

17 NOV A felicitous mix of geography and geology positions, the British Virgin Islands (BVI) is sailing's magic kingdom. It's got a year-round balmy climate, steady trade winds, few tides or currents, a protected thoroughfare in the 56km-long Sir Francis Drake Channel, and hundreds of anchorages. These factors make the BVI one of the easiest places to sail. There are three options: a sailing school; a bareboat charter (no crew but fully equipped); or a luxurious crewed charter.

Caribbean hurricane season runs June to November, but by mid-November, the weather is starting to settle and high-season prices haven't kicked in. — *www.bvi.gov.vg*

Explore the Sinai

EGYPT

WHY NOW Summer is too hot, winter often sees snow – so visit in between
WHERE Sinai Peninsula
DATES November

18 NOV Biblical and beautiful, Egypt's Sinai is a desert land conversely famous for its water activities. Sitting like a cork in the neck of the Red Sea, the Sinai's south coast features amazing underwater scenery and is a diving and snorkelling paradise. Ras Mohammed National Park offers the Red Sea's finest diving. There are 20 dive sites within the park, including wrecks, Eel Garden and Shark Observatory.

Sinai's interior is a more arid affair; a land of jagged mountains and desert plains. The most famed peak is 2285m Mt Sinai, reputed to be where Moses received the Ten Commandments. Hike via the 3750 Steps of Repentance to the summit. — *www.egypt.travel*

Toast the toilet!

INDIA

WHY NOW It's World Toilet Day! And the Indian capital loves the loo the best
WHERE New Delhi
DATES 19 November

19 NOV

It stinks of a world-gone-mad but, yes, today is indeed World Toilet Day. It's not as whimsical as it sounds: the World Toilet Organization, which established the special day, is dedicated to lobbying governments worldwide on improving sanitation, and this is its call (or flush?) to action.

Arguably, the best place to love the lavatory, big-up the bog and celebrate the crapper is the Sulabh International Museum of Toilets in New Delhi, a collection of privies, chamber pots, bidets and more, dating from 2500 BC to the modern day; there's even a replica of King Louis the XIV royal loo. — *www.worldtoilet.org; www.sulabhtoiletmuseum.org*

Go for an undersea stroll

MAURITIUS

WHY NOW Go for a properly wet walk before the approaching rainy season
WHERE Grand Baie and Belle Mare
DATES Mid-March to early May

20 NOV

The novel activity of undersea walking – or 'snuba' – allows even nondivers the chance to experience the colourful life below the waves in complete safety.

Wearing a weight belt and diving helmet, you're guided down to the sea's sandy bottom (about 3–4m deep), so you can eyeball the fish in their natural habitat. Breathing isn't an issue – solar-powered pumps on the boat above feed oxygen down so you can stay underwater for a 15- to 25-minute 'walk'. You can even keep your glasses on – your head doesn't get wet at all.

Winter (May to early December) is the best time to visit Mauritius – it's cooler and drier. — *www.tourism-mauritius.mu*

RIGHT: **Straw-colored fruit bats at Kasanka National Park, Zambia, fly in colonies of 100,000 or more**

BELOW: **Local dancers parade through Surin during the annual Elephant Festival**

See the elephant round-up

THAILAND

WHY NOW Cheer elephant antics
WHERE Sri Narong Stadium, Surin
DATES Third weekend in November (21–22 Nov 2015; 19–20 Nov 2016; 18–19 Nov 2017; 17–18 Nov 2018)

21 NOV

Welcome to Thailand's biggest elephant show. In Surin, the massive mammals play soccer, sprint at up to 35km/h and pick up tiny objects with their trunks. One elephant takes on 70 beefy soldiers at tug-of-war.

The animals start filling the city and parading the streets during the preceding week. At one point they enjoy an 'elephant breakfast', the world's largest ele-feeding frenzy. The festival ends with an eight-act play and a finale featuring 2000 performers and hundreds of elephants.

Although it may sound like the animals are being exploited, Thais hold them in great esteem and even believe Thailand is shaped like an elephant's head. — *www.tourismthailand.org*

Marvel at 5 million bats

ZAMBIA

WHY NOW There are huge numbers of bats during the fruiting season
WHERE Kasanka National Park
DATES November and December

22 NOV It's funny how some of the greatest wildlife spectacles go unnoticed for years. That's the case with the straw-coloured fruit bats in Zambia's Kasanka National Park. These large bats of equatorial Africa migrate great distances in search of fruiting trees, a journey that brings them to Kasanka every November and December, coinciding with peak production of musuku fruit. An estimated 5 million fruit bats gather here on a single hectare of swamp forest, with so many roosting at once that large tree branches are known to break under their combined weight.

Each evening at sunset the entire roost lifts off, and for 25 minutes observers at the park's Fibwe Hide will be treated to the unforgettable image of giant bats spreading across the sky. Fruit bats spend the night flying over many sq km eating fruit and spitting out seeds everywhere they go, playing an ecologically significant role as seed-dispersers for these trees. During the day, bats can be watched as they huddle many-deep on tree trunks and branches. — *www.kasanka.com*

Hike the Simiens

ETHIOPIA

WHY NOW Come early in the dry season for green landscapes and wildflowers
WHERE Simien Mountains
DATES October to May

23 NOV Far from Africa's beaten mountain paths is a range unlike any other on the continent. The Simien Mountains are made up of several plateaus, separated by broad river valleys. A number of peaks rise above 4000m, including Ras Dashen (4543m), Ethiopia's highest peak, and the 4th-highest mountain in Africa. At the range's northern edge is a 60km-long escarpment overlooking a land of rock pinnacles and mesas for some of the finest views in Africa.

No matter how you look at them, the Simien Mountains are awesome. And this massive plateau offers plenty of tough but immensely rewarding trekking. It's not just the scenery (and altitude) that will leave you speechless, but also the excitement of sitting among a group of gelada monkeys or watching magnificent walia ibex joust on rock ledges.

All treks begin and end in Debark, in the Amhara region, where the park headquarters are located. The most popular trekking routes are along the western side of the massif, taking in the most impressive sections of the escarpment. The most spectacular scenery is around the Geech Abyss, while the classic Simien trek continues past Geech to the summit of Ras Dashen; allow eight to 10 days for the return hike.

— *www.tourismethiopia.gov.et*

RIGHT: **ALEXEI KALMYKOV – GETTY IMAGES**

Watch silent lightning

VENEZUELA

WHY NOW Sightings of the stormy spectacle are at their best
WHERE Río Catatumbo, Lago de Maracaibo
DATES September to November

24 NOV

The unusual occurrences that take place in Catatumbo National Park might come as quite a shock... Centred on the mouth of the Río Catatumbo at Lago de Maracaibo, a strange phenomenon unfolds, consisting of frequent flashes of lightning with no accompanying thunder. The eerily silent electrical storm, referred to as Catatumbo Lightning, can be so strong, bright and constant that you will be able to read at night. It is also said to be the world's largest single generator of ozone gas.

Various hypotheses have been put forth to explain the lightning, but the theory that holds most weight is that it's due to the cold winds descending from the 5000m-high peaks of the nearby Andes Mountains clashing with the hot, humid air evaporating from Lago de Maracaibo. This produces the ionization of air particles, which is responsible for the lightning.

On average the skies here are quietly electrified on around 160 nights a year; displays tend to be best in September and November (during the wet season) when there can be up to 150 to 200 flashes per minute, visible from up to 400km away.

Tours to Catatumbo National Park can be arranged from Mérida, western Venezuela. It's worth lingering here, as the city is home to many historic squares, charming colonial houses and churches and leafy parks.
— *www.venezuelaturismo.gob.ve*

Pushkar Camel Fair

INDIA

WHY NOW To buy a camel
WHERE Pushkar, Rajasthan
DATES Coincides with Purnima full moon
(25 Nov 2015), usually October or November

25 NOV Drawing in 50,000 camels and 200,000 people, Pushkar Camel Fair is ostensibly a time when Rajasthani farmers gather to buy and sell their camels, cattle and horses. However, most of the trading is completed in the days leading up to the fair; when the festival proper begins, the camels go to the outer as moustache competitions and sporting events take centre stage.

For the seven days of the festival proper, there's a programme of events, most taking place in the festival ground: think tugs-of-war, kabaddi matches, turban-tying contests. If you prefer to see camels than people, visit just before the festival. Trading has no set start date, though cameleers usually arrive a week before festivities begin. — *www.rajasthantourism.gov.in*

Be grateful at Thanksgiving

USA

WHY NOW To eat turkey and watch parades
WHERE New York City, New York
DATES Fourth Thursday in November (26 Nov 2015; 24 Nov 2016; 23 Nov 2017; 22 Nov 2018)

26 NOV Thanksgiving is the USA's most renowned festival. The celebration, which takes place in Canada on the second Monday in October, has its roots in the New World's colonial beginnings. In 1621 the Pilgrim Fathers held a feast at Plymouth, in present-day Massachusetts, to celebrate their first American harvest and to thank the aboriginal people who helped them settle in. In modern times the US President issues a proclamation and pardons a turkey.

Today, TV viewers are torn between the boss' wise words and American football games. Off the couch, towns fill with patriotic parades, the biggest of which attracts 2.5 million spectators to Manhattan: the famed 4km parade of 'falloons' (balloon-cum-floats) finishes on 7th Ave, near Macy's. — *www.nycgo.com*

241

LEFT: **Lightning at the mouth of the Catatumbo River**

BELOW: **Camels look their best at Pushkar's Camel Fair**

Cruise up close to penguins

SOUTH GEORGIA

WHY NOW It's the beginning of one of the most fabulous wildlife gatherings on earth
WHERE South Atlantic Ocean
DATES Late November to February

27 NOV

Plonked in the South Atlantic, 2150km off the southern tip of South America, South Georgia is one of the world's loneliest outposts. Buffeted by fierce sub-Antarctic storms and thrashed by choppy seas, this rugged island is difficult to visit and receives few visitors. Fortunately, specialist cruise ships do stop by.

South Georgia is at the edge of the Antarctic Convergence, a productive upwelling of nutrients, and is thus a prime spot for breeding seabirds and marine mammals. There are 400,000 nesting king penguins and 3 to 5 million macaroni penguins. Add in vast numbers of other seabirds, plus 300,000 southern elephant seals and 3 million Antarctic fur seals, and you have perhaps the greatest concentration of wildlife in the world.

The two real showstoppers are the king penguins (the second-largest of all penguins) and the wandering albatross – half the total population of these vast birds nests here from mid-November, when they fly in to perform elaborate courtship displays. — *www.sgisland.gs*

Solve Coopers Capers

USA

WHY NOW Investigate hijacking hijinks
WHERE Merwin Village Rd, Ariel, Washington
DATES Saturday after Thanksgiving (28 Nov 2015; 26 Nov 2016; 25 Nov 2017; 24 Nov 2018)

28 NOV Coopers Capers is a celebration/deliberation of America's only unsolved hijacking. On 24 November 1971, a man held up a Boeing 727 with a bomb threat and parachuted into the night with US$200,000 strapped to his waist. DB Cooper was gone.

The lakeside town of Ariel in Washington State, where authorities initially thought Cooper had landed, became the base for the search. Every year, conspiracy theorists and storytellers gather here to exchange views about what became of Cooper; there's a prize for the most imaginative hypothesis, as well as a lookalike competition and parachute jumps.
— *www.legendofdbcooper.com*

LEFT: **A creche of king penguin chicks on South Georgia**

BELOW: **Tribal clothing in Northern Thailand**

Trek to hill tribes

THAILAND

WHY NOW The weather is refreshing, there's little or no rain and wildflowers are in bloom
WHERE Around Chiang Mai and Chiang Rai
DATES November to February

29 NOV The hills of north Thailand aren't just scenically spectacular. They are home to an array of traditional communities, visits to which can enrich your walking. You need to pick a hiking trip responsibly, though – it can feel awkward playing voyeur in these remote villages, and good local tour operators have become more conscious of the need to tread carefully here, limiting the number of visits to particular areas and making sure they bring benefits to the tribes themselves.

Chiang Mai and Chiang Rai are the main trekking hubs. Guides aren't essential, but provide deeper insight. Try to arrange homestays en route. — *www.tourismthailand.org*

Raft the Zambezi

ZAMBIA

WHY NOW The Zambezi River's white water is running at its best
WHERE Victoria Falls
DATES Mid-August to December

30 NOV Victoria Falls' thundering curtain of water is a wonder of the natural world. Over this 1.7km-wide precipice, an average of 550,000 cubic metres of water plummets 100m into narrow Batoka Gorge every minute.

Victoria Falls is Africa's adventure capital, offering a staggering array of activities – including some of the world's best white-water rafting. The Zambezi River below the falls is said to have the highest concentration of Grade V rapids on earth. Wild, low-water runs of around 22km operate from mid-August to late December. All operators walk around Grade VI rapid nine, which is nicknamed Commercial Suicide.
— *www.zambiatourism.com*

Hike Torres del Paine

CHILE

WHY NOW The shoulder summer season of December is one of the best trekking times
WHERE Torres del Paine, Patagonia
DATES December

01
DEC

Soaring more than 2000m above the Patagonian steppe, the Torres del Paine (Towers of Paine) are spectacular granite pillars that dominate the landscape of what is arguably South America's finest national park. For hikers, 181-sq-km Parque Nacional Torres del Paine (see *right*) is a dream, with a well-developed trail network and *refugios* (mountain huts) and camping grounds at strategic spots.

For most trekkers the question is whether to Circuit or to 'W'. Circuiting takes around eight days, while the W trek, named for the route's in-and-out shape, takes around five. Most hikers start both routes from Laguna Amarga – the W climbs to the spectacular Torres del Paine Lookout, immediately below the towers. With their mighty columns ringed by shelf glaciers, this is one of Patagonia's classic scenes. The W goes on via Los Cuernos and Lago Pehoé to Lago Grey, where the unstable, 200m-thick snout of Glaciar Grey continually sends blocks of ice – some as big as a house – plunging into the freezing waters. Walking the complete Circuit takes in the W plus the more remote back side of the massif. — *www.torresdelpaine.com*

RIGHT: **WALTER BIBIKOW – GETTY IMAGES**

December

Be awed by orca

NORWAY

WHY NOW The herring are amassing, and so too are the hungry orca

WHERE Vesterålen, Arctic Norway

DATES November to February

02 DEC

Late October signals the arrival of migrating herring in Norway's Nordland, north of the Arctic Circle. And behind those herring come hundreds of hungry orcas. The killer whales spend months stalking these chill waters, nosing into fjords and chasing herring; they hunt by bait-ball feeding, herding the silver fish into a lump, whacking them with their tails and then chomping on the stunned shoal.

As the orca chase the herring, wildlife watchers chase the orca – this is a prime spot to see the sleek black-and-white mammals. To do so you can remain in a sturdy whale-watching trawler or disembark into a small Zodiac (rigid inflatable boat) for a surface-level view.

Andenes, on the northern tip of the Vesterålen group of islands, is a prime spot to see them. Even better, a boat safari here might reveal sightings of fin and humpback whales too. — *www.visitvesteralen.com; whalesafari.no*

Feel floaty

JAPAN

WHY NOW Watch huge *hikiyama* (floats) hauled up hill at the festival of Chichibu Yomatsuri
WHERE Chichibu, Saitama Prefecture, Honshu
DATES 2 to 3 December

03 DEC Now, this is how you brighten up a cold winter night. The historic Chichibu Yomatsuri is officially one of the Three Great Float Festivals of Japan, and sees two fabulously festooned *kasaboko* (huge parasol-like objects) and two *yatai* (house-shaped floats) paraded through the dark city streets. Proceedings are particularly exciting on the night of 3 December, when the mighty floats (which can weigh up to 20 tonnes) are carried up a steep slope, to a chorus of drum-beats and flute-whistles, and the raucous cheers of the crowds. A battery of fireworks accompanies the efforts, bringing brilliant illumination to the chill, inky skies. — *www.jnto.go.jp*

LEFT: **A killer whale, or orca, spy-hops in a Norwegian fjord**

BELOW: **Two huge houses, decked in lanterns, are pulled on festival floats during Chichibu Yomatsuri**

Track lowland gorillas

CONGO

WHY NOW It's the beginning of the short dry season in this seldom-visited sanctuary
WHERE Nouabalé-Ndoki National Park
DATES December to February

04 DEC Shrouded in mystery and political unrest, the Congo Basin sees few visitors. Yet a vast area on the border of Congo and the Central African Republic promises one of the premier wildlife experiences in all of Africa.

Congo's Nouabalé-Ndoki National Park is the most visitable part, and large populations of lowland gorillas and forest elephants remain here. Since 2001 the Wildlife Conservation Society and Congo government have done a fine job of protecting wildlife and building a tourist infrastructure. Trails, viewing platforms and quality lodging are now available at the Mbeli Bai forest clearing, where up to 180 habituated lowland gorillas gather. — *www.wcscongo.org*

Beat up Santa at Klausjagen

SWITZERLAND

WHY NOW Watch hordes of Swiss whip and chase Father Christmas
WHERE Küssnacht, Lake Lucerne
DATES 5 December

05 DEC On the eve of St Nicholas Day, the folk of Küssnacht drag out their whips and cow bells for an unusual parade. Dating back to the Middle Ages, when evil spirits were chased away with cow bells, this rite was banned in the 18th century after it became too raucous. It was revived as Klausjagen when St Nicholas was co-opted in to hide the pagan overtones.

The parade begins on Seebodenstrasse and is led by whip-crackers. Behind them come men wearing *iffele* (paper bishop's hats) lit from within by candles. St Nicholas himself is next, 'chased' by groups of up to 500 people clanging cow bells. It's enough to make Santa want earplugs for Christmas. — *www.klausjagen.ch*

Cruise the Sunderbans

INDIA

WHY NOW Tiger sightings are most likely, and the weather is cooler and drier
WHERE Sunderbans Tiger Reserve, West Bengal
DATES October to February

06
DEC

The lush, vast Sunderbans Tiger Reserve sits within the world's largest estuarine forest and delta. This chunk of Gangetic West Bengal is cloaked in mangrove and saline mud flats, dotted by 54 tiny islands and laced by myriad streams. It's also home to one of the planet's largest tiger populations.

The Royal Bengal tigers (estimated to number 250) wander the impenetrable mangrove forests and even swim in the channels. They're known to have an appetite for humans, but are typically shy; sightings are the exception, not the rule. There's plenty of other wildlife though: look for chital deer and rhesus monkey amid the trees, crocodiles lurking on the mud banks and many fish, crabs and birds.
— *www.westbengaltourism.gov.in*

RIGHT: **Cruising past Petzval glacier in Paradise Bay, Antarctica**

BELOW: **Deer are on the menu for the tigers in the mangroves of the Sunderbans**

Light up the night

COLOMBIA

WHY NOW Spark up for the Día de las Velitas – the Day of the Candles
WHERE Villa de Leyva
DATES 7 December

07
DEC

Call in Christmas, Colombian style. On the eve of the Feast of the Immaculate Conception (8 December, a national holiday), people across the country honour the Virgin Mary by lighting a load of candles and paper lanterns, and placing them everywhere – in their homes, on statues, in parks and public squares, on family tombs. It is a religious observance, and a clear signal that the festive season is officially about to begin.

The Día de las Velitas is observed countrywide, but a good place to be is Villa de Leyva, in Boyacá department. The pretty colonial village turns the event into a three-day festival, with processions, Christmas choirs, fireworks and flickering lights – a magical sight.
— *www.colombia.travel*

Sail the White Continent

ANTARCTICA

WHY NOW There's up to 20 hours of daylight each day and the chance to see hatching penguins
WHERE Antarctic Peninsula
DATES December

08 DEC

Antarctica, the earth's most isolated continent, must be earned, through either a long, often uncomfortable voyage or an expensive flight. Weather and ice set the schedule, and itineraries are subject to the continent's changing moods. What you'll find, however, is a spectacular wilderness of snow, ice and rock, teeming with wildlife.

You'll most likely visit Antarctica on an expedition ship. The most popular trip involves an exploration of the Antarctic Peninsula, one of the continent's richest breeding grounds for seabirds, seals and penguins. Trips leave from Ushuaia, on South America's Tierra del Fuego; your first landing will probably be at one of the South Shetland Islands, a chain of isles at the northern end of the Antarctic Peninsula with spectacular scenery and abundant wildlife.

On the Antarctic Peninsula, likely landings include the former British base at Port Lockroy; Neko Harbor, where a glacier often calves with a thunderous roar; the US Palmer research station; and Paradise Harbor, described as 'the most aptly named place in the world' due to its majestic icebergs and reflections.

The Antarctic tour season is short – about four months, with each month offering its own highlights. Coming in December, at the height of the austral summer, you'll find penguins hatching eggs and feeding chicks, and you'll have up to 20 hours of sunlight a day.

— *www.antarctica.ac.uk*

Get wet at Iguazú Falls

ARGENTINA

WHY NOW It's wet season – but that's when the falls are at their fullest and most impressive
WHERE Iguazú National Park
DATES December to February

09 DEC

Iguazú means 'big water' in the indigenous Guarani language. It's a description that does what it says on the tin: it's the world's most spectacular waterfall. Here on the border of Argentina and Brazil (with Paraguay nearby), the Iguazú River turns south then north as it spreads out and plummets over an immense U-shaped 80m-high lip of hard basalt.

At this point the river is 1500m wide and, depending on water levels, forms anywhere from 160 to 260 separate waterfalls around a huge thundering bowl of mist, rainbows and tropical rainforest. If you visit during the rainy season (December to February) you might get wet, but you'll see the falls in their fullest flow.

The stunning visual presence of this place is accentuated by an abundance of great dusky swifts. With incredible energy and athletic grace, flocks of several hundred swifts arc and wheel like daredevils through the billowing clouds of foam and mist. The best time to see the swifts is towards the end of the day when they return from their daily feeding flights over the 2200 sq km of rainforest protected by Argentina's Iguazú National Park and Brazil's cross-border Iguaçu National Park. The swifts' goal is to roost behind the veil of waterfalls where they are safe from predators; watch them cut through waterfalls and disappear behind the water. — *www.iguazuargentina.com*

RIGHT: **MICHAEL RUNKEL – GETTY IMAGES**

Ski at the Cedars

LEBANON

WHY NOW Feel festive by skiing on the nearest snow to Bethlehem
WHERE Cedars Ski Field
DATES December to April

10 DEC

Lebanon likes to boast that it's the only country in which you can ski in the morning and swim in the Mediterranean in the afternoon. It's an appealing prospect.

Lebanon's highest and oldest ski field, the Cedars, is located less than 30km from the Med coast and 130km from Beirut. People have been skiing here since the 1920s; it got its first ski lift in 1953. There are runs suitable for all levels as well as numerous off-piste opportunities.

The runs begin at over 2000m, so the season usually starts in early December (sometimes November), ahead of other resorts in the country. With good snow, it can run through to April. — *www.skiinglebanon.com*

Eat chocolate at l'Escalade

SWITZERLAND

WHY NOW The festival positively encourages you to eat loads of smashed up Swiss chocolate
WHERE Geneva
DATES 11 December

11 DEC

Need an excuse to eat chocolate *before* Christmas? At l'Escalade, the city's largest festival, marzipan-filled *marmites en chocolat* (chocolate cauldrons) are smashed, gathered and devoured to commemorate the defeat of an attack by the Duke of Savoy on 11 December 1602. One legend suggests the assault was repelled by a housewife who whacked a trooper with her *marmite* (cauldron) then raised the alarm.

There's also a torchlit parade, an 8km l'Escalade run around the old town, and a fancy-dress run too. Indeed, with December nights in Geneva averaging as low as 0°C, you might want the furriest costume possible. — *www.compagniede1602.ch*

RIGHT: **Pre-Columbian pole-dancing in Chichicastenango**

BELOW: **Dervishes whirling away at Konya, Turkey**

Whirl with the dervishes

TURKEY

WHY NOW Watch Sufi mystics spin and twirl at the Mevlâna Festival
WHERE Konya, Anatolia
DATES 10 to 17 December

12 DEC

In the Islamic world the 13th-century Sufi poet Celaleddin Rumi, or Mevlâna (Our Guide), is all but considered a saint.

One of the world's great mystic philosophers, he believed union with God was possible through dance. After Mevlâna's death, his followers formed the Mevlevi brotherhood, or whirling dervishes, with dance as one of its foremost worship *semas* (ceremonies).

The Whirling Dervishes Festival commemorates Mevlâna's death on 17 December 1273. At the festival, the dervishes do their famous whirl, a smooth, pure, elegant trance-like performance, their full skirts splayed, their minds with God. — *mevlana.net*

Party at Fiesta de Santo Tomás

GUATEMALA

WHY NOW Enjoy the fair and fireworks and watch others risk a limb on the flying pole
WHERE Chichicastenango
DATES 13 to 21 December

13
DEC

The highland city of Chichicastenango (Chichi) celebrates its patron saint in a death-defying way. For a week, festivities are limited to typical festival events – parades, traditional dances, fireworks – but on 21 December (St Thomas'

Day) things look up, literally. On this day, wooden poles as high as 30m are raised in the plaza beside the Iglesia de Santo Tomás and the dance of the *palo volador* (flying pole) begins.

Two ropes hang from the top of each pole and the *palo volador* dancers ascend in pairs, scaling the poles on wooden steps and tying the ropes to their bodies. Then they leap, swirling around the pole at high speed, the ropes unravelling as they go, lowering them to the ground. Some hang onto the rope with their hands, and others tie it around their ankles. It's like bungee jumping for the faithful.

As Chichi has few accommodation options, arrive a few days early if you want to stay through the festivities. Failing that, popular Panajachel is about 1½ hours away by bus.
— *www.visitguatemala.com*

Raft the source of the Nile

UGANDA

WHY NOW Rafting is good year-round, but this is one of Uganda's drier months
WHERE Jinja
DATES December

14 DEC The source of the Nile has been long disputed. Over the centuries, many have gone looking for the start of Africa's mighty river. Now, they come to get tossed about on it.

The Nile leaves Lake Victoria at Ripon Falls near Jinja, Uganda, which has made this unsuspecting town one of the world's best white-water rafting destinations. This is the place to come to tackle the 'big four' – the source's four Grade V rapids – rather than the 'big five' animals usually sought on African safaris.

Rafting trips operate out of Jinja, which is about 1½ hours by bus from the Ugandan capital, Kampala. The growing list of white-water accoutrements is turning Jinja into one of Africa's burgeoning adventure destinations. The brave-hearted can try riverboarding, in which you take on the Nile armed only with a boogie board. Or, after a bit of instruction, you could tackle the white-water in a kayak; the less brave could ride a tandem kayak instead of piloting their own. Or simply leap down into the water from the 44m-high Nile High Bungee. — *www.visituganda.com*

Watch elephant seals fight

USA

WHY NOW Males are battling for dominance, and guided tours begin
WHERE Año Nuevo State Reserve, California
DATES 15 December to 31 March

15 DEC

From mid-December, 2700kg male elephant seals haul onto the beach at Año Nuevo and start some of the fiercest battles in the animal kingdom. Rearing up 3m, they slash at each other with dangerous canines and thunderous blows; battles may last 45 minutes and continue until combatants can barely move. The prize for all this effort is a dominant position within the colony and access to harems of females that come ashore from late December.

About 5000 elephant seals haul up at Año Nuevo, the world's largest mainland breeding colony. You can see them on guided walks, which run from 15 December to 31 March.
— *www.parks.ca.gov/?page_id=523*

LEFT: **Running the Nile's rapids at Bujugali Falls, north of Jinja, Uganda**

BELOW: **Male northern elephant seals battle it out at Ano Nuevo State Reserve, California**

Crawl to see St Lazarus

CUBA

WHY NOW Make a pilgrimage to a saintly shrine when the weather is fine
WHERE Santuario de San Lázaro, El Rincón
DATES 16 December

16 DEC

For a pilgrimage worth bloodying your knees to see, head for El Rincón, near Havana, to watch (or join) up to 50,000 faithful descend en masse on the venerated shrine of Lazarus, a saint known for his ministrations to lepers and the poor. Once banned under Castro's Cuba, the Procession de San Lázaro was given government approval again in 1961.

The tougher the approach to the shrine, the greater the supposed rewards. Pilgrims crawl on bloodied knees, walk barefoot and drag themselves prostrate – all in the name of good karma. Along the route, offerings are made to San Lázaro, who is depicted on crutches, with his sores being licked by dogs. — *www.gocuba.ca*

Boulder at Fontainebleau

FRANCE

WHY NOW The sandstone is at its best during the French winter
WHERE Fontainebleau
DATES December

17 DEC

Look past the elegance of Fontainebleau, the former royal residence 67km southeast of Paris, and you'll find its antithesis, the gritty world of bouldering, at play in the Forêt de Fontainebleau. To boulderers (who climb near to the ground without ropes) this is the enchanted forest, a place where they can't see the trees for the rocks.

'Font' is prized for its diverse routes and its collection of circuits, in which problems are linked together into a single route. The circuits might feature up to 75 problems; one stretches for 10km. Each circuit is colour-coded according to its difficulty, with yellow the easiest and black the most tendon-tearing. — *www.bleau.info*

Coo at snow monkeys

JAPAN

WHY NOW You'll see monkeys 'hot-tubbing' on a snowy winter day
WHERE Jigokudani Monkey Park, Honshu
DATES December to February

18 DEC

Amid the steep mountains, ski resorts and volcanoes northwest of Tokyo, there lurks another natural attraction: the snow monkeys of Jigokudani Yaen Koen ('Jigokudani Monkey Park'). These Japanese macaques live further north and at far colder temperatures than any other nonhuman primate. During north Japan's frigid winters these monkeys survive on a meagre diet of bark and tree buds, and struggle to stay warm.

However, snow monkeys possess an uncanny capacity for passing on new ideas. In fact, the famous '100th monkey' dictum – that new ideas spread spontaneously once they reach critical mass – arose from a scientific study in which a single snow monkey started washing her food in the ocean and within a few generations every monkey was doing the same thing.

This same behaviour led a snow monkey to plonk herself courageously into one of Nagano's steaming hot springs in 1963. On a bitter-cold day, those 50°C waters must have felt like heaven because it wasn't long before this 'hot-tubbing' behaviour spread to all 270 monkeys that live in Jigokudani ('hell valley').

This collection of hot springs is outside Yudanaka, a town of ancient architecture, cobbled streets and 19 hot spring spas and guesthouses. — *www.jigokudani-yaenkoen.co.jp*

Shop for Christmas

GERMANY

WHY NOW Indulge in festive retail therapy at the country's most traditional Christmas Market

WHERE Hauptmarkt, Nuremberg, Bavaria

DATES Friday before Advent Sunday to 24 December

19 DEC

In Germany 'tis the season to be shopping. Across the country, Christmas markets spring up throughout this month, but most famous is Nuremberg's, which fills the city's main square with almost 200 stalls. It opens with a 'Christmas angel' in a golden gown reading a prologue that concludes with the words, 'do rejoice when Christ child now invites you all to see this market. Whoever comes to visit shall be welcome'.

It's thought that the first Christmas markets were held in Hauptmarkt in the 16th century. After a decline in popularity in the 19th century, they were revived by the Nazis in the 1930s.

Known as the 'Little Town from Wood and Cloth', the market is a one-stop shop for Christmas goodies: tree ornaments, cribs, candles, toys, gingerbread, fruit cakes, Christmas bratwurst. For something uniquely Chriskindlesmarkt, pick up a few *Nürnberger Zwetschenmännle* (Nuremberg Prune Men), small figurines made from dried fruit – ideal if Christmas lunch leaves you a little plugged up...
— *www.christkindlesmarkt.de*

Wake up with the birds

PANAMA

WHY NOW You can enjoy the best mix of resident and migrant birds
WHERE Canopy Tower, Soberanía National Park
DATES December

20 DEC Imagine waking up to canopy-level birds scolding you right outside your bedroom window... Mornings like this have made the Canopy Tower in Soberanía National Park one of the world's most memorable avian sites. This strange abandoned radar tower-turned-hotel puts you right up there with hundreds of birds that are otherwise very difficult to observe.

If you get a hankering to see even more species, you're in the right country at the right time of year. For 20 years running, Panama led the world in having the highest numbers of any Christmas Bird Count, posting sightings of around 350 species seen in a single 24-hour period. — *www.canopytower.com*

LEFT: **You'll love the gingerbread at Nuremberg Christmas Market**

BELOW: **Negotiating a crevasse on Cotopaxi**

Dive with manta rays

MICRONESIA

WHY NOW This Pacific Ocean paradise gets even better when the mantas cruise by
WHERE Manta Ridge, Mill Channel, Yap
DATES December to February

21 DEC The total land area of the 2000 Micronesian islands is so small that many world maps don't even dot them in. But, with its clear, 27°C waters teeming with coral and tropical fish, they are on every diver's map.

Take Yap: it has good diving, with excellent coral, vertical walls, sea caves, channel drifts, schools of grey sharks and barracuda, sea turtles and shipwrecks. Its big draw, however, is manta rays. From December to February a school of mantas cruises Mill Channel. These gentle creatures, up to 3.6m across, swim through as divers cling to a ledge. The manta rays often come close enough to brush divers with their wingtips. — *www.visit-micronesia.fm*

Climb Cotopaxi

ECUADOR

WHY NOW The best climbing conditions: this is one of the driest times, and the least windy
WHERE Cotopaxi, Avenue of the Volcanoes
DATES December to February

22 DEC The symmetrical cone of Volcán Cotopaxi (5897m) is Ecuador's second-highest peak. It's also a popular climb, due to its proximity to Quito (55km) and its classic form. It's not a technical ascent by mountaineering standards, but the route is crevassed; glacier skills are essential.

The ascent starts from a *refugio* (hut) on the mountain's north slopes soon after midnight; the aim is to summit in the early hours, before cloud descends, and to get down before the snow softens. It takes 5–7 hours to reach the summit, three to descend. The view from the top includes Chimborazo (6310m), Ecuador's highest peak. — *www.ecuador.travel*

Join the Sahara Festival

TUNISIA

WHY NOW Bed down in a Bedouin tent on the edge of the Sahara for camel racing fun
WHERE Douz
DATES 23 to 27 December

23 DEC While the Christian world is occupied with Christmas, Saharan nomads flock to Douz, Tunisia's gateway to the desert, for a celebration of their culture. The sandy town hosts camel races, hunting for rabbits with Saluki dogs, and fantasias – military displays, when riders on Arabian horses skilfully canter, turn, stop and shoot their rifles.

Up to 50,000 visitors from across North Africa pitch their tents on the outskirts of town. In the evenings, there are dances by Tunisian, Algerian and Palestinian companies and recitals of poetry. Having begun as a Berber marriage market, the festival also features public weddings. Food-wise, expect the odd camel tagine and Tunisia's finest dates, which are harvested in Douz at this time of year. — *www.cometotunisia.co.uk*

Attend Midnight Mass

VATICAN

WHY NOW Join the Pope for the ultimate Christmas Eve blessing
WHERE St Peter's Basilica, Vatican
DATES 24 December

24 DEC Amid all the tinsel, over-eating and rampant consumerism, it's easy to lose sight of the real roots of Christmas. In order not to do so, spend Christmas Eve with the Pope. Every year, the Holy See hosts a midnight mass at St Peter's Basilica, in the Vatican City, the resplendent fulcrum of the Catholic world.

Anyone can attend, for free – though capacity is limited (this cavernous church can hold about 15,000). For a chance to secure a ticket, you need to apply several months in advance, by fax.

While you're there, soak up the festive atmosphere in the rest of Rome: visit the Christmas market in Piazza Navona, look for the *presepi* (nativity scenes) that crop up around the city and breathe in the aroma of roasting chestnuts. — *www.papalaudience.org*

RIGHT: **Father Christmas, aka Santa Claus, at Rovaniemi in Finnish Lapland**

BELOW: **Horse riders at the Sahara International Festival in Douz, south-western Tunisia**

Meet Santa in Lapland

FINLAND

WHY NOW Enjoy kitsch Christmas festivities and fun in St Nick's backyard

WHERE Rovaniemi, Lapland

DATES December

25 DEC The Finnish city of Rovaniemi, which straddles the Arctic Circle, is the self-styled home of Santa Claus. Here, you'll find the Santa Claus Tourist Centre, the Santapark amusement park and Santa Claus Village (take a reindeer sleigh ride between the latter two) and a school for Santa assistants.

Rovaniemi's airport is even classified as Santa's official airport by the International Aviation Association. In short, this is the place to play out all your childhood Chrimbo fantasies.

However, when you've had your fill of the fat man in the red suit (is 5 minutes enough?), you'll discover that Rovaniemi is also a convenient base for a huge range of snowy activities. Luckily, the fact that Lapland is cloaked in polar night (expect around 4 hours of twilight each day) is no inhibitor to having outdoor fun.

From Rovaniemi you can head off to remote wilderness lodges, go reindeer-sledding, skiing, snowshoeing and ice-fishing. You could mush your own team of exuberant huskies across sparkling fields of white or rev a zippy snowmobile over a frozen lake. And always remember to look up: that dark winter sky is the ideal canvas for the magical Northern Lights – the ultimate Christmas illuminations. — *www.rovaniemi.fi*

Watch baby warthogs

KENYA

WHY NOW It's the best time to see youngsters, and the weather is warm and dry
WHERE Amboseli National Park
DATES Mid-December to March

26 DEC

Warthogs are one of the most fascinating characters on the African plains. They are especially fun to watch when they have young – you might spot a whole line of babies trotting along behind their mother with heads high, manes flowing and tails aloft.

Sounders (a female and her brood) depend on burrows for survival. When pursued by lions, cheetahs or hyenas, they bolt with astonishing speed for the nearest hole, babies heading in first and the mother backing in while slashing with her tusks.

You can catch warthog antics at many of Kenya's parks and reserves, but why not watch them at Amboseli against the picturesque backdrop of Mt Kilimanjaro? This park has easy access and an excellent infrastructure. Plus the park will be green following the 'short rains', which end in mid-December, giving way to a hot, dry season that lasts until March.
— *www.kws.org*

RIGHT: **GRANT DIXON – GETTY IMAGES**

Paddle the Franklin River

AUSTRALIA

WHY NOW Spring rainfall means good river levels
WHERE Franklin River, Tasmania
DATES December to March; trips take 8 days

27 DEC

After a successful campaign to prevent it being dammed in the 1980s, Tasmania's Franklin River is a byword for Australian environmentalism. Today, this wild river is a rafting hotspot, offering a 100km-plus expedition-style adventure through Tasmania's pristine Southwest World Heritage region.

Experienced rafters can tackle the Franklin independently. For novices, tour firms offer rafting packages. Trips start below the Lyell Hwy, on the Collingwood River, and end at Sir John Falls. The greatest rush comes in the Great Ravine, a 5km-long gorge bubbling with invitingly named rapids such as the Cauldron (see *left*), Thunderush and the Churn. Other highlights include the deep Irenabyss and iconic Rock Island Bend with its waterfall.

Water levels on the Franklin rise and fall like the stockmarket, and will have a major effect on your trip. High-water will do much of your paddling work but can make the Great Ravine treacherous. — *www.parks.tas.gov.au*

Go on an elephant trek

CAMBODIA

WHY NOW Humidity levels are low, there's little rain and a cooling breeze whips across the land
WHERE Mondulkiri Province
DATES December to January

28 DEC Nestled against the eastern border, Mondulkiri is Cambodia's most sparsely populated province. This has helped make it a great spot for elephant trekking.

The villages of Phulung and Putang, near Sen Monorom, are easy places to arrange a trek. However, for a truly original elephant experience, spend a day at the Elephant Valley Project, 11km from Sen Monorom. Here you can learn the art of the mahout: hike out into the trees beside the pachyderms, watching them interact as family groups; take an afternoon ride on elephant-back; help wash the animals in the river; and understand the unique roles they play in local life. — *www.elephantvalleyproject.org*

Drive a banger to Africa

ENGLAND TO GAMBIA

WHY NOW The first cavalcade of old cars attempting the Plymouth–Banjul Rally sets off
WHERE Plymouth to Banjul
DATES Late December

29 DEC You don't have the necessary money or speed to enter the famed, high-rollin' Paris–Dakar Rally? Then try the Plymouth–Banjul Rally instead. To do this annual, noncompetitive and bargain-basement rally, your vehicle must have cost less than £100 and you must have spent no more than £15 on preparing and fixing it up. Then all you have to do is nurse it across six countries (England, France, Morocco, Mauritania, Senegal, Gambia) and 6000km to Banjul, where it will be auctioned for local charities. Cars usually leave Plymouth just after Christmas; it'll probably take around three weeks, depending on how often you break down... — *www.dakarchallenge.co.uk*

RIGHT: **Renew your acquaintance with Edinburgh on New Year's Eve**

BELOW: **Aussie band The Cat Empire performing at the Woodford Folk Festival, Queensland**

Join the folk festival

AUSTRALIA

WHY NOW Escape from the rest of the world at Australia's biggest folk festival
WHERE Woodfordia, Queensland
DATES 27 December to 1 January

30 DEC The Woodford Folk Festival is a wicked way to welcome in the new year. For six days, the temporary wonderland of Woodfordia – 70km north of Brisbane – springs up in rural Queensland, and over 2000 performers put on around 450 events to entertain some 130,000 fans. It's a post-Christmas camp-out for everyone, from raging hippies to city hipsters to huge families.

There is folk music, obviously, but also street theatre, films, comedians, acoustic jams, political debate, circus acts, craft workshops and late-night cabarets. It all culminates on New Year's Day, with an incendiary evening send-off. – *www.woodfordfolkfestival.com*

Say hooray for Hogmanay

SCOTLAND

WHY NOW There's a wee party going on in the Scottish capital

WHERE Edinburgh

DATES 29 December to 1 January

31 DEC For Scots, the New Year has always been a more important celebration than Christmas, and largely they've managed to convince the world of the same through the enormous Hogmanay celebrations that engulf Edinburgh, which pulls in 250,000 partying punters.

Hogmanay events begin on 29 December with a free procession: people with flaming torches head along the Royal Mile and onto Calton Hill, where a replica Viking longship is set alight. On 30 December, the 'Night Afore', there's more live music than you can poke a bagpipe at.

New Year's Eve is when Hogmanay truly explodes, with Edinburgh's city centre becoming a gigantic street party. Concert stages line the streets, or you can pick up tickets for events such as the Hoog dance party or the headline Concert in the Gardens, staged below the castle.

New Year's Day is Edinburgh at its silliest. Check out Dogmanay, which sees dog sleds racing across Holyrood Park, or join hundreds at Loony Dook, plunging into the icy waters of the River Forth in fancy dress.

— *www.edinburghshogmanay.com*

Index

INDEX

INDEX

ACKNOWLEDGEMENTS

PUBLISHED IN OCTOBER 2014
by Lonely Planet Publications Pty Ltd
ABN 36 005 607 983
90 Maribyrnong St, Footscray,
Victoria, 3011, Australia
www.lonelyplanet.com

Publishing Director Piers Pickard
Commissioning Editor Robin Barton
Author and Compiler Sarah Baxter
Art Director Daniel Tucker
Layout Designers Arun Aggarwal, Lauren Egan
Editors Karyn Noble, Sally Schafer
Image Researchers Shweta Andrews, Lauren Egan
Pre-Press Production Tag Response
Print Production Larissa Frost

Thanks to Ruth Cosgrove, Brendan Dempsey

ISBN 978 1 74360 165 5
© **Lonely Planet 2014**
© **Photographers as indicated 2014**
Printed in China
10 9 8 7 6 5 4 3

LONELY PLANET OFFICES

Australia
90 Maribyrnong St, Footscray,
Victoria, 3011
Email talk2us@lonelyplanet.com.au

USA
150 Linden St, Oakland, CA 94607
Email info@lonelyplanet.com

United Kingdom
240 Blackfriars Road, London, SE1 8NW
Email go@lonelyplanet.co.uk